The Formation
of the British Liberal Party

The Formation of the British Liberal Party

JOHN VINCENT

CHARLES SCRIBNER'S SONS ▪ New York

Acknowledgements

I wish to acknowledge the gracious permission of Her Majesty the Queen to make use of an extract from papers in the Royal Archives at Windsor.

I am also deeply grateful to the Baines and Clark families for generous hospitality and access to family papers, and to many museums, libraries, public bodies, and societies for making available various materials in their hands.

Contents

Contents

Introduction

Introduction

No single source or type of source was used predominantly. The problem was rather one of fitting together evidence from several kinds of source, most of which were in themselves well-known and unrewarding, but which, by being considered as a whole, could be brought to yield new information. The chief groups of sources used were (1) the well-thumbed canon of Victorian political biography; (2) the papers of such Cabinet politicians as Palmerston, Russell, Gladstone, and Clarendon; (3) the papers of Radical Parliamentarians, like Cobden, Mill, and Bright, and of notable local leaders like Cowen, Mundella, Leader, Baines, Rathbone, Melly, George Wilson, and J. B. Smith; (4) the papers of local party organizations and of militant societies such as the Liberation Society and the Peace Society; (5) the pollbooks for various English borough elections, which throw some light on the structure of the Liberal vote, and (6) local newspapers and miscellaneous items from the local history collections of municipal libraries. No new major source was discovered, though some minor ones were, such as the Baines papers, and some obvious sources were deliberately neglected, particularly in the case of aristocrats and administrators whose preoccupations, though worthy, did not make them of high priority in a study of popular Liberalism.

This book breaks new ground in its description of what kind of people the Liberals were, what they did and why they did it, and in relating leadership and policy to the nature of the party. It is at least original in the simple sense that for much of its length, it deals with topics which have not previously been systematically studied in the light of the sources now available.

One outstanding debt, however, is to Professor H. J. Hanham, whose *Elections and Party Management: Politics in the Time of Disraeli and Gladstone*, (1959), forms an essential starting-point for all work in Victorian party history—*sto magni nominis umbra:* another, for guidance and suggestions, is to Dr Kitson Clark, who first saw the statue in the marble.

*   *   *

The Liberal Party had two contexts: its place in the nation, and its meaning for the individual. The meaning of the Liberal Party for the individual Liberal will be dealt with later; for the nation, the party was an answer to the most important question of modern domestic politics in all countries. That question is, what group should, or rather can, rule when the landowners have ceased to be able to do so by themselves, as an aristocracy? The specific groups which might be nominated as successors to the aristocracy, are hard to find appealing or adequate. The army, business, an organized working class, social leaders without the old social functions of landed aristocracy, an intelligentsia—none of these, taken as they are usually found to be, can run a country with the easy command that the landowners once had. And yet however much a country may lack a natural social base for a government, it is impossible to have a political system in which power does not derive from being for or against well-marked kinds of people or institutions. The peculiar interest of the post-aristocratic situation, the essence of which is that force of circumstances is unusually weak in determining the social character of a régime, is that it was what people made it, that excitement, ardour, skill, great men, great gambles, great temptations, could so significantly alter the situation.

The Liberal Party of Victorian England provided a four-fold solution to this interesting and important problem. First, they insisted that aristocratic rule could not go on for ever, but must be transformed into something else. They did not overthrow it, for in England the decline of the aristocracy was simply a decline in the areas of national life where it had influence and authority, and a decline in will to govern; political opposition from those 'groaning beneath the aristocratic yoke' was less important. Second, they ensured that the successor group to the aristocracy was a section of the aristocracy, reinforced with outside talent to form an administrative intelligentsia. Third, this successor group had the flexibility and tact to form fruitful diplomatic relations with many other groups wholly unlike or quite repugnant to itself, while engaging in hearty conflict with the people most like themselves, the general body of the landowners. Fourth, it assuaged the feelings of poor and powerless people and helped them to accept a most inequitable distribution of wealth and authority, by presenting to them conflicts in which their representatives made a great body of the rich do things they did not want to do, and by making reforms, not important themselves, which conveyed a disproportionate sense of a will to justice. This brings us to the meaning the Liberal Movement had for the individual.

But let us sum up thus the Liberal answer to the question, what to do when the landowners cannot govern by themselves? It was not to replace the old ascendancy by a new one, nor yet to ignore the existence of clusters of power, but to combine rule by consent over individuals, with rule by consensus between clearly marked groups, by keeping matters in the hands of those most skilled in adjusting minute particulars to make provisional agreement possible—those trained under the old dispensation. Power lay with nobody, not even with the presiding body which created the system in which continual negotiation was possible, but only in the ebb and flow of tensions within the system itself. In Whig politics, as in Whig economics, market forces were sovereign.

*   *   *

For the nineteenth-century man, the mark or note of being fully human was that he should provide for his own family, have his own religion and politics, and call no man master. It is as a mode of entry into this full humanity that the Gladstonian Liberal Party most claims our respect. In Stalybridge, indeed, where only the Radical manufacturers might throw their ashes into the stream, the cause of the liberation of humanity might fall to a popular Tory Party: but in the mass, emancipation from traditional bondages and restraints found its political expression in being a rank-and-file Liberal. Despite the nerveless Liberalism of the purse-proud and of the one-party vestries, despite the marring social fear, the traditional claim of the Liberals to have some peculiar moral significance holds true: not as they thought, as regards the

heights of politics, not because of their programme, but
because, over whole areas, to vote Liberal was closely tied
to the growing ability of whole new classes to stand on their
own feet and lead independent lives. The great moral idea of
liberalism was manliness, the rejection of the various forms
of patronage, from soup and blankets upwards, which had
formerly been the normal part of the greatest number. Thus,
being a Liberal (rather than just promiscuously recording a
Liberal vote) was something that could not come about without great changes in the circumstances and horizons of classes
hitherto outside the political nation—changes creative of
moral pressure which overflowed into a traditional parliamentary culture, full of banality, and very little ready to be
moralized. That is the paradox of Liberalism. The view of
Arnold, that at a parliamentary level, Liberal politics were
little more than the 'good cries' of Tadpole and Taper super-
ficially modernized and moralized, is in fact compatible with
respect for the claim that deep moral feeling might be involved in being Liberal.

The discrepancy between intention and profession, and
results, between what a Nonconformist writer called the
'party of Christ' and the actual ordinariness of what that
party did, is a great fact, far too great to be bridged by throwing down a plank called hypocrisy. It is a problem which
brings us up against the limitations both of our imaginations
and of theirs: but it cannot be solved without a great deal of
respect for the suffering flesh and blood whose Liberalism
was the political extension of their general effort to tread the
road of improvement.

For instance, there is a defect of sympathy, natural and
easy now to fall into, which treats of any activities besides the
sedentary holding of abstract opinions on the merits of the
'questions of the day', and the orderly expression of these
opinions at the polling booth, as irregular, primitive, animal,
and corrupt, and above all as not really political at all, as
those elections were more or less the same as the wakes. A
medium-sized borough had more of the Greek city state about
it than that.[1] The rediscovery of what Victorian elections

[1] In Macclesfield 20,000 people went to the nominations in the
Market Place in the 1850's and 1860's: even on one occasion when there

were actually like—through the evidence in corruption cases
—suggests a low view of electoral human behaviour. This is
fair enough, but for most people politics was the politics of
the town in which they lived their lives,[2] and for them, and
in their own terms, elections were a rational business, in
which the real issue was not the Parliamentary representation
of the borough, but the relative positions of the electors
within the town. The ceremonies, processions, banners,
posters, music, bands of 'lambs' and supporters, colours,
favours, and seating arrangements at the hustings, were much
more a drama enacted about the life of the town, the precedence, 'pecking order', and social sanctions which held it
together, than a means of expressing individual opinions
about the matters of the day to which candidates confined
themselves—in their speeches. Elections were for the England
of 1860 what drama, sport, and liturgy have been for earlier
and later times: there was nothing else which brought an
entire population together and demanded they determine
their relation to each other.

Thus, elections considered as national politics were frivolous and primitive: considered as local politics, serious and
rational.[3] As typical of this contradiction one may mention
the Whitby fishermen of 1868, active Reform Leaguers, vic-
toriously carrying Gladstone's son round the local 'Khyber
Pass': what they were to gain from a Liberal ministry must
be rather obscure, but at any rate their position in the town
could never be the same again after ousting the Tory landlord
from the Whitby seat. They had raised themselves, and that
was the central thing.

Though at first glance Victorian politics might appear a
raft of superficiality and cant floating on an ocean of brutality

---

was no contest. There was 'grave moral danger to the young' in the
carnival atmosphere on these occasions, 'boys and girls dancing together
in the streets'.

[2] The breakdowns of Bright and Mundella under ostracism suggest
the intensity with which purely local reverses were felt.

[3] 'Every milkman and every grocer in Leeds voted against me, I was
told, though I was as innocent of the (Food Adulteration) Act as you.'—
Edward Baines to his brother-in-law, 18 March 1874. (Baines mss.,
'Interesting Papers' bundle.)

and corruption, in fact there was an area of intense moral
effort behind the Liberal situation, centred on the hopes, now
for the first time rational, that society as a whole might be improved, the view so conscientiously avoided by earlier generations; by the elder Ruskin, by Newman Hall's father, by the
old Wesleyans of Bunting's school, by the old 'Tories of the
school of Homer'. Moral improvement had an economic and
a Christian dimension. The economic dimension is clear:
above all, the industrialization of the inland coalfields, and
the development of single-class suburbs,[4] were the logical
results of the railways. But such changes chiefly matter after
the 1860's, while Liberalism was the natural political expression of an England much as it had always been—of tight,
teeming towns, isolated industry, and agricultural shires,
stirred up and fattened, but not essentially changed, by the
railways.

Much harder to believe in, and more necessary to insist
upon, is the Christian dimension of Liberalism: it is something which has rather to be inferred and supplied, from
scanty and unsuitable testimonies; and one has then to guess
how far this estimated quantity affected or accredited Liberalism. In its work, England was workmanlike in a new way in
the nineteenth century: in work there is little discontinuity
of attitude between then and now: but what was England
working for? For ends, some of them, that 'good society' or
Bagehot's 'educated class' had, for a very long time, not been
in the habit of conceiving: while, at the other end, the ideas
which moved, even dominated, the literary and official classes
of the metropolis, were often only trace elements among the
urban middle classes. The men who made the North what it
is, very frequently took orthodox, traditional Christianity as
the conscious expression of their modernity and their sense
of belonging to a revolutionary *élite* working for a newer
and better civilization. Their sects were often odd—George
Wilson of the Anti-Corn Law League was a Sandemanian—

[4] In an article in the *Journal of Transport History*, May 1955, H. J.
Dyos shows there were no real changes in housing patterns in London till
the 1880's, when workmen's returns came in. But in Sheffield, John
Brown moved his works down to the Rotherham railway in the early
1860's with 'Radical' results in Brightside politics as early as 1868.

but they were orthodox in the sense that at a deathbed, the centre of their religion, they would turn to consolations more like those of the European peasant than of a Whig political economist. When George Eliot wrote in the 1860's of the quaint and homely religion of her youth ' which ran in families', the implied contrast is always not with the atten- uated honest doubt of the histories of thought, but with a modern religious world enormously grown in strength, so far as strength lay in being ecclesiastically and theologically cer- tain, militant, and articulate. Educated society, including Gladstone, almost invariably avoided mentioning God in its correspondence: the middle class, on the other hand, if at all typified by the Baines family, referred to God's wishes at all points of their political and domestic life.[5] This discussion of the Christian element in Liberal politics cannot go very much further than this caution, that, for many Liberals, politics was not an autonomous activity, but one deriving from a religious centre in a way we cannot often trace:[6] and the Liberationist side of Dissent did not have the independent existence that writers, both for and against it, claimed it had.[7]

The following words of Sir Edward Baines to his family help to give these points some social concreteness:

> To our young grandchildren I wish to say that we have had the great advantage of pious ancestors on both sides for several generations; we have also had the happiness of connecting ourselves with an unusual number of truly Christian families, several members of which have been distinguished as Ministers of the Gospel, several filling positions of honourable usefulness in public life, several by their scholarship and contributions to literature, several by

[5] Edward Baines in a typical phrase ended a letter to Gladstone: 'Devoutly praying for the guidance of Divine Wisdom to the helmsman of the State, I am, etc.' (24 April 1880, Baines mss., 'Interesting Papers' bundle).

[6] The subdued rational Christianity of a man like Cobden is easily lost sight of—especially by a Morley. There are papers showing Cobden's belief that he had witnessed direct Divine inspiration once in his life.

[7] Miall, for instance, saw clearly the problems facing the Churches in an industrial society. But the means he chose to solve them, Liberation- ism, grew into an end in themselves.

large services to charity, education and religion. Among
them I may mention names that have been respected, or
even eminent, for two or three generations. At the head of
this list I place my grandfather, Matthew Talbot, and my
father Edward Baines: and then follow the names of Pye,
Smith, Conder, Read, Huigh, Reynolds, Bence, Blackburn,
Willans and Crossby. We bequeath this relationship to our
successors as an honourable legacy and hope that the re-
membrance of them will be a continual motive to spotless
virtue, to intellectual culture, to Christian usefulness, and
to the carrying down of the line of piety to a remote
posterity.[8]

That similar aspirations, without similar opportunities,
might be found far below the fine flower of bourgeois society,
the novels of Mark Rutherford afford testimony, though for
an earlier and more excited period: but otherwise, the ten-
pound shopkeeper or publican 'who governed England', has
left only the puniest traces of individual existence. There is
a hole at the centre of the picture, but the thousands of
nineteenth-century chapels entitle one to fill up the hole in
the written evidence in a fairly definite way.

The foregoing pages have tried to establish the way much
of the politics of the Liberal rank and file was serious, as
serious as the life from which it grew, even though its inspiration was mainly local, and its expression rather rowdy. To
talk about a party from the base upwards, is to bring out the
immense gap between the real political life of the people, and
the political life of those to whom politics was a career (the
Parliamentary class), and the casual and arbitrary connection
of the two forms of politics. Their lives ran in different
channels from start to finish. In religion, politics, culture,
wealth, there is almost no community of experience, no possible human solidarity, to unite the 'top ten thousand in

[8] Address to His Family, 9 September 1879, on his golden wedding:
Baines mss. This plethora of spotless virtue made Leeds society as exclusive as that of any ancient city: see *Memoirs of Sir Jacob Behrens*,
35 ff., for his comments on his move to raw, wide open Bradford in 1836.
Similarly, at Manchester in the 1850's a Lord Mayor was blackballed
from a Mosley Street club because he had not 'come over with the
Arkwrights'. (*Rochdale Standard*, 24 January 1857.)

Sheffield',[9] with metropolitan 'good society', that is, with the world of Trollope, Thackeray, and Bagehot, with its extensions in the upper levels of Barsetshire society.[10] Or, in an individual case, the difference between the two largest employers of labour in the Potteries: Earl Granville, born into the world of European diplomacy, trained for the highest responsibilities and assuming them in comparative youth, and Mr Roden, M.P., likewise an employer of some thousands of souls, but, outside Stoke-on-Trent, not really counting for much.

The choice of evidence for this book has been governed by the assumption that most of what is usually said about the evolution of mid-nineteenth-century society is limited in value by its being written by, for, and about, one single, specialized, geographically-limited, sociologically-imprisoned group; 'good society', as unrepresentative in one way,[11] as the Primitive Methodists in another. Fallacy upon fallacy results from our taking our history of the century from the testimony of this class, what they saw when they peered in the mirror being distorted by the anxieties of their exposed and isolated position.

The educated mind has always dwelt on Parliamentary history, the Parliamentary party, and its politics. It is its natural limitation. In this view, the Liberal Party came into being in 1859 through the agreement at Willis's Rooms brought about by the Italian question: and so on in that vein. Whereas, what was really new was not the slow adaptations of

[9] The phrase is used by Arnold in a letter to Mundella's daughter. It is when the term 'middle class' is used with such persons in mind, that it becomes as useful and as precise to us as it was in its evocations then. At Oxford there were lectures on *The Middle Class, Its Condition and Prospects.*

[10] To take education alone, 100 English boroughs of over 5,000 people had no endowed grammar schools at the time of the Taunton Commission. This is a large proportion of the 170 odd English parliamentary boroughs.—Woodward, *The Age of Reform*, 468.

[11] Once again an instance from Arnold illuminates: 'It is true, the *Saturday Review* maintains ... that we have found our philosophy, that the British nation has searched all anchorages for the spirit, and has finally anchored itself, in the fulness of perfected knowledge, on Benthamism.' If numbers matter at all, one must say Spurgeon's Tabernacle (1861) was the preferred anchorage of the Zeitgeist.

the Parliamentary party: but the adoption of that Parliamentary party by a rank and file. The great frontier is not the division between Whig and Tory in Parliament, but that separating the Parliamentary parties from the national party.[12] Thus the sudden arrival of the national party in the third quarter of the nineteenth century, passed at the time, and since, largely unrecognized. This was partly because it had no organizational counterpart (the educated mind tending to overestimate the need of the uneducated for organization), and also partly because, at Parliamentary level, the Peelite tradition in administration gave a rather misleading sense of continuity. More important in contributing to the oblivion of the formation of national parties as communities of sentiment, was the fact that it came about at a social level which has left few historical records. But admitting the existence of the national party as a new kind of thing in the 1860's, one at once comes to questions different in scale from the usual ones. How could all these millions of people, who knew nothing of each other's lives, find themselves acting, with some warmth, in common? How was it possible to unite millions in sentiment (but *not* by organization) in the 1860's, when previous decades had seen such difficulty in uniting a few hundred M.P.s for or against a ministry? To answer such questions a fresh assessment of the lineaments and proportions of the whole of England becomes necessary.

The study of a truly national community like the Liberal Party, most of it outside the educated class, brings out how much English history is not what it has been thought to be, how much of English life has never come to the knowledge of 'those who know' at all. There is one supreme exception, one unifying, all-seeing authority: McCalmont's *Poll Book*. This,

---

[12] The best description of the old Parliamentary parties is that of Arnold: 'These parties, differing in so much else, were yet alike in this, that they were both, in a certain broad sense, *aristocratical* parties. They were combinations of persons considerable either by great family and estate, or by court favour, or lastly, by eminent abilities and popularity: this last body, however, attaining participation in public affairs only through a conjunction with one or other of the former. These connections, though they contained men of very various degrees of birth and property, were still wholly leavened with the feelings and habits of the upper class of the nation. They had the bond of a common culture. . . .'

rightly read and understood, is the *comédie humaine* of the experience of a people, in convenient and coded form: with Domesday Book, it is the sociological document *par excellence*, abundant and diverse, the irrefutable corrective of received ideas, partial views, and *a priori* constructions. Below are some examples of this ignorance of a people about themselves.

As before stated, England was a Christian country, in which the discussion of public questions was conducted, whether in Parliament or in print, by a specialized group which, in life and thought, tended to be more alienated from orthodox Christianity than any other set of men in broadcloth in the country, and to be least impressed by the forms of manners to which the provincial Christian revival attached special importance.[13]

The national institutions only begin to express the Christian earnestness of the country fully, long after the educated mind has moved into the region of difficulties and doubts. The effects of militant religion on politics increased remarkably steadily between 1857 and 1886, and the Parliament of 1885 reflected the religious state of the country in 1857, more accurately than did the Parliament of 1857 itself. When Benjamin Whitworth entered Parliament in 1865, he and Edward Baines were the only total abstainers in the Commons: in 1885, there were as many as thirty-six abstainers.[14] Likewise, it was perfectly politically possible for Cobden and Gladstone to make confident plans for the Englishman to drink *vin ordinaire* (to wean him from spirits) at the time of the French Treaty, though in the same year, Mr Tweedie, the temperance publisher, wrote:[15]

I should say that there are at least 4,000 Temperance

[13] Of the Peelites, Gladstone wrote: 'There was not a dandy or a coxcomb among them.' But though the administrative rigour of the Peelite tradition was impregnated with religious revival, the impression is that the saving remnant in Parliament was as small as usual, and not in itself powerful. Palmerston's misjudgments of public feeling about Sunday opening of museums and bands in the parks, showed how inadequate mere Parliamentary sensitivity had become.

[14] A. Arthur Reade, *The House of Commons on Stimulants* (1885).

[15] Speech of E. Baines on Borough Franchise Bill, 10 April 1861.

Societies in the United Kingdom, and not less than 3,000,000 teetotallers, including all ages, three quarters of whom are not likely to belong to any society, and perhaps more than half of whom are under fifteen.

Thus the Liberal Party in the country from the beginning lived in a milieu where religious revival led on to the adoption of 'good causes', and thence to political militancy: and in the new national party, the Militant became as prominent a phenomenon as the old Notable or Wirepuller. It fell almost entirely to Mr Gladstone to attract the forces of religious revival behind an accommodating but unredeemed party not connatural with its supporters.

If it took the religious tone of the age in general a whole generation to develop a Parliamentary cutting edge, so also the great expansion of Nonconformity was very slow to develop its political potential. To the Primitive Methodists, for instance, the Act of 1884 gave political effectiveness for the first time:[16] while the great Wesleyan body moved slowly forward from the disruption of the 1850's (led, not surprisingly, by the Methodists of Rochdale and Sheffield), to become predominantly Liberal only by the time of Home Rule.[17] The educated mind, which had reacted heartily against the Liberationist intervention in 1857, and whose Church Defence Associations brought gains to the Tories in 1859, had caught on to the affiliations of Dissent and democracy, at the first appearance on the political scene of organized Nonconformity. Because there was always a traditional link between Dissent and the Whigs and Liberals, it has been assumed that this affiliation was a constant, not a dynamic and growing one. In fact, the Gladstonian Liberal Party had,

[16] Results in some counties in which the Primitives were strong, in the 1885 election (boroughs excluded): Durham and Northumberland, 12 Lib., 0 Cons.; Cornwall, 6 Lib., 0 Cons.; Suffolk and Norfolk, 9 Lib., 2 Cons.

[17] The founding of the *Methodist Times* in 1885 by Hugh Price Hughes marked 'a convenient date for marking the beginnings of a dominant Liberalism within the Methodist church'. M. Edwards, *Methodism and England* (1943) 168: quoted by J. F. Glaser, 'English Nonconformity and the Decline of Liberalism', *American Hist. Review*, January 1958, 356. In Haslingden, Lancashire, in 1961, eight of the nine Liberal councillors were Methodist lay preachers.

chiefly because of the very tenacity with which the Methodists and the counties hung on to their Toryism, an enormous expanding social frontier throughout its life.

This was fortunate for the Liberals, for in their traditional strongholds they reached their limits early and thereafter began to recede. In the great towns, the only change possible was a move towards Conservatism, such as occurred in fact in Lancashire after 1852, in London after 1859, in the great cities of Yorkshire after 1885.[18] The extraordinary stability of the Liberal representation in the great cities can be seen from the following table:

Variation in number of Liberal members returned 1832–80
(for constituencies with population over 100,000 in 1851)

1832—31	1847—30	1865—30
1835—30	1852—29	1868—32
1837—30	1857—30	1874—23
1841—26	1859—31	1880—25

In the great cities, that is, the Liberals stayed exactly where they had been in 1832, for the whole generation up to 1868, except for 1841: and in 1868, they held their own, in absolute numbers, but declined relatively owing to the increase in the total number of seats. Most significant, the Tories kept in 1880 most of the gains they had made in this class of seat in 1874 (unlike all other classes of borough seat). Whether or not Disraeli intended it, the electoral régime of 1868–85 was marked by a strengthened Tory grip on the counties, and a weakened Liberal hold in the great towns.

Despite the rise of a popular Tory Party in the great towns between 1859 and 1885, despite the Parliamentary impotence of the Liberalism of the great towns, 'public opinion' never felt anything but deeply nervous of the new industrial England. The educated mind, blinkered by the metaphor of the inclined plane, reasoning from a falsely eschatological significance given to the Manchester School and the League's

[18] In Sheffield in 1885 the classical modern pattern appeared; the residential districts of Hallam and Eccleshall were heavily Tory, the central business district moderately so, the working-class districts at the East End—Brightside and Attercliffe—strongly Radical. This was the first clear case of political division following from class housing patterns.

'victory',[19] largely lost its enjoyment of politics and its power of seeing things as they were. A great deal of social fear need never have arisen, if the electoral system had been properly understood, and if people could have come to see industrial life as something perfectly viable and commonplace in its own way.

The corollary of the obsession with and antipathy to that brand new Benthamite world of the manufacturing districts with which the educated mind used to frighten itself, was neglect of the fact that the historical process showed no sign of stopping in districts which had nothing to do with heavy industry. Yet it was the great rural and small-town Radical tradition which really made history in the great landslides: 1832, 1857, 1880, 1885, and 1906. What, electorally, made and unmade governments, were the small and medium boroughs and the counties. These alone could really register the feeling of the country—an immediate tremor in the aristocratic opinion that governed the country, or some deeper, irreversible current of social evolution, or both at once, as when the aristocratic feeling for Palmerston coincided with the Liberationist intervention in 1857:

Population of Constituency in 1851 (England only)	*Gains or Losses in Liberal M.P.s at general election*	
	in 1857	*in 1859*
Under 10,000	+ 12	− 11
10,000–20,000	+ 11	− 3
20,000–30,000	− 5	0
30,000–50,000	+ 2	− 2
50,000–100,000	− 1	0
Over 100,000	+ 1	+ 1
English counties	+ 23	− 8

[19] Cobden did not take a millennial view of the League, recollected in tranquillity, '. . . but a blundering, unsystematic series of campaigns, in which we were partly indebted for victory to the stupidity of our foes, and still more to the badness of their cause'. (13 September 1853, Cobden to Prentice, Cobden mss., Chichester, Letter book 51.) But the millennial view of the League prevailed all the same. When the Manchester School amounted simply to two distinguished Parliamentarians with their circle of personal acquaintances, it was still common to talk of it as the spearhead of a pyramidal and homogeneous Radicalism.

As between Tories and Liberals, that is, the larger boroughs were practically mute in the business of moulding governments: similarly, taken by areas, the historically determinative area was not the North:

Area (England only), Counties and Boroughs	Gains or Losses of Liberal Members in 1857	in 1859
West	+ 9	− 6
South	+ 14	− 3
East	+ 10	− 7
Midlands	+ 10	+ 3
North	− 6	− 1

Where there was a marked national trend, the North was either against it, or did not register it to a significant degree. The northern tail was not wagging the dog; the dog was certainly wagging the tail.

There is a distinctive regionalism in English history, not at the level of idiosyncrasy and local colour, but arising from the differing circumstances of broad blocs of people. The educated class, meeting its like everywhere, naturally antedated the arrival of national political homogeneity, and assumed political behaviour in the country ran on much the same lines as in London and the Home Counties. The broadest distinction is between those areas where social evolution and electoral reform increased Liberal strength, and those where it diminished it. Lancashire, London, and the Home Counties move away from Liberalism, whilst Scotland, Wales, the agricultural counties, and the great central provincial belt of the coalfields,[20] move towards Liberalism from Toryism, or towards a more Radical form of Liberalism. These regional differences correlate significantly with the distribution of Dissent, which was relatively weak in Lancashire, London, and the South East, and not strong in the West Riding.

[20] This is the belt running from Northumberland and Durham through the woollen districts and Sheffield to the Black Country and the East Midlands towns, and onwards into S. Wales and Bristol. The political structure and evolution of this region was fairly uniform over the period 1832–92. Certainly, it is what must be borne in mind when considering the typical political effects of the Industrial Revolution— not Lancashire.

A. NUMBER OF LIBERAL M.P.S RETURNED FOR ENGLISH COUNTY CONSTITUENCIES[21]

1832	102 out of 144
1835	71 ,, ,, ,,
1837	45 ,, ,, ,,
1841	20 ,, ,, ,,
1847	36 ,, ,, ,,
1852	30 ,, ,, ,,
1857	53 ,, ,, ,,
1859	45 ,, ,, ,,
1865	51 ,, ,, ,,
1868	47 out of 172
1874	27 ,, ,, ,,
1880	54 ,, ,, ,,
1885	134 out of 234
1886	64 ,, ,, ,,
1892	103 ,, ,, ,,

It will be noticed that the Liberals did less well in the counties in 1868 and 1880 than in 1857, 1859, 1865, if the increase in seats is taken into account.

In 1885, 1886, and 1892, outside the Home Counties, almost no county remained completely Tory: only Westmorland, Rutland, the Isle of Wight, and the East Riding (with one Liberal in 1892) did so. Yet Middlesex, Surrey, Sussex, Kent, and Berkshire returned a solid bloc of thirty Tories for their county seats at these three elections. The Home Counties had become an autonomous political entity, yet they were not the only example where a strong local current moved in contrast to the national trend. Lancashire and Yorkshire, as the table on page xxvii shows, sometimes, but not always, differed markedly: but at least enough to prevent one speaking of the North as a fairly homogeneous political region.

Where even Lancashire and Yorkshire had such diverse political experiences, any accurate national history must take a very full account of the marked and contradictory political 'personalities' of the regions.

Another fundamental point of discussion about nineteenth-century politics is the position of the middle class. There was

[21] Compiled from McCalmont, *Parliamentary Poll Book*.

B. A STRONG CASE OF REGIONALISM: ELECTORAL DIFFERENCES BETWEEN LANCASHIRE AND YORKSHIRE, 1832–86[22]

Year	Lancashire		Yorkshire	
	Liberal	Conservative	Liberal	Conservative
1832	20	6	34	3
1835	15	11	24	13
1837	15	11	23	14
1841	14	12	18	19
1847	18	8	26	11
1852	19	7	25	12
1857	16	10	22	15
1859	15	11	24	13
1865	15	12	26	13
1868	11	22	28	10
1874	7	26	21	17
1880	21	12	30	8
1885	27	38	36	16
1886	19	46	32	20

in no sense in the mid-nineteenth century, a real middle-class alternative to aristocratic government, as is occasionally supposed. On this point such observers as Mill, Arnold, Cobden, and Gladstone were fully agreed. Nor was there an insurrection of 'bourgeois' ideas against the old ways of thought. The middle class did exist, socially, in the sense of 'broadcloth-wearing' inhabitants of the towns: but it could not be identified with any particular set of social or political ideas. Everybody knew, then, whether a person was middle class or not: and what were the thousand corollaries of that status. But the limited education and the still small businesses of such people restricted their competence to take part in public life. The middle class, indeed, was an irreducible and primary social fact, of tremendous negative importance; but many a social fact does not become a political fact. The middle class in business were entering politics by absorption, not by conquest, and were typically doing it through the mines, banks, railways, the City, and the shipping interest, that dominant part of the business world with which committees of the Commons were so entangled and in which the best blood of the land had long co-operated with complete equanimity. In

[22] Computed from Bean, W. W., *Parliamentary Representation of the Six Northern Counties* (Hull, 1890).

other words, the Northern textile masters were an isolated occupational group even in the business world,[23] and even this self-conscious salt of the earth did not, as a body, run to a programmatic and ideological idea of politics. The Free Traders were not in fact essentially crusaders for *laissez-faire*.[24]

The large capitalists, then, were initially only a fractional part of the middle class: of this fraction, only amongst one subdivision, that of the textile masters, was there anything like a general feeling of alienation from the conventions of aristocratic government: and even amongst the textile masters, the attempt of the Manchester School to turn this feeling into a collective support of a distinctively bourgeois policy was a resounding failure.[25] As for the other sections of the provincial and business *élite*, it is no easy matter even to find out who were the upper classes of Norwich, Bristol, Hull, the North East, the coalowners, or the City, let alone define their political tone, which rarely obtruded beyond their borough walls.

The real corpus of thought uniting the middle class, or the

[23] As they bought and sold on exchanges in free competition, and their main problems were speculation in raw material prices and amortization of fixed capital, their attitude was bound to be entirely different from the ordinary capitalist interested in contracts and goodwill. Hence the 'forthrightness': they could afford it. The Liberal mill-owners of Lancashire may be guessed at 500 families (from the trade directories): not enough to batter at the English constitution very effectively. Cobden's daughter wrote a novel suggesting they were unlikely to do anything very effectively: and she knew every one of them.

[24] E.g. John Bright was a Philistine about economics as about anything else except Milton. '... I suspect this scientific political economy is something like metaphysics and what has been called philosophy—there is no bottom to it and the writers upon it can scarcely define or understand what they mean,' he wrote to his daughter.

[25] The *Hard Times* school of critics of the Free Traders never make the necessary reservations in favour of the spirit of intelligence, immensely masculine, of considerable integrity, of great capacity for getting to the bottom of social issues and sparing no pains, which characterized the League generation at its best. Later generations in Lancashire could well have done with some of this social intelligence which socially minded critics so easily wish away—to judge from various testimonies from Arnold's *Cotton Famine* to Bowker's *Lancashire under the Hammer* (1928), a tract of genius.

Liberal section of it, was not a Benthamite, utilitarian, or natural-law view of the world, not American or economical principles, but something of a different order: a view or recollection of English history. The Dissenters above all, were formed in a historical culture of almost Judaic narrowness, and their political views were grafted on to an interpretation of seventeenth-century politics quite as much as those of the great Whigs were. One must think of the great Bicentenary celebrations of 1862, the revival of the cults of Cromwell and Milton,[26] the woodcuts of Bunyan in Bedford gaol provided for the readers of the *Liberator*—even John Bright reading his favourite Hallam aloud to his wife—to get some idea of the culture that the middle class would draw on to interpret their politics. The really important attitudes had nothing to do with the industrial revolution, much to do with the English Civil War,[27] and a change in deference extending far outside the areas of industrial progress, had caused these attitudes to flourish as never before. The national institutions embodied memories of oppression; for instance, it was found in 1873 that the predominantly Dissenting county of Huntingdonshire had no Dissenters on its county bench.[28] From such ancient memories and present reminders,[29] Liberalism gained a stamp of generality, a historical perspective, and a unity of outlook, that it could never have won from a purely modern industrial background.

Sir Richard Tangye, the great Birmingham manufacturer and inventor of the hydraulic press, is a case in point. The way he thought about politics had nothing to do with capitalism or hydraulic presses, or rather, he saw even those as epiphenomenal to the energy of spirit built up over centuries of sectarian conflict. He thought instead of the family cow that was distrained in summer, and the flitch of bacon carried off in the winter, when his grocer father refused to pay Church rates. To his dying day this mild humanitarian could never

---

[26] Bright's 'the greatest man who ever lived'.

[27] Arch's ancestors had fought at Edge Hill: it all seemed very recent.

[28] *Hansard,* vol. 253, col. 372, 18 June 1880.

[29] Cobden tried to get up a libel case against Macaulay on behalf of William Penn: Gladstone in 1870 gave Wales its first Welsh-speaking bishop in two centuries.

forgive the State Church for so putting people under the harrow. History spoke a message to him. It was his invincible persuasion that the English people owed more to Oliver Cromwell than to any other of their rulers. He saw in Cromwell the man who made civil and religious liberty possible, and he collected and venerated his relics. And even in the conduct of his business, he found the same reading of the forces in history applied. When he developed a ten-seater steam bus with a cruising speed of 20 m.p.h., the landed interest quietly put it down by Act of Parliament.[30]

When their moment of historical opportunity came, the leaders of the Radical rank and file were prepared and confident, because their collective outlook had been two centuries in preparation. Leadership of the type of Gladstone's, far from 'riding the chariot of reform only to apply the brakes', far from weakening the party, as is often supposed, by avoiding the social commitments which would have gained industrial working-class support, in fact was able to maximize the revolutionary potential available in the country, given the electoral system of that time. The Gladstonian formula was the most extreme one practicable: Chamberlain's rejection of it was a triumph of will over intelligence.

A harmfully valetudinarian idea has prevailed of a brief heyday of middle-class rule in the mid-nineteenth century, being inevitably swamped by Demos. This has no place in history. What really happened is that in their attitude to politics, the middle class began by defining itself against the landed aristocracy and those who were associated with them. This prevalent feeling however did not, in a large way, affect the structure of Parliamentary politics, in the way that the later feelings which arose when the middle class defined itself in opposition to the working class, became central in the electoral system. Rather, Demos and the middle class really arrived on the political scene at about the same time, both were penned in and tied down by the social realities of an aristocratic constitution, and both had to work a parallel passage to a commanding position, by gaining from the aristocratic sphere, before they could turn to face each other.

The conquest of public opinion by the Parliamentary

[30] Stuart J. Reid, *Sir Richard Tangye* (1908), 8, 79 and 201.

parties preceded the development of systematic party organization by a generation. There were no orders from above to create a party. Community of sentiment had to exist before organization could be possible: where such community existed, not much organization was necessary. The real units of opinion and organization remained the mill, union, pub, street, high street, estate, farmers' ordinaries, and so on. The various forms of Liberal Association, local and central (both going back long before Chamberlain) have their interest, and will be treated later. They left things much as they were, as usual tending to become uninspired machinery. The national party was a reality of a quite different order from the national party organization, which has been regarded with such superstition, but which was naturally least of all interesting in its bumbling origins. One returns to the futility of contrivances in the face of the deep currents of social evolution.

There is a more philosophic meaning to the inconsequence of party organization. It is, that the notables, the traditional holders of power, already had the kind of expression of their strength that they wanted, in their hold over the institutions of local government and Parliament, and therefore found a parallel form of organizing their power superfluous, except for electioneering purposes. Conversely, while the middle classes had great aggregate strength, they had not developed, or were only starting to develop, strong collective institutions similar to those of the traditional holders of power. The great national institutions of the middle class were the new provincial daily press, and the great militant societies. (The municipalities and chambers of commerce were far less significant: associations of employers and investors were even more remote from being politically effective bodies.) The middle class in the 1860's was beginning to have political institutions exempt from the grasp of the traditional educated class, institutions which were to be a permanent feature of the political scene. Even so, the middle class remained without strength in proportion to its numerousness, hardly standing ahead of the working classes organized in their cooperative societies, trades unions, and the briefly effective National Reform League.

This introduction is intended to show that, when every

allowance is made for Bagehot's view that Parliamentary parties were associations of the wealthy for carrying out the ideas of the wealthy, the emergence of national political parties cannot be explained except by showing that they performed a function, and that a respectable one, in individual and local life, at all levels of society. Further, it is suggested that most of what has been said about English history at this time, was in fact true only for the small and specialized group who said it. To correct this, and to state one's own views, it was necessary to give in detail some of those religious, moral, regional, electoral, and organizational developments which, though an important part of the national experience, were little represented in its recorded experience.

The value of taking extended views is particularly true in the case of the Gladstonian Liberal Party. Though an analysis of the Parliamentary party is necessary, its chief importance is negative, in revealing how far it was from being a 'movement', and how impossible it would have been, with such support alone, to have done the things Mr Gladstone did do. It was from outside Parliament, and from the world outside the World, from the milieus described in this introduction, that the Liberal Movement drew its social strength and social meaning. These mainly provincial milieus have been underestimated because of the strong barriers existing against their obtaining their due influence in Parliament. Despite these barriers, however, the rank and file were able to make themselves heard through the newly representative function given to party leadership by Bright and Gladstone. Though this system of dual monarchy required exceptional skill to operate, it did give additional leverage to the leadership against either the Parliamentary party or the national rank and file, thus justifying the traditional emphasis placed on Gladstone, and it enabled the administrative intelligentsia which he personified to impose its compromise solutions on questions of policy, with something like disinterestedness. The very situation demanded a type of man and policy of which it may fairly be said: *Honi soit qui mal y pense.*

* * *

The following chapters attempt to give an account of the

social structure and moral aura of the Parliamentary Liberal Party, its leadership, and its provincial rank and file. Though the limits 1857 to 1868 have not always been adhered to, the change in the 1860's from Palmerston to Gladstone was chosen as the decisive moment in the party's history, and it has been possible to obtain a fairly comprehensive view of nineteenth-century Liberalism from one decade of its heyday alone.

The chief historical problem lay in the evolution from the Parliamentary party system to the national party system. The sudden adoption by provincial society of the official parties as the expressions of their political feelings, by no means a natural development, occurred with such speed in the 1860's that it has been largely lost sight of. This mutual convergence of provincial feeling and Parliamentary politics was not accompanied by, still less brought about by, changes in central or local party organization. A chapter on the subject attempts to bring out the insignificance of official party machinery in creating that largely unorganized community of sentiment called a party. The creation of a (predominantly Liberal) cheap daily press outside London, the action of organized labour and militant Nonconformity, the Reform agitation of the 1860's, and the representative significance of Gladstone, were the chief influences in changing the context of the Parliamentary Liberal Party. Up to 1865, that party had been the expression of personal rivalries and political differences within the aristocracy, broadly defined. After 1865 the Liberals, without important changes in their Parliamentary personnel, came to represent great and dynamic social forces in the country, by reason of their vitalizing connection with their rank and file. The representative of that connection was Gladstone. The energy thus imparted was sufficient to allow the Executive to start building up an authoritative State responsible for the great matters of national life, and to diminish the extremely unfruitful ascendancy exercised by Parliament over the State between 1847 and 1868.

The following sections describe the Parliamentary party, the rank and file, the leaders, and policy. In the first, the Parliamentary Liberals are analysed according to their occupation, class, and opinions.

The tendency to regard the Liberals as composed of opposed wings of Whigs and Radicals is shown to be incorrect. The great bulk of the Liberal M.P.s were neither Whigs nor Radicals but simply commonplace wealthy Englishmen whose political actions were bound neither by affiliation to great houses nor by theoretical intransigence. The idea of the 'Manchester School' as representing a pyramidal and homogeneous Radicalism is shown to be a mere bogy of the Press. Both Whigs and Radicals as such were not among the forces that shaped events. The only intransigence of historic proportions in the party was that of the rich Nonconformist employers, Radical chiefly by reason of their Dissent. It is claimed that this small group exercised a beneficent and a profound influence on the party, though Liberal M.P.s in the 1860's were very strongly tied to the classes traditionally holding power in England. Half of them, for instance, were large landowners, or their sons.

The second section offers studies of the Press, of organized Dissent, and of the working-class Liberal—the three pillars of provincial Liberalism from its start in 1860 to its end. It concludes with a 'microscopic' analysis of the Liberal rank and file in Rochdale, supported by miniatures from Whitby and Leeds. An interesting discovery is the nearly equal division of voters, within each class and each occupation, between Liberal and Tory.

The section on leadership includes studies of Palmerston, Mill, Bright, Russell, and Gladstone, based on their papers. The questions there are why Gladstone achieved a unique predominance, what other leaders missed by not having the breadth of support that Gladstone had, and how far others sowed for Gladstone to reap.

The chapter on policy is concerned with the relation between the social structure of opinion within the Liberal Party and the formation of State policy. Only a broad treatment is possible, and only on the great questions: democracy, peace and war, and the condition of the people. It is urged that while Liberal reforms of State institutions were less imposing than tradition has it, Liberal social policy was, however, less hidebound than is usually thought. In foreign policy, it is alleged that the importance of the coalescence of Parliament

and people lay not in the immediate shifts of diplomacy in the 1860's, but in a long-term change in the social structure of opinion on peace and war. The conventional wisdom of the nation on this subject, which had been sharply divided by class at earlier times, was consolidated by Liberal teachings in the period 1850–70. On questions of political reform, the disingenuousness of the Liberals must be emphasized. The Liberals, flatly, were not democrats, their Reform Bill of 1866 was an exclusion Bill, and when they adopted democracy after 1867 for political purposes, they knew neither its feelings nor its justifications.

1 The Parliamentary Liberal Party

The Parliamentary Liberal Party

Victorian idolatry of Parliament was unfortunately accompanied by a singular lack of close reasoning about its social
elements, although great weight attached to certain loose and
oracular surmises on the subject. In an age distinguished for
renewed mental vigour in other fields of social thought, it was
remarkable how little the informed mind of the day felt any
need to subject its Parliament to a process of examination and
enquiry.

In reviews of the composition of the House of Commons,
one tendency in particular stood out. The facts were organized in the light of a particular analogy, at first sight a most
promising one. For a generation profoundly conscious of upward expansion everywhere, stopping no man knew where,
something that could not be named simply industrial or
demographic or democratic, but seeming to come from the
heart of things, a satisfactory explanation of Parliamentary
life had to be one given in terms of this general stream of
tendency.

In practice, this meant organizing one's account of British
political history, and still more the Liberal Party, round a
Parliamentary left wing that scarcely existed, and round an
equally over-dramatized and inadequate picture of intransigent conflict between the aristocracy and the middle class.
Friends and enemies alike agreed that the intellectual
Radicals, the Northern businessmen, and the militant Dissenters, were the green shoots on the tree of history; the tree
itself escaped attention. Mixed together in the blur of historical perspective, varied impressions of change became
generalized as the bourgeois theory of nineteenth-century
politics:

The predominant part of both [Houses before 1832] was
taken from the same class—from the English gentry, titled
and untitled. By the Act of 1832, this was much altered.

The aristocracy and gentry lost their predominance in the House of Commons; that predominance passed to the middle class . . . The spirit of our present House of Commons is plutocratic, not aristocratic.[1]

No fatal error of fact overthrows Bagehot's thesis. Big business, small business, and Dissent, did increase their representation in Parliament,[2] and this had a certain connection with the increasingly 'popular' tone of the Liberal Party. Yet this whole influential, familiar construction of our history in terms of progress and reaction, was an imposition of a mind looking at everything but what was before it, deriving its interpretation, with a shrinking heart, from overmuch dwelling on the democratic vista. This chapter is written in dissent from the kind of view exemplified by the quotation from Bagehot given above.

The relations between the Parliamentary Liberals and the National rank and file, and the mediating role of Gladstone's leadership therein, can well enough be described in terms of conflict between the old and the new England. But within the Parliamentary party, these terms do not mean very much,[3] that is, differences of social kind did not imply, in any general way, differences of political quality. The growth of industry and of towns that made up the Long Revolution, was far too broad and general a thing to be registered in a direct way in the social composition of Parliament. For instance, there were more Jews than Methodists in Parliament in 1868, though the Jews came from a traditional area of English life, the City, and the Methodists generally from modern industrial backgrounds. Though the landscape of England showed a huge and simple division between old and new, the kind of divisions which Parliament registered, were those not of

[1] Bagehot, *The English Constitution* (1872 edition) xxiii.

[2] The traditional holders of power also expanded their influences as things grew fatter. Lord Lansdowne became Chairman of the Great Western, Lord Salisbury of the Great Eastern Railway—the beginning of a new theme in English politics.

[3] Two Liberals of the 1860's (Buckley of Salisbury and Packe of Lincolnshire) had fought at Waterloo: one had become a railway chairman. The panics of 1859–60 involved many people to whom the Napoleonic threat was not a historic, but a personal memory.

social fact in general, but between politically functional groups, each only partially embodying a limited area of society. The wine was really in different bottles altogether.

An analysis of the Liberal Party in the House of Commons brings out its general character clearly, without at all explaining why it did what in particular it did do. 456 Liberal M.P.s sitting between 1859 and 1874 for English constituencies may be grouped as follows:

I	Large landowners[4]	198
II	Gentlemen of leisure[5]	49
III	Lawyers[6]	84
IV	Radicals[7]	20
V	Big businessmen	74
VI	Local businessmen[8]	43
VII	Militant businessmen[9]	34
		502

As will be seen, the total number of entries exceeds the number of persons analysed by forty-six, forty-six members therefore falling within two of the above categories. These were chiefly lawyers who were also businessmen or landowners, and those who were equally landowners and businessmen.

A number of further enquiries were made about these 456 Liberals sitting for English seats between 1859 and 1874. Only twenty-eight could honestly be described as Whigs by birth and connection. The picture built up by Chamberlain in the 1870's of straightforward opposition between two large blocs of Whigs and Radicals was worth nothing as a descrip-

---

[4] i.e. listed as having over £2,000 gross annual rental in Bateman's *Great Landowners of Great Britain* (4th edition, 1883): or their sons.

[5] i.e. men with no traceable professional qualifications, business interest, or landed property over £2,000 gross annual rental.

[6] i.e. all members who received a legal education and practised for some years.

[7] All Radicals who were not actually capitalists and large employers of labour.

[8] Including members of professions—accountants, doctors, solicitors—whose background was provincial municipal life.

[9] Those with a sense of mission.

tion of what the Liberal Party actually was. Not narrowly
aristocratic, the Liberal Party was, however, widely tied to the
land, the Church, and the services, which were the informal
and real basis of the aristocratic constitution and the object of
Radical attack. Of our 456 English members, 47 were patrons
of livings, and 122 held or had held rank in the services or the
militia. Both figures are in a sense minimum figures. Many
members not patrons of livings had fathers who were: many
of the non-military would later in life enter the yeomanry,
many were incapacitated by age and health, so that the men
of military inclination formed an even larger element in the
party than the figures indicate. The figure of 196 large landowners is equally an understatement of the propertied
element in the party, since it omits some mines and forests, all
Metropolitan property, all estates under £2,000 gross annual
rental, all members who alienated their estates between their
sitting and 1883, and a fair number of estates which can
plausibly, not certainly, be attributed to the family of a
member of common surname and uncertain address.

The English Liberals had then a massive and homogeneous
landed right wing, amounting to about half its numbers in
England (and to a similar proportion in Ireland and Wales,
and a greater one in Scotland). 113 relatives of peers, 47
patrons of livings, 198 large landowners, 122 men of military
connection—such figures do not of themselves return a freez-
ing no to the identification of the Liberal Party with progress,
but it is not ungenerous to construe them as tokens of strong
involvement with the (aristocratic and territorial) *status quo.*

However, about half the Liberal Party had no direct territorial connections. But this half of the party by no means met
the other half with an equal and opposing force. It was not
in any straightforward way middle class: a great number of
lawyers and big businessmen had acquired an aristocratic
education and tone and belonged as much to the aristocracy
as if they were landed proprietors. That is, they were
unshakably established in Clubland. Nor did middle-class
intrusion into Parliament proceed chiefly by way of political
radicalism. This other half of the Liberal Party, can only be
described as a random collection of residual elements whose
sole common feature was their landlessness. Amongst those

who had neither landed nor business interests, the eighty-
four lawyers and the forty-nine gentlemen of leisure dwarf
the mere twenty genuine Radical politicians and agitators.
Similarly among the business interests, the great majority had
no militant desire for real change. Against thirty-four Radical
businessmen of the Samuel Morley type, must be set seventy-
four big businessmen and forty-three local businessmen,
whom it is impossible to conscript as groups into the category
of middle-class Radicalism.

The Radical campaign within the Liberal Party was sustained by extremely few members of Parliament: chiefly, in
fact, by the twenty Radical politicians and by the thirty-four
Radical employers. No other group gave consistent support
to a policy of change, though each naturally had a peppering
of individuals willing to co-operate with the Radicals. It is
seriously arguable that the front bench was the most practically effective Radical group in the party, not in its speculative opinions, perhaps, but because of its greater contact
with imperious administrative and electoral necessities. The
territorial citadel of the Liberal right wing was quite intact
in the 1860's. Its strength was augmented by the way the bulk
of the non-territorial section of the party looked for political
and social leadership to the territorial section and identified
their interests with its own. Most of the middle-class intruders
blended into the aristocratic landscape—or wished to. The
important division in the Liberal Party was not an equal one
between business and land in the House of Commons, but
between the great majority of all social elements in the
House, and a minute Radical minority of about ten per cent
acting in spasmodic conjunction with 'the people', 'public
opinion', and the front bench, to achieve a little progress.
Eppur si muove; the overwhelming majority, with their spirit
of accommodation and repose, were overcome by the remnant, and calculation, reason, and Gladstone, liberated the
party from what, in any social analysis, seemed to be its very
self.

*   *   *

The Liberal peerage were a class on their own, fairly aloof
even from those groups most akin to them like the Whig

M.P.s in the Commons, the Liberal landed gentry, and the administrative class. The parent stem of the Liberal peerage was the old Whig oligarchy, with a few new branches dependent upon it, united with similar Whig connections in Scotland and Ireland. Its structure can be illustrated by a table:

THE LIBERAL PEERAGE IN THE 1860's[10]

Group		Total Rental £	Average Rental £
I	32 English Whig magnates	1,736,000	54,000
II	39 English Whig gentry	710,000	18,000
III	21 Scottish landowners	682,000	32,000
IV	33 Irish landowners	527,000	16,000
V	13 Anglo-Irish landowners	277,000	21,000
VI	2 families of commercial origin	69,000	35,000
VII	7 promoted politicians	51,000	7,000
VIII	2 revived peerages	21,000	11,000
IX	6 Whig cadets	47,000	8,000
X	7 judicial peerages	11,000	1,500
XI	6 military and official titles	No traceable land	
XII	16 English landowners converted since 1845	650,000	41,000
	184 titles	4,781,000	26,000

Some points bearing considerably on the structure of the Liberal Party may be made from this table. Firstly, there was very great inequality of wealth within the peerage. Secondly, the Whig magnates, especially in England, had an undiluted ascendancy and cohesion which no new group even remotely threatened. Thirdly, as many as a quarter of the Liberal peerage held land in Ireland; in addition to whom, there were many Irish peers not members of the House of Lords who, like Palmerston, were also Irish landowners and Liberals. Many of the Irish Liberal peers rallied cheerfully round Gladstone in 1869–70; but the involvement of so much of the

[10] This table is based on Bateman's *Great Landowners*, 4th edition, 1883; G. E. Cokayne, *The Complete Peerage*; and *Dod's Parliamentary Companion*, 1860–70.

peerage in Ireland was in general a handicap to the Liberal Party. Fourthly, the numbers of converts to the Liberal Party during the generation of its greatest success was not very large. Those converted between 1845 and 1870 (Abingdon, Ailesbury, Audley, Calthorpe, Camden, Chichester, Churchill, Cleveland, de Grey, De Tabley, Dudley, Harris, Harrowby, Newcastle, Sydney, and Wodehouse) were converts worth having. There were ten other cases of conversion, involving Irish and Scottish families (Airlie, Argyll, Carysfort, Clare, Essex, Fife, Huntly, Kingston, Massereene, Portsmouth). Nevertheless, only twenty-six out of 184, or about one seventh, of the Liberal peerage arose from a change of family allegiance between 1845 and 1870.

It would therefore seem the Liberalism of the peerage was generally a family heirloom.[11] The attraction of the permanent majority party for men of nebulous views, important in building up the Liberal Party in the Commons, did not count for much in the Lords; indeed, the great Whig families had been better party men in adversity than they were in their mid-century prosperity. It was not contemporary feelings,[12] but allegiances acquired between 1794 and 1832, and not easily cast aside, that kept together a large Liberal Party in the Lords till 1886. There is certainly much evidence for the political enervation of the Liberal peerage. There was an extraordinary want of dignity in the pleading tone that Granville, the Liberal leader, had to adopt to men still *in statu pupillari*. Lansdowne went straight from a scapegrace university career to the Liberal front bench; Rosebery, about the same period, was asked to second the Address while still an undergraduate.[13] The use of these expedients to keep a party together suggests that, in a hopeless position, the Liberal leaders sought at best to maintain a travesty of a political party in the House of Lords. The casualness of some of the proceedings at this level was extraordinary.

[11] The Catholic peerage, for instance, was traditionally Whig, in memory of 1828.

[12] Party pride—as distinct from belief—was strong. In 1867 the whole body of Liberal peers walked out of the House on a point of honour.— Lord E. Fitzmaurice, *Life of Granville*, I, 515.

[13] Crewe, *Rosebery* (1931), I, 41.

[Lord Brownlow] . . . also wished to join the Liberal Party, but strong a Liberal though my father was, he persuaded him to abandon the idea, for he said, one vote more or less in the House of Lords was not worth dissensions in a happily united family.[14]

There was a great deal of nominal Liberalism on the Liberal benches. Some Liberals, like Monteagle and Clanricarde, were in a perpetual state of disaffection: many of the Palmerstonians, like Lord Overstone,[15] whom Palmerston nearly put in his Cabinet, were supporting Tory candidates by 1865. Those men of 1832 who felt strongly about what Overstone called 'the old and true constitutional creed of the Liberal Party' were exactly those who were most averse to Gladstonian Liberalism; while those who could accept Gladstonian Liberalism, like Rosebery and Lansdowne, often did so initially more from willingness to oblige than from any political motive. In either case, the Liberal peerage represented a purely negative element in any calculations of what was to be done.

The detachment of the Liberal peers was heightened by their rather loose connection with the party in the Commons. Out of 456 Liberal M.P.s sitting for English seats between 1859 and 1874, only 114 were related to the peerage; only fifteen out of seventy-one Scottish members in the same period were related to the peerage.[16] Of these, obviously a great many were not related to the Liberal peerage in a politically significant way. Hence at least half, and probably three quarters, of the Liberal large landowners in the Commons, were not politically connected with the Liberal peerage. The history of the Liberal Right can no more be written in terms of an aristocratic connection, than that of the Left in terms of doctrinaire Radicalism. The Liberal Right represented a very broad sweep of national opinion; the peerage was an undigested, aloof group within it. Its most positive and interesting characteristic was its enormous

[14] Sir G. Leveson-Gower, *Years of Content, 1858–86* (1940), 12.

[15] *Life of Lord Wantage, by his wife* (1907), 167.

[16] i.e. members who (a) were sons of a peer, or of a daughter or sister of a peer, (b) who married the daughter or sister of a peer.

income—about ten per cent of the whole national rental—and its most important action was its refusal to put that income at the disposal of the party. Any one of two dozen Whigs could have met the whole expenses of the party, yet their combined contributions left the party seriously short of money, to its certain electoral loss.[17] Of the Marquess of Westminster, one of the richest Whig peers, his son wrote: '. . . he does not take any interest whatever in politics, and now less than ever.' Though of the twenty-eight noblemen owning over 100,000 acres in Great Britain and Ireland, as many as thirteen or fourteen were Liberal[18] in 1870, the Tories were in fact very much better supported by their rich men.

The papers of the Liberal Whips show the Whig nobility in a poor light, as expecting to take office and honours without giving anything in return. Argyll, for instance, gave £100 to the election fund:[19] his gross rental was about £50,000. Glyn wanted a fund of £10,000 to £15,000 for the election, but on the eve of the election he had only £5,000, all of which was appropriated: '. . . hitherto Brooks Club has done what was needful, but the times are changed.'[20] It saddened him to see 'the utter apathy of those who are rich and who have had all they can get out of the party and who will do nothing. . . . I wish Brooks Club was shut up—it does positive harm.'[21] The Liberal peerage, even in Palmerston's day, did not support their party as the Tory peers did theirs.

The Whig peers, tenuously connected with their own party in the Commons, stratified among themselves by enormous inequalities of wealth, were further detached from Liberal politics by their economic interests and by a technicality of constitutional law. On the first count, it must be noted that the peerage still almost completely excluded industrial wealth,[22] the Strutt peerage of 1856 being a flash in the pan,

[17] v. H. J. Hanham, *Elections and Party Management* (1959), 26–7.

[18] Calculated from G. E. Cokayne, *Complete Peerage*, VI, 713, and *Dod* for 1870.

[19] Glyn to Gladstone, 16 September 1868; B.M. Add. mss. 44,347 f. 169.

[20] Glyn to Gladstone, 4 September 1868; ibid., f. 151.

[21] Glyn to Gladstone, 22 September 1868; ibid., f. 175.

[22] See R. E. Pumphrey, 'The Introduction of Industrialists into the Peerage', *American Historical Review*, LXV, 1959, 1–16.

and that not only was its capital invested in land, but its fortunes had arisen in the first place from land.

A peculiarity of the constitution served to isolate the Liberal peerage. It was claimed by Lord Granville in 1867 that:

> . . . with regard to this House, he [Derby] has a power almost superior to the Queen's prerogative of making peers . . . by practically having the selection of Scottish and Irish representatives . . . That power, I may add, he has exercised with merciless severity towards the minority of both these Peerages; for no individual, whatever his position, character, or ability, has the slightest chance . . . unless his political opinions perfectly coincide with those of the noble Earl.[23]

So far as this allegation was true—it cannot easily be checked —it would mean that the Tory peerage had an automatic majority of forty-four votes. Hence, though the Tory working majority in the Lords in 1868 was said to be about sixty to seventy,[24] the English peerage was much more nearly equally divided than the votes would indicate. The Liberal peerage was significant not for what it did or did not do, nor for its retardative effect, but as an emblem of the hold of a mechanical Liberal orthodoxy over a typical body of rich and unadventurous men, and of the way a large party may be built up round a very small core of belief. Piquantly, the chief cause of lukewarm orthodoxy[25] in 1860 was the espousal of violent heterodoxy by one's family sixty years before; but this hereditary twist apart, the situation in the Lords registered well enough the general force of convention drawing the normal man of wealth towards the Liberal Party.

[23] E. Allyn, *Lords versus Commons* (1931), 83.

[24] Roy Jenkins, *Mr Balfour's Poodle* (1954), 12: quoting Fitzmaurice, *Granville*, II, 16.

[25] '. . . poor old Liberal hacks . . . , whose real self belongs to a kind of negative Hellenism—a state of moral indifferency without intellectual ardour . . .'—M. Arnold, *Culture and Anarchy* (1935 edition), 173.

THE PUBLIC MEN

It is extraordinarily difficult to strike a just balance between adulation and disparagement when discussing the Liberal front bench. In their austere rectitude and their regard for the conclusions of argument, they represent a high-water mark of the conception of public duty; yet with the objectivity and disinterestedness of their administrative manners went a habit of procrastination and of calculating the minimum of concession with the least show of determination. In putting public before party ends, they took real political risks and showed their fundamental detachment from party ethics: as Clarendon wrote about Irish lands: '. . . whether we do little or much we are sure to discontent everybody in Ireland and we had better therefore satisfy our consciences by doing what is just and right between the contending parties.' Nothing could be more admirable than the way ministers stuck to their principles at the cost of much-needed votes:

> We were no doubt financially right in putting an end to the Galway contract, but I fear we shall prove to have been politically wrong. . . . The Irish members must act as they choose, and we are quite ready to face the result.[26]

The other cases where political interest and administrative honour clashed were also settled in favour of administrative honour, the refusal of Wood and Villiers to turn India and the Poor Law upside down for the benefit of Lancashire being the main example. Lowe embodied zeal for truth and right reason in public administration in a peculiarly unqualified way, but his politically suicidal ideas of public policy differed only from those of colleagues[27] through his want of dullness, Gladstone, for instance, supporting his Revised Code of 1862 as a 'great and salutary reform'.[28]

Criticism must turn, not on this admirable, and scarcely

[26] Palmerston to Russell, 25 May 1861: Russell Papers, P.R.O. 30/22/21.

[27] The Cabinet memoranda on Lowe's Revised Code are in the Russell Papers.

[28] P. Guedalla, ed., *Gladstone and Palmerston: Correspondence 1851–1865* (1928), 293.

infringed loyalty to a political ideal, but on the nature, adequacy, and extent of application of that ideal. Unfortunately, that ideal, served with a devotion worthy of a greater cause, was essentially negative: it was an ideal of purity, of justice which merged into indifference, which represented a fear that the old evils might, like the cholera, some day return, rather than an honest attempt to press ahead with the suppression of electoral bribery and appointment by patronage. That men of enormous wealth, with every pleasure at their command, should undertake excruciatingly dull public work in time they could well have used in attending to their estates (the Newcastle, Clarendon, Gladstone, and Devonshire estates were in a parlous state), was one of the glories of Victorian public life, but it was glory that shed its light unevenly. Broadly, where the State, public finance, administration, and Imperial government were concerned, the Executive brooked no infringement of the highest standards, whether attempted by vested interests or by party politicians. In this area of public life, as Lowe said, the ideal of the Liberal Party 'consists in a view of things undisturbed and undistorted by the promptings of interest or prejudice, in a complete independence of all class interests, and in relying for its success on the better feelings and higher intelligence of mankind.'[29] To an extraordinary extent, the discussions of the Cabinet did take this tone (so untypical of the ardour and animosity of party Liberalism); as was once said of Argyll by his son, they were generally willing 'to adopt a policy of examination and inquiry'. In questions of administration, the administrators might be more radical than the Radicals.[30] But where party advantage, the condition of England, and class interest were at stake, men who dismissed clerks and put down contractors with warm conviction, rarely did more than take residence in the capacious doctrine of circumstances.

[29] A. P. Martin, *Life and Letters of the Rt. Hon. Robert Lowe, Viscount Sherbrooke* (1893), II, 445.

[30] e.g. in the case of Bright's curious opposition to opening the Civil Service to competition in 1870 (Morley, *Gladstone*, 1903, II, 315). Bright was 'not very keen' on a corrupt practices bill in the 1880's: A. Ramm, *Pol. Corr. of Granville and Gladstone 1876–1886*, I, 339.

The Liberal front bench had two creeds: one of sound and pure administration in what touched the State—its aggressive creed; one of fatalism and opportunism as regards everything else. Party Liberalism—the popular slogans for which the executive had reluctantly to act as impresario—it did not believe. It believed, very strongly, in the old aristocratic ideal of 'civil and religious liberty', but this was no longer a *casus belli* in politics. The great new nostrums of popular provincial Liberalism, Free Trade apart, could never appeal to the aristocratic leadership as pure libertarianism had done, and Cabinet and party were bound together more by mutual advantage than by common cause. For the party, the Cabinet were the necessary and irreplaceable men; for the Cabinet, party was a lever to gain support for policies essentially administrative in inspiration. The Cabinet were not so much opposed to Reform, National Education, the Ballot, Church Rates Abolition, and all the other panaceas of party politics, as unable to see such matters as bearing on Imperial government till they became irresistible. Their quarrel with the Tories arose from their sense of responsibility, not their Liberalism; they simply could not believe the Tories were competent to guide the destinies of a great empire, and maintain a high standard of departmental administration. They had some grounds for this belief.

What the incorruptible fatalists on the Liberal front bench found so objectionable in Tory opportunism, was their free and genial exploitation of the state for party ends, just as the Tories were rightly shocked by the Whigs' exploitation of popular politics to serve the ends of state. The Liberals, hardened by office, regarded the outside world with cordial hostility and suspicion. Gladstone's phrase about the Ulster Presbyterians 'nosing about for public money' hit off this attitude, as did Bright's agreement: 'Ireland is never unanimous but on one thing—getting something from the Imperial Exchequer.'[31] Ungenerosity became a passion and a cause. All contemporaries agreed that the Tories were more accommodating with subsidies and appointments, contracts and magistracies; that, unlike the Whigs, they were not born with no on their lips, that they did not have the professionalism,

[31] Bright to Gladstone, 15 October 1869: B.M. Add. mss. 44,112 f. 90.

the smell of ink and paper, that hung about the Liberal front bench. For instance, the Liberals were wont to assume that young Lord Stanley, being a natural bureaucrat, was therefore not a Tory at all. The natural irresponsibility of Tory ministers seeking easy popularity in a short term of office— and not facing such results as the £9,000,000 bill for the Abyssinian War—greatly helped Liberal ministers to feel that by making reforms they hardly cared for, they were preserving the *sine qua non* of good government, a Liberal ministry: 'You know I have no party feelings and care only for the *res publica*, so I have done and shall continue to do all in my power to prevent mischief.'[32] Gladstone's reluctance to spend money was matched by equally reluctant attitudes in other departments: 'I am most anxious not to make the appointment of Magistrates a political or party question. Nothing . . . can tend more to degrade the bench . . .'[33]

When the Conservatives did take office, the Liberals felt it their duty to guide their prentice steps: a Conservative politician was loud in his praise of the way

> they had helped the incoming Conservatives with information, each in the department which he had managed, to transact their business at starting, really anxious, not for party advantage, but for the proper transaction of the business of the country.[34]

Time and again Liberal ministers gave up to mankind what was meant for party.

The paradox between this attitude of being *au-dessus de la mêlée* and their strong party loyalty was only apparent, their party loyalty being not to the popular Liberal Party in general, but to their colleagues. Some analysis of their *esprit de corps* is called for. It was based, firstly, on their detachment from pride of order, from colossal wealth, and their freedom

[32] Clarendon to the Duchess of Manchester, 21 March 1859: *My Dear Duchess, Social and Political Letters to the Duchess of Manchester, 1858–1869*, ed. A. L. Kennedy (1956), 45. Here Clarendon, often caricatured as hungry for office, was in fact against a factious dismissal of the Tories.

[33] Duchy of Lancaster papers, Liverpool file: Sir George Grey to Mr Ewart, 11 August 1860.

[34] *Letters of Lord Blachford*, ed. G .E. Marindin (1896), 276.

from belonging to any wider national group. The great bulk of the front bench were landowners or relations of landowners, or belonged to the professional class, like Lowe, which had identified itself with the landed class.[35] Even the plutocratic element, Goschen, Childers, lacked nothing of aristocratic *ton*. Gladstone, Cardwell, Milner-Gibson, and W. E. Baxter, though commoners, were all large landowners. Yet, although the poorest of the front benchers, Clarendon, Sir George Grey, and Milner-Gibson had about £3,000 a year in landed income alone, or thirty times the wage of a skilled artisan, most public men compared themselves with the Whig peers, with their Himalayan incomes, and consequently genuinely felt themselves poor. They stood to the great Whig families as Burke did to Rockingham.

> Lord Canning is certainly not a rich man. . . . The Duke of Somerset is far from wealthy—Lord Russell we know has very limited means. Lord Shaftesbury has a very slender income. Lord Fitzwilliam . . . is of course well able to pay any Price . . .[36]

Clarendon, the most right wing of the Whigs, could nevertheless write of 'the hideous selfishness which wealth generates, and which has always made me content with being poor'.[37] Gladstone and Bright certainly looked upon themselves as relatively poor men. Childers and Goschen gave up their prospect of great wealth on taking up office. To sum up the argument, though their incomes were nothing to complain of, though they were the equals socially and in education of the greatest houses in the land, the administrators felt themselves to be bound in common by ability alone, to represent the ascendancy of intelligence alone and not of property, and in a curious way, since they were often the poorest in the

[35] Even Lowe, the militant bureaucrat, much preferred 'the invaluable superintendence of the gentry and clergy' in education to 'indifferent or incompetent local bodies' or central direction: Martin, *Life of Lowe*, II, 215–16, quoting an article by Lowe in the *Quarterly Review*, July 1867.

[36] Palmerston to Gladstone, 21 January 1862: P. Guedalla, ed., *Gladstone and Palmerston*, 198.

[37] Maxwell, *Clarendon*, II, 348. Clarendon in 1867 still called the ballot 'that greatest of abominations'.—ibid., II, 334.

circles in which they moved, they had a fellow-feeling for the resentments of others.

Though the social tone of the Cabinet was set by their connection, direct or indirect, with the landed class, they were rarely, unlike the Tories, landowners and nothing else. Only Argyll and Somerset represented the pure types of magnate and country gentleman respectively, and Argyll's case is complicated by a streak of intellectualism in him which prevented him from simply mirroring the position of such Dukes as Richmond and Buccleuch in Tory cabinets. Gladstone was a considerable coalowner, Granville was not a landowner at all but an ironmaster and the largest employer of labour in Hanley,[38] with a pocket interest in the French treaty. Hartington was the heir to a property which was at least as much industrial as agricultural. Cardwell and Gladstone retained Liverpool business connections. Clarendon, Russell, Palmerston, and Milner-Gibson were town politicians first, landowners second. Lowe, who wrote for *The Times* till 1867, was thought of by his colleagues as its representative.[39] The front bench, in short, recruited from a variety of different milieus, and the only common quality being ability, formed a detached milieu of its own without outside allegiance.

There was no real bar against business. Childers was advised by old Sir Charles Wood, 'to aim at the London and North Western chairmanship. No impediment to office, rather the contrary.'[40] Childers in fact became in the intervals of a political career, chairman of an English bank and an Indian railway, deputy chairman of an Australian bank and a director of several English railways. Similarly, though there

[38] 'The sanguine Puss, however (who as an Iron Master is enthusiastic about the Treaty) . . .'—Clarendon to the Duchess of Manchester, 6 February, 1860; *My Dear Duchess*, ed. A. L. Kennedy (1956), 89. For Granville's position in Hanley, where he paid a weekly wages bill of £5,000 at this time, see E. J. D. Warrilow, *A Sociological History of Stoke on Trent* (1960), 265. Delane wrote of Granville's spirits falling with the price of iron (Delane to Dasent, 29 August, 1864; Dasent, *Life of Delane*, II, 122). In the 1880's Rosebery and others helped to save Granville from bankruptcy due to German competition.

[39] For the opinion of Granville and Wood to this effect, see Walpole, *Russell*, II, 409.

[40] S. Childers, *The Life and Correspondence of the Rt. Hon. Hugh C. E. Childers, 1827–1896* (1901), I, 99.

were endless objections to Goschen's appointment in 1866, his business background was never mentioned as one of them. Goschen and Childers together epitomize what may be called the Liberalism of the Executive—the assumption, on the part of men with little interest in Liberal Party politics, that State business was most safely transacted by the Liberals.

Again, just as the man of Cabinet rank left his background and economic interests behind him on advancement, so political background was very largely disregarded by Palmerston, Russell, and Gladstone, in whose hands appointments lay. The problem for them was not, as outsiders thought, to secure jobs and power for political friends, but how to make the best use of the talents of all sections for the purpose of public business. Palmerston especially looked at appointments in an impersonal light:

> Hartington's bearing and his being the son of the Duke of Devonshire, will tend to keep in order the Tory Colonels and Generals who keep barking at us . . . To satisfy our friends below the gangway, I propose to fill up the office at the Admiralty vacated by Hartington by some one of their number who will be a pledge to them that due economy will be observed in that Branch. I am inclined to think of Stansfield . . . It was he who moved the vote of economy last year. . . .[41]

When Sidney Herbert threatened resignation on a point of expenditure, Palmerston argued the case in terms of the public interest rather than of political character: 'We must not part with him for so small a sum. He is by far the best administrator of Army Matters I have ever known, and I am sure I should not know where to look for another half as good.'[42] It was Palmerston of all people who opened the way to the front bench for the Radicals. His appointments of Forster, Villiers, Gibson, Stansfeld, and Gilpin led on to those of Bright, Ayrton, Baxter, Playfair, Winterbotham, and Harcourt. Radicalism became in the 1860's a high road, not to

[41] Palmerston to Russell, 20 October 1863: Russell Papers, P.R.O. 30/22/14.
[42] Palmerston to Gladstone, 12 April 1860: *Gladstone and Palmerston*, ed. P. Guedella, 131.

the wilderness, but to office. The personal quality of the Radicals changed rapidly from lunatic fringe to a cluster of brilliance and ambition, once office lay ahead: young and ambitious men like Dilke and Trevelyan saw their course clearly. After 1868, Gladstone was prone to appoint Whigs over the heads of better men, in order to carry out his theory of aristocracy: but in the Whig heyday, there was no such double standard. Where the aristocrats could expect favour, was in the age at which they entered office. They had a twenty years' start. But once in office, the same standard of competence was expected from all. The Cabinet carried very few passengers or cronies; the position of such weak appointments as Clanricarde, Vernon Smith, or Stanley of Alderley was an uncomfortable one. Appointments which smacked of favour were often nothing of the sort. Lowe complained: 'that the Cabinet was reserved exclusively for men of particular connection and family. Had he been a Radical, he might indeed have had it, but for a man of moderate views, the Cabinet was closed.'[43] In fact Lowe was valued especially by a Whig section in the Cabinet, and the promotion of Lord de Grey to the War Office on Sidney Herbert's death, which had violently annoyed Lowe, was probably due, not to birth, but to the reputation de Grey—Florence Nightingale's candidate—had gained as a military reformer. Those who entered the Cabinet less on the strength of their individual character, than as representatives of some group within the party, were few and unimportant. Molesworth, Gibson, M. T. Baines, Goschen, Sir Benjamin Hall, were the chief appointments of this type. The great exception was Bright: what Bright brought to the Cabinet was not weight in counsel or departmental ability, but political support. But in general the composition of the Executive was decided by administrative, not by party political criteria. This assessment by Gladstone of one of his 'new men' was typically non-political: 'I have seen Childers, who pleases me exceedingly, not only by his capacity for work, but by the general manliness and unselfishness of his character as it comes out in affairs.'[44] The result of the catho-

---

[43] Hardinge, *Carnarvon* (1925), I, 337.
[44] Gladstone to Russell, 31 January 1866; Russell Papers, P.R.O. 30/22/16.

licity of the front bench was its near monopoly of talent. This, and the lack of competition within it, gave it great collective strength *vis-à-vis* its followers, whom it could quietly ignore even when the great majority of them were opposed to the policy of the Executive. Gladstone looked on the solidarity of the Executive as a matter of rule: 'The next most serious thing to admitting a man into the Cabinet, is to leave a man out who has once been in.'[45] And the same attitude underlay his remark on Goschen's appointment:

> My opinion is very strong against the disturbance of the order of promotion in the official body, unless upon grounds of unquestionable superiority of talent or service . . . Now you have lately introduced into the Cabinet a most able man: but you cannot be unaware that the cohesion of the corps is somewhat weakened.[46]

The Liberal Party in no sense chose its leaders. In the compact which arose from the meeting at Willis's Rooms in 1859, the Parliamentary party only ratified by acclamation an arrangement already made between the leaders. Only in the Cabinet changes of 1872–4 did the idea of altering the Cabinet to suit the electoral needs of the party make its appearance. The election of Hartington as leader was a colossal innovation, though the impossibility of connecting Hartington with innovation minimized the shock. It was a big stage towards absorbing the front bench in party and reducing its prime responsibility to the crown.

The whole tradition of the Executive led them to look more to the good opinion of their colleagues than of their supporters. Granville, for instance, 'always felt the Cabinet to be a great bond between him and those with whom he has served' and only Graham remained a stranger to him after being in a Cabinet together.[47] Their solidarity was put to good use in putting through policies and legislation, chiefly on Imperial and social matters, on which the political party

[45] Morley, *Gladstone* (1903 edition), II, 416.
[46] Gladstone to Russell, 1 February 1866: Russell Papers, P.R.O. 30/22/16.
[47] *Journals and Letters of Reginald Viscount Esher*, ed. M. V. Brett (1934), I, 60.

had no real opinion. An Executive simply drawing on current political ideas to interpret its work would have had no policy at all over half the range of government. This inadequacy in party politics set the Executive free to act as the representative of expert and informed opinion on the one hand, and of interests and opinions unrepresented in Parliament on the other. The lines of policy which actually emerged are described below, in the final section of this book, and the limited role played in policy making by party politics further analysed there. Considering the front bench here simply as a political group, we have tried to show only how both its internal constitution and its external ties inclined to make it, as it appeared to Bagehot, the embodiment of government by rational discussion.

THE WHIGS

There were three distinct groups of Whigs: the first formed the bulk of the Liberal peerage, the second an important section of the party leadership, the third section, however, being a quite unimportant section of the House of Commons. The back-bench Whigs were unimportant because they were very few in number, because they had nothing in common apart from their relationship with the historic Whig houses, and because they personally lacked weight. The Cabinet Whigs in no sense owed their position to the support of a strong Whig bloc on the back benches, nor did they show much sign of caring how many of their cousins sat behind them. Chamberlain's imputation of the existence of a cohesive and militantly aristocratic Whig caucus within Parliament was only the rhetoric of ambition; the true explanation of Whig predominance, which lay in their power of serving the State and in their immense concentration of official experience, was not acceptable to Radical self-esteem. In fact the back-bench Whigs represented all shades of political opinion, and were in general politics a marginal, not a directive force.

There were two exceptions to their general unimportance.

The back-bench Whigs had one historic moment—1866: and they had one historic function—it fell to this one small group of far from extraordinary young men to make or mar the experiment of government by a progressive aristocracy under a popular constitution. In 1866 it was definitely by Whigs sitting for seats under aristocratic influence that the Reform Bill was defeated. But that is to put it too simply. Really, it fell to the Lansdownes and Grosvenors, with their safe seats and self-confidence, to represent a much more general reticence about Reform within the party—a reticence sincerely opposed by Radical Whigs like Amberley and Lord Frederic Cavendish—and having expressed this reticence, the Adullamite Whigs returned to the Liberals, who had largely agreed with them. The Irish Church debate of April 1868 showed that, of all the thirty or so Adullamites, only Lord Elcho still remained voting with the Conservative ministry, and the Liberal Party again became of one mind.[48]

If the Whig opposition to Reform in 1866, however decisive, did not represent a secession of extremists, their conduct over the period 1860–85 was equally far from guerrilla warfare against their party, and in the general drift of the upper class towards the Tory Party, the Whigs did not lead the way, but were preceded by *The Times*, the suburbs, and a great part of the business world and the universities. In the 1860's it was the smart thing in Society to be Palmerstonian. The 1860's, G. O. Trevelyan said, were the last decade to see anything of Society in the old sense of the word —'not a mere juxtaposition in one city of parallel sets of wealthy people, but one supreme set recognized by all others as being Society *par excellence*'.[49] That one supreme set was a Whig set. On the Tory side, Disraeli indicated the rusticity of his colleagues by saying none of them knew how to give a good dinner; on the Whig side, there was what the American Motley called the perfection of human society. The break came in the middle of the 1860's. With Palmerston's death, the great salons of Lady Palmerston, Lady Molesworth, and Lady Waldegrave, with their connections with the great quarterlies, the *Morning Post*, *The Times*, and the Holland

[48] J. E. Denison, *Notes from My Journal when Speaker* (1900), 223.
[49] G. M. Trevelyan, *Sir G. O. Trevelyan, a Memoir* (1932), 66.

House *littérateurs*, lost their political centrality at the same time as a new social world, essentially opposed to all they held dear, emerged around Marlborough House. But until that happened, the Whigs held the key to society, and their price was a political one:

> [Lady Palmerston's] Saturday evenings were exclusively Whig, and she was served by an able staff of aides-de-camp. Mr Abraham Hayward, chief of the staff, kept her informed of everybody who came to London and ought to be invited to her house, whose political support was worth having, and whose claims must not be overlooked. . . .[50]

After 1868 the Whigs in the House of Commons, if they remained with the Liberals, were likely to do so on a basis of conviction. No longer riding on the crest of fashion, affected by the idealism of the new university teaching and impressed by Gladstone, the younger Whigs particularly stood distinctly to the left of 'Society'. In all the great branches of Whig activity—political entertaining, selfless administration, and the propagation of the Whig cast of mind—the Whig back benchers played a very small part. If there was a Whig legacy, it was in foreign policy. It was the Whigs, not the Tories, who preserved and popularized the foreign policy of the aristocratic epoch. When Russell spoke of 'keeping up the traditional policy of England', he was not thinking of Fox. But this instilling of the traditional wisdom of Whiggery into the public mind was performed more by the Whig historians than by the Whig politicians. The back-bench Whigs were chiefly remarkable as the raw material from which Gladstone tried, as Disraeli had dreamt of doing in his novels, to turn the theory of Platonic aristocracy into English fact.

Gladstone's real attempt to create an ideal aristocracy did not and could not work: but so far as circumstances and the men available allowed, Gladstone gained a great personal success, though one on too small a scale to affect policy. His appointments of Whips and Private Secretaries from the young historic Whigs reflected his predilections even more than his choice of Cabinet, and his relations with the young Spencers, Cavendishes, Primroses, Seymours, and Leveson-

[50] Lady St Helier, *Memories of Fifty Years* (1909), 80.

Gowers—and with his own sons—provided some of the happiest pages of reminiscences about the Grand Old Man. In 1868, two processes were only just beginning—the general drift away from the Liberals by the upper classes as a whole, including the Whigs: and the creation, by Gladstone's policy of aristocracy and personal attractiveness, of an ideal Liberal nobility, so small in fact as to be almost an extended household, which ended in a Jacobite forlornness in 1886.

The real thorns in the flesh of the Liberal Party were the self-seeking lawyers and contractors, the trade union-hating employers, shipowners, like Norwood of Hull, and mine-owners who opposed legislation from interested motives, intriguers for office, and the fanatical hawkers of Radical panaceas. Compared with these, the obstructive power of the Whigs was nothing, save on the one occasion in 1866 when they spoke honestly what half the party hid in its heart. The Whigs erred and strayed from more venial causes. Always, in the background, lay the enervation of the aristocracy through the new ease of travel, the creation of a new life of pleasure centred on London, and the divorce of the highest social life from politics about 1870. The standards of ambition and industry were lowered, as standards of pleasure and the range of interests open to a man in society increased, and the lower self of the Whigs appeared—not so much hostility to improvement as a mildly recalcitrant dilettantism—a lower self nevertheless infinitely more agreeable than those other thorns in the flesh referred to above. Gladstone, as early as 1865, 'expressed a poor opinion of the industry of the titled young generation in Parliament, and thinks they do not attend sufficiently or apply enough to their duties'.[51] Their chief fault was often simply youth.

The public were as willing to support the Whigs as Gladstone was to promote them, their wealth, in fact, making them very suitable candidates for expensive popular seats like the West Riding or Westminster. Far from being edged out of politics by Radical attrition, the Whigs went down in a blaze of popularity, greater in the 1860's than they had known at any time since the honeymoon of 1832. Macaulay in one field, Hartington in another, showed how clear the way ahead was

[51] *Records and Reminiscences of Lord Ronald Gower* (1903), 93.

for a Whig seeking public favour; and how much public demand, for the first time, exceeded supply. At a moment of unprecedented opportunity, there was an extraordinary dearth of first-rate men wanting to come to the front: the end of the Whigs was as simple as that.

*　　*　　*

The back-bench Whigs sitting in the three Parliaments from 1859 to 1874, for English and Welsh seats only, were as follows:

Amberley, Viscount—Nottingham
Bury, Viscount—Berwick, Norwich
Cavendish, Hon. G. H.—North Derbyshire
Cavendish, Hon. W. G.—Buckinghamshire
Cavendish, Lord F. C.—West Riding
Coke, Hon. H. C. W.—Norfolk
Euston, Earl of—Thetford
Fitzmaurice, Lord E.—Calne
FitzRoy, Lord F. J.—Thetford
FitzWilliam, C. W. W.—Malton
Fortescue, Hon. D. F.—Andover
Gower, Hon. E. F. Leveson—Bodmin
Grosvenor, Earl—Chester
Grosvenor, Lord Richard—Westminster
Grosvenor, Lord Robert—Flintshire
Hartington, Lord—North Lancashire, Radnor
Howard, Hon. C. W. G.—Cumberland East
Howard, Lord E. F.—Arundel
Leveson-Gower, G. W.—Reigate
Milton, Viscount—West Riding
Paget, Lord A. H.—Lichfield
Paget, Lord C. E.—Sandwich
Ponsonby, A. G. J.—Cirencester
Raynham, Lord—Tamworth
Russell, A. J. E.—Tavistock
Russell, F. C. H.—Bedfordshire
Worsley, Lord—Grimsby

(Total, 27)

Of course, all landowners, or all those on the Liberal side

who were not popular Radicals, were and are sometimes
referred to as Whigs. This is to make the term so inclusive as
to be meaningless. Similarly, it would be quite impossible to
define the Whigs in terms of subscription to anything so
nebulous as Whiggery. The course followed, therefore, has
been simply to list above those who were Whigs by connection with a historic Whig family. This classification reveals
some important points. It shows that only about one eighth of
the eighty-one County representatives on the Liberal side
between 1859 and 1874 were themselves from historic Whig
families. It shows that the massive support of the lesser
country gentlemen was as important to the Whigs as to the
Tories; more so, perhaps, as the great Whigs were so prone to
withdraw, sulking. Also, the Whigs did not even occupy all
the seats that patronage gave them,[52] let alone those the
public would probably have given them had they come
forward. Whig influence, consequently, was felt as much
through territorial influence as through direct family representation in the House. Above all, these figures make it clear
that Whig influence in Parliament could never have rested
on numerical power. In fact the Whig stronghold was the
Cabinet, not the nomination seats, and their power derived
from their competence, their social prestige, and the esteem
of their colleagues and their party.

GENTLEMEN OF LIBERAL VIEWS

What in the parties of the French Revolution was called 'the
Plain' must of its nature be difficult to describe. Its character
was to have no character, its plan to fall in with the plans of
others. Whether every party must carry such ballast is an
open question, but half the Parliamentary Liberal Party of
the 1860's may fairly be called, without any imputation on
the private character of its members, politically nondescript.
This was all to the good; since the class character of the

[52] There were twenty-three English and Welsh seats in the hands of
Liberal patrons in 1868: before 1868 there were several more.—H. J.
Hanham, *Elections and Party Management* (1959), 412.

Parliamentary party could not change with speed proportionate to the changing balance of power in the electorate and the increasing demands on government, the next best thing was that it should be nullified by an extreme unassertiveness. The weight of the few Liberals with beliefs drew along the numbers without; and the support rendered equally to Palmerston and Gladstone by the same back benchers, derived not from inconsistency of principle but from this indeterminacy of character.

An extraordinary monotony of opinion pervaded the Liberal lawyers, landowners, and businessmen, the three great castes within the party, being indistinguishable in political colour. Unlike the aristocratic right, the dissenting left, and the serious front bench, all of whom performed an educative function, the centre did not try to proselytize any brand of Liberalism. What it professed was not the views of a party, but the accepted commonplaces of the country as a whole; and office usually subtracting ability and ambition from its ranks,[53] it depended on combination with the minority sections for action and articulateness.

These ordinary back benchers who sat between 1859 and 1874 were drawn from the 198 large landowners, the eighty-four lawyers, and the forty-nine 'gentlemen of leisure', a term that will be explained in due course. But from the numbers of the landowners must be deducted the aristocratic Whigs, the front benchers who owned land, and the great industrialists and financiers who were only secondarily landowners. Some abatement, too, must be made in the number of lawyers on account of those who retired from the Bar early in life in order to manage their land or their business. A slight deduction must be made from the numbers of the gentlemen of leisure, since some of those in this category would doubtless belong in other groups if sufficient were known about them. Taking the lowest estimates of the size of these groups in the Liberal Party between 1859 and 1874, it may be concluded that out of 456 English Members analysed, about 150 were landowners, or sons of landowners, with estates of rentals of £2,000 a year or more, who neither held office nor were con-

[53] 'We have effectually subtracted the brains from below the gangway ...' wrote Bruce in 1873: Morley, *Gladstone* (1903), II, 463.

nected with the historic Whig families; about forty were gentlemen of leisure, having income, education, and position, without commercial or landed responsibilities, professional training, aristocratic connection, or government office; and about forty to fifty members were professional lawyers. Some of the more genteel and well-established businessmen, like Gurney, Grenfell, and Glyn, also belonged to the plain of the party, representing the same conventional Liberalism, the same detachment from particular interests, and bringing with them no new intellectual or social element. Perhaps 250 M.P.s altogether constituted the plain of the English party, homogeneous in its public school and university education, its social advantages, and its Anglicanism, and this preponderance of numbers made its mark on the party character. It prevented it from being a revolutionary, a democratic, a crusading or doctrinal party: but gave to the party that spirit of equity and disinterestedness, uninflamed by ardour, that was its real merit in the 1860's. The alliance of the front bench and the Radicals was more than a match for such elements of recalcitrance in the party as the aristocratic right and the self-seeking businessmen, and the function of the plain was to act as audience and jury in cases where the verdict was sure to go to those Liberal ideas which had been found to embody the spirit and experience of the age. Now, though individuals everywhere may have disinterested views on public questions, disinterestedness in the bulk necessary to supply a Parliamentary majority can only come from some specially favourable milieu. Given the conditions of mid-Victorian England—a country equally divided between agriculture and industry, with its national education sharply cut off from the life of the great towns—the mass of easy-going landowners, lawyers, and gentlemen of leisure who made up the inert majority of the Parliamentary Liberals were better fitted to be the instruments of justice towards, at least, the urban populations, than any other section of the rich. What, in terms of an ideal electoral system, was an anomalous and unjust predominance of property in general, and certain kinds of property, education, creed, and profession in particular, worked for the best in terms of the total national life.

THE SECULAR RADICALS

The Radicals found their way into Parliament through two distinct causes. One group, the secular Radicals, were individuals, in a small minority in all classes, who became Radicals through their identification with some Radical tenet. The second group were the great Radical capitalists, predominantly Dissenting, who represented the social challenge of an order collectively Radical and economically and politically powerful, no less than they stood for the uncompromising doctrines of a kind of political Calvinism. If the truculence of the Samuel Morleys, if not their quality and power of action, was only to be expected, it is less easy to account for the paucity and ragged disorder of those who, with every opinion to choose from, chose Radicalism simply because it seemed to them the truest view of things. What Chamberlain remarked in 1878 was true of almost any previous period:

> There is no party of Radicals below the gangway: their only point of agreement is the fact that each one differs in some respect or other from the leaders: but their differences among themselves are really greater than those which separate them from the front bench . . .[54]

In the 1830's men eaten up by ideas were as common as blackberries: with every subsequent decade of Liberal ascendancy, their numbers in the House dwindled to a lunatic fringe. Only in 1865, after Palmerston had opened the way to office to able Radicals, did men of birth and talents again come forward with views systematically more extreme than those of their party. Between 1840 and 1865, the theoretical secular Radicals were a symptom more of confusion in the ideas of the age, of its proneness to eccentricity, than of any vehemence of the populace. Real personal differences of view within a class, the source of the aristocratic Radicalism of the 1830's, were more and more overshadowed by the Radicalism of the great interests: of the League manufacturers, of the Dissenters, and finally of labour.

The secular Radicals of the 1860's were not a homogeneous

[54] Chamberlain to Collings, 26 February 1878: Chamberlain Papers, JC 5/16/78.

group: they perhaps never had been even in the 1830's. They were divided by generation and by background, and each background and each generation was divided by a diversity of opinion. Since the death of Joseph Hume, the Radicals had followed no Parliamentary leader: [55]

> The old Radicals who were in the House long before him [Cobden], such as Sir B. Hall, Williams, Brotherton, etc. are extremely jealous, I suspect, of his popularity and influence, and carefully abstain from doing anything that might seem to encourage the idea of his being the leader of the extreme Liberal party.

There were three generations of Radicals: the survivors of the 1830's, the League and aldermanic Radicals of the 1840's and 1850's, and the cocksure intellectuals of the 1860's. The members from the 1830's were aristocratic, Byronic, almost adventurers, like Roebuck, Berkeley, Tom Duncombe, and Villiers, perfectly disinterested nuisances in a tradition going back to 'the intrepid Fox' of the Westminster elections. There was also by contrast Slaney of Shrewsbury, a man like Chadwick, full of schemes of practical improvement, an enthusiast for drains and model cottages; and in this generation as later, the Radical economic pedant and the Radical sanitary enthusiast cancelled each other out. Surviving as institutions or jokes, as Berkeley, with his annual motion for the ballot, was considered, they had little influence on the course of events.

The new recruits to the theoretical Radicals in the 1840's and 1850's came from the Manchester School on the one hand —Cobden, Bright, Villiers, Gibson, Fox, Gilpin—and on the other from a group of Dickensian aldermen, chiefly elected by London boroughs, whose choice of principles was less happy. Duncombe, one may charitably suppose, opposed measures of sanitation from sheer exuberance of nature; but to Mr Cox, inveighing against acts which compelled householders to divert their cesspools into the sewers, principle was the royal road to popularity. Or again consider the view of Alderman Lusk, M.P., on the notorious London vestries: 'Mr Ald. Lusk said, he was in favour of local self government. The

[55] H. Richard's diary, 1853, quoted in C. S. Miall, *Life of Henry Richard* (1889), 95.

House ought not to distrust the local authorities who after all, were our own flesh and blood. The Bill unfairly reflected upon them.'[56] To such low estate, the great principles of 1832 could, and regularly did, fall.

In the 1860's there was a change for the better. Radicalism entered into a connection with labour, especially organized labour, that had been lacking before, to say the least; and it gained enormously in intellectual respectability and social prestige. Under the universal influence of Mill, Radicalism had at last become at least a possible conclusion one could carry away from university studies. Men like Dilke, Trevelyan, Fawcett, John Morley, Goldwin Smith, and Thorold Rogers, could enforce not very novel principles[57] with the whole Victorian cultural apparatus behind them, thus bridging the gap between popular Radicalism and the educated public, and placing the real case of Radicalism inescapably before such decorous and sophisticated minds as that of J. D. Coleridge. Neate, the member for Oxford, Tom Hughes, Peter Taylor of Leicester, the younger Cowen, and Jacob Bright, were outer members of the general Radical group, and, chiefly through the influence of thorough discussion, had come to feel the incontrovertibility of the Radical claim to regard every institution as merely provisional and open to argument. In all their arguments, their point of departure was *how* best to secure to the individual certain advantages. At this level, their disquisitions on oppressed nationalities, the rights of women, democracy, and the principles of church establishment, were impressive. What they lacked was any theory as to *what* they were dealing with, what their principles had to be applied to, and what forces were at work in history. This lack was serious and fraught with consequences: between 1860 and 1920 it was generally accepted that, whatever actually happened in politics, the 'principles of Liberalism' were a miscellany of vaguely humanitarian enthusiasms, chiefly for the relief of the individual from metaphysical rather than material distress. The Liberals generally

[56] *Hansard*, vol. 185, col. 1864, 14 March 1867.
[57] Mill and Fawcett were the only expert economists in the party, and they disagreed. The 'brilliant men' of the Liberal Party were fundamentally amateurs in everything.

had the better cause in these matters: but sailing under this flag, all the great part of life that could not be conscripted under the categories of humanitarianism had to be dismissed as complications or mere matters of administration. The contrast with the philosophy of the Manchester School was complete.

A coherent interpretation of the world and of history might have been found for Liberalism in the thought of Cobden. The choice, indeed, was between Cobden and nothing: for coherent thought among leading Liberals was as rarefied as the atmosphere on the moon. Consider the field of contenders. Lord John Russell enunciated epigrams concerning the constitution and national liberty; but to follow third in debate after Burke and Fox is to seem small. Mill based a pyramid of analysis on a pinpoint of information. Gladstone had tortuous theories on current politics as well as on church affairs; he combined an almost Marxist view of 'the Christian superiority of the poor' with a belief in aristocracy worthy of Sir Walter Scott or Disraeli the novelist, and he worked out for himself a system of casuistry governing the conduct of public men acting through parties. Palmerston, curiously enough, did indulge in general analysis rather like that of the Manchester School, his ideas coming from the social theories taught in the Scottish universities of his youth, but the drawback in his case was that the endeavour to comprehend was subsidiary to an attempt to justify a policy otherwise conceived, and was not linked with any corresponding theory of beneficial action. Whatever the merits of all these theories, no politician could gain from them any addition to his information about the world he had to deal with, or learn to pick out the great issues of policy and place them in relation to a vision of history.

As it was, Cobden could not fill the gap. Faced, like Gladstone and Bright, with the necessity of changing the class basis of his support late in his career, he was held back by his health, and died when on the point of leading a trade union Reform agitation. His great popularity with the masses at his death had only been won by jettisoning earlier supporters:

[Manchester] . . . was a good cradle for the League, for there were strong purses, and their owners thought they

would be replenished with Free Trade. It was one aristocracy pitted against another . . . But you know we had
but little sympathy from the 'workers' till the work was
done.[58]

The various shadow movements based on Manchester between 1847 and 1857 merely beat the air:

> . . . year after year we met and paraded ourselves as 'the
> Manchester party' but I was myself never inspired with
> much faith in our proceedings. I attended our annual
> gatherings and talked as loudly as the rest; how could I
> refuse our friend Wilson's invitation? . . . and so we went
> on till we knocked on the head last month.[59]

Family and financial troubles made him accept defeat and
absence from Parliament in 1857–9 with equanimity. 1857
was virtually, and might have been actually, the end of his
career as a Radical M.P.: 'I was sorry to hear of my election
for Rochdale. It will confer neither credit nor comfort on me.
My parliamentary and public life is over.'[60] For six months
of the year it was unsafe for him to venture out of doors or
to speak: and even in the summer, an asthmatic hoarseness
impeded his delivery. From about 1857 Cobden was, as he
wrote: 'almost as much a creature of atmosphere and tempera-
ture as a gnat or butterfly . . .'[61] He and Bright spoke far less
frequently in Parliament in the decade after the Crimean
War than in the one before:

	Cobden	Bright
1850	58	120
1855	16	57
1856	0	4
1857	0	0
1858	0	40
1859	2	44

[58] Cobden to J. B. Smith, 12 August 1857: Smith Papers, Manchester
Central Library.

[59] Cobden to J. Vaughan, 23 May 1857: Cobden Papers, Chichester,
Letter Book No. 28.

[60] Cobden to his wife, 24 May 1859: Cobden Papers, Chichester.

[61] Cobden to Gladstone, 23 February 1862: B.M. Add. mss. 44,136,
f. 178.

	Cobden	*Bright*
1860	0	87
1861	1	53
1862	29	17
1863	34	18
1864	16	25
1865	0	15

(The numbers refer, not to set speeches, but to interventions of any kind recorded in the indexes to Hansard.)

The Manchester School played no part in the formation of the Liberal Party. Its theory was none the worse for that. Cobden's pamphlets were its *Das Kapital*: Cobden its Marx. It combined a statistical patriotism (rather like that with which Chatham regarded France): 'Our only chance as a nation is in knowing in time what is sure to come from the United States' [62], with a passionate internationalism bitterly opposed to all orthodox patriotism:

> Our history must be rewritten for the last two centuries before the people will be able to deal out justice to the two aristocratic parties who have done their best to ruin a country so favoured by nature as almost to defy the effort to destroy its prosperity. [63]

Cobden's view of the English past was exactly that of Macaulay, turned upside down; his view of the future involved considerations no other man in public life could take into account. He regarded the abolition of war as Marx did that of capitalism, as the key to all other improvements, social, political, and economic. The springs of invention, the sources of pauperism, the prospects of Reform and of national education, all depended on the abandonment of the old system of aristocratic government, where the prime purpose of national organization was to indulge in wars not touching the solid and permanent interests of the country.

The principle of non-intervention, adopted by the Liberals in the 1860's in fair degree, was for them simply a natural aversion to unprofitable, remote, unrighteous, or impossible

[62] Cobden to Bright, 1 November 1853: Cobden Papers, Chichester, Letter Book 2.

[63] Cobden to J. B. Smith, 27 October 1852: Smith Papers, Manchester, Central Library.

wars. This aversion arose spontaneously, and not from either the proselytism or the political strength of the Manchester School. It was not a conversion, but an adjustment to circumstances. There was no vision behind it. How different from this kind of non-intervention was the foreign policy of Cobden:

> . . . I can already see before me as on a map, the dawning disclosure of those proceedings which perhaps by their own instrumentality, will bind together the *Countries* of Europe, as so many *Counties*, and thus convert monarchies into baronies—separated, but not divided by ring fence boundaries.
>
> . . . Into thy hands is the regeneration of this miserable system gradually falling . . . Recent events in this country have shown . . . thou hast laid down the fulcrum and seized hold of the lever which shall abolish this miserable system of exclusion and warfare, and establish that sort of intercourse which shall interweave the social sympathies of every country by and through the medicine of the selfish interests —no impracticable thing—but how enormous an object. Thy mission is this or nothing. . . .[64]

Cobden sought to change, not only the tariff, but through the tariff, the world. Instead of crying peace, he established, in the French Treaty, a *modus operandi* for creating it. Gladstone dismantled what Cobden had built.

*   *   *

Anyone wishing to find in Victorian Liberalism some aid to comprehension, some not eccentric prophecy on the world and on history, must find themselves confronted at last with Cobden. Only Cobden bound the whole miscellaneous information of his age into a few guiding generalities. No master of the Victorian cultural apparatus, he was unable to pass on his vision even to sympathizers, and in general he earned the hearty contempt of the educated. His teaching was heeded no more than the valueless radicalism of the currency reformers and the opponents of drainage. It was not embodied by the

[64] Ashworth to Cobden, 22 July 1846, presumably in reply to some manifesto not now preserved: B.M. Add. mss. 43,653, f. 93.

Nonconformist capitalists. It meant nothing to Gladstone. In painting the endless landscape of Victorian Liberalism, its only prophet must be omitted entirely from the scene.[65] By holding to his simple and puzzled version of rustic morality, without any of the strenuousness in integrity that character-ized Radical heroes like Bright, Cobden cut himself off from power and influence, but put himself in a position to say unusual things about the meaning of history in his time:

> Great is the crime in man or woman,
> Who steals the goose from off the Common,
> But who shall plead the man's excuse,
> Who steals the Common from the goose.[66]

DISSENTERS AND BUSINESSMEN

> And it is not only in moments of depression and weariness, but far more when the mind is clearest, and faith and hope in what might be strongest, that I feel intense discontent with myself and the class of educated men above the pinching of poverty. It seems as if it would be so easy to make this world so different.[67]

With these words of William Rathbone, the Liverpool mer-chant prince who was an ardent Gladstonian, astute machine politician, and founder of the District Nursing Movement, we come to the heroic element in Parliamentary Liberalism, its Radical industrialists. It is the world of Samuel Smiles, in its second generation, the fortunes having been made, but social assimilation by polite society having still to do its deadly work. Despite a constant ambiguity attaching to these authori-tarian lovers of liberty, they provided whatever element of

[65] Palmerston and the Liberal Whip agreed that a proposal for a pension to Cobden would stand no chance in Parliament.—Palmerston to Russell, 18 February 1862, in Palmerston Papers, 'Private Letter Book, 1862'.

[66] He murmured this rhyme as he lay dying.—A. Cobden-Sanderson, *Richard Cobden and the Land of the People*, 12.

[67] Diary of William Rathbone, 2 July 1871: Rathbone Papers, Liver-pool University Library.

distinct purpose there was in the party, and the general will of the populace could only express itself in agitation under their aegis.

Nearly all the English Dissenters in Parliament were businessmen, though some were also, in a secondary degree, landowners. A large part of the businessmen in Parliament were, however, not Dissenters; worse still, even in the 1860's there were a large section who were content to rest on their oars and attend to their business interests. These apostates came from three groups: the small-town businessmen of aldermanic type, out of their depth in Parliament, the big businessmen, London bankers and the like, who had made their way into Society and found life agreeable enough as it was, and those of middle rank who, militant Liberals in 1832, had come to fear for their property by the 1860's. Doulton, the porcelain manufacturer who sat for Lambeth, and Crosland, a woollen manufacturer sitting for Huddersfield, for instance, voted against Gladstone's Reform Bill in 1866, probably from consideration of their interests as employers. There were also businessmen whose personal position was not favourable to high-mindedness, like the Rothschilds and the three or four representatives of the China firm of Jardine, Matheson, and Co. who sat amongst the Liberals. There were also a few scapegrace individuals, contractors who canvassed, speculators who broke the 'eleventh commandment' and had, like Alderman Carter of Leeds, to leave hurriedly for New York, but the rogue element was remarkably small. In total numbers, the quiescent party among the businessmen—the rustics, the worldly, the fearful, and the personally interested —may have been in a majority: but it had no collective force, no spokesmen, no ideas, no institutions, no confidence or prestige, with which to arrest the mass of the Radical attack. Business as a whole was of much the same political timbre in the 1860's as later; it was only when translated into terms of Parliamentary force and of influence upon policy, that the Radicals in the business world, though few in number, became the colour most visible in the spectrum. Without doubt, there were about thirty to forty great capitalists, Dissenters almost to a man (Mundella and Platt were the principal exceptions), who, like Rathbone in the passage quoted above, sighed for a higher and better civilization, which they conceived chiefly in terms of the material welfare of the labouring classes, and saw in Liberal politics a chief means of achieving this. Education would combat intemperance, pauperism, and perhaps trade unionism, and education on a sufficient scale depended on peace and democracy. The great employers, who were the most extreme individualists in the party, defined their Liberalism in terms of social welfare more than did any other group in the party—more prominently than the working-class leaders themselves. Samuel Morley, for instance,

> was overwhelmed by a fear, not that communism will proceed to universal confiscation (I have no fear of this) but lest wealthy, and perhaps you will allow me to add, educated Englishmen may not promptly devote themselves to solve the problem how the poverty, disease and vice of so many of our own flesh and blood can be diminished and resolved . . . this can best be accomplished by improvement in our laws . . .[68]

So far as the question of ultimate definition of purpose went, the great employers were at one both with Lord Shaftesbury and the Socialists. If in fact a very great part of their attention was absorbed by the traditional good causes of middle-class radicalism, this was because of the whole bias and limitations of the culture and information of the age, and because of the actual merits of the 'good causes' themselves, rather than from too contracted sympathies. The working-class leaders themselves did not press strongly for collectivist or welfare measures, but for political ones. So it was that the middle-class radicalism of the 1832 vintage reached its high-water mark in the 1860's on the shoulders, as it were, of working-class agitation. The Radicals in Parliament had a remarkably broad range, and, though their approach was individualist, their work did touch at points the relief of ignorance and misery. Though the Anglican Liberal M.P.s were no less charitable than the Nonconformist Radicals, they did not carry such activities into politics. The Radicals were not only involved in controversial social commitments, but they

[68] Hodder, *Life of Samuel Morley* (1887), 250.

developed an equally distinctive way of carrying out their good causes. This generally took the form of lifelong commitment to a particular question, with a shadowy National Society providing outside backing, and a war of attrition carried on in Parliament in question time and in motions on the adjournment. Rathbone chose as his target a Bankruptcy Bill, Peter Rylands the reform of the diplomatic service, Stansfeld the repeal of the Contagious Diseases Act. Fildes, a Manchester stockbroker sitting for Grimsby, entered Parliament to promote the abolition of capital punishment, a cause popular among the Manchester business class at this time. The Society for the Abolition of Capital Punishment had fourteen M.P.s, all of whom were Liberals, on its Committee in 1868. That Reform came in 1866 and not later, and that the education bill was brought in in 1870 and not later, owed much to the obduracy of W. E. Forster. In another direction, Peter Taylor, who was a partner in Courtaulds, a business which had been active in the campaign against Church rates, joined with Cowen and Stansfeld in sympathizing with Italian and other European revolutionaries. Dixon and Reed of Hackney worked steadily for national education. Taylor, Bright, Gilpin, Samuel Morley, Hugh Mason, Baines, and Titus Salt were members of the Executive Committee for the prosecution of Governor Eyre. Morley, Brogden, Dixon, and Salt, all great employers, were among the largest subscribers to the fund which enabled the trade union paper, the *Beehive,* to be reduced to a penny in 1870. Bass, the great Burton brewer who sat for Derby, was very active in promoting trade unionism on the railways. The world of controversial humanitarianism, and the world of radicalism, were linked in one way by a common tender-mindedness in primary social attitudes, and in another by a stage army of interlocking directorships. The Parliamentary Liberal Party as a whole was not tender-minded or noticeably different from the Conservatives on humanitarian and social matters, but even in the 1860's it had to behave differently in adjustment to the Nonconformist conscience.

Their energy, money, popular connections, and lack of distracting interests made the great employers formidable as the theoretical and aristocratic Radicals had not been. In their home towns, they were necessary men and nothing could go forward without them. Their ascendancy might grow from almost nothing in a few years. In one generation, Crossley's carpet factory in Halifax became the largest in the world, employing 6,000 persons. Platt's textile machinery works in Oldham had 400 employees[69] in 1837; 2,500 in 1854, and 7,000 in 1872. In such a setting, a kind of industrial feudalism was perfectly natural to master and man alike. In taking on the responsibility for making a civilization, they bound themselves to commit errors. What was striking was that they took on the responsibility of setting public affairs to right as much as they did. Much of their social creativity and dynamism came from what was bound to pass away; the euphoria created by the success of the Anti-Corn Law League, the dying down of intransigent class politics, the sense of resentment and social exclusion felt by commercially educated Dissenters, the identification with the life of the town rather than the country estate, and an abundance of indisputably righteous causes to champion. Though all the mental apparatus of what was later a diehard Right[70] can be found in the outlook of the Radical employers, in the 1860's they were truly the intransigents of the party, the one group which surprised by a fine excess.

THE LAWYERS

Every century has found to its chagrin that the House of Commons became a fifth Inn of Court. In the nineteenth century, too, the House was closely connected with the legal profession, but, given the special interest attaching in the nineteenth century to questions of patronage, reform, and

[69] W. Ogwen Williams, 'The Platts of Oldham', *Trans. Caernarvonshire Hist. Soc.*, xviii, 1957.

[70] Of the rigid economic creed of a man like W. E. Forster, it may well be said, as of the Calvinists, '. . . these men did not idly believe in such cruelty. They were forced into their beliefs by the demands of their understanding, and their assent was more meritorious than the weak protests of so-called enlightenment.'—Mark Rutherford, *Revolution in Tanner's Lane*, 9th edition, 140.

social change, the enormous representation commanded by the Bar takes on a special colour. In an age of declining patronage, the attitudes or expectations of the old ways lingered on unaltered among the legal sixth of the House, whose professional hopes depended considerably on the Executive. In an age where special interests were thought to be trampled down by the general will, law reform was left to the mercy of those who were to be reformed. In an age when social change was held to derive from the growth of trade and manufacture, the largest non-landowning group in the House was, by far, the ancient profession of the Bar. Also, in addition to the process by which the local plutocrat replaced the local Norman blood in the constituencies, the lawyers were already carpet-bagging, in a modified form, among the towns of their circuit—and with a success which anticipated the enormous growth of non-local representation after 1885.

The number of lawyers in the Commons in the 1860's may be taken to be over 100. The *Financial Reform Almanack* (1872) printed this table:

Barristers,	active	82
„	retired	17
Solicitors,	active	6
„	retired	2
		107

For the following Parliament, the useful *Parliamentary Directory of the Professional, Commercial and Mercantile Classes* (1874), gave more detail:

Barristers		104	
„	of whom Liberal or Home Rule	60	
„	of whom Q.C.s	33	(19 Liberal and Home Rule)
„	serjeants	2	
Solicitors		11	(6 Liberal and Home Rule)
Total legal interest, 1874		115	

Since both tables probably derived from *Dod's Parliamentary Companion* (though no sources are given), the figures throughout are likely to be somewhat on the small side, though not greatly so. But there is no doubt of the main points: that lawyers were a sixth of the House or so, and that, even in 1874, more than half were Liberal. Their social composition is less easy to determine. As in other professions, they tended to be recruited from the higher social levels, though, unlike in other professions, the prospects of the poor but brilliant man were excellent at the Bar: but in any case social origin was only one element in the social position which the individual lawyer derived mostly from his profession and his professional standing. Altogether this, the largest non-landowning group in Parliament, had the least quarrel, and the greatest affinities, with the aristocratic constitution and its operators.

The interest of all this lies in its application to the distinct subjects of executive patronage and of law reform.

As to patronage, there was certainly much quiet and decorous corruption not in harmony with the canons of Victorian rectitude. A certain number of facts can be brought together, but the resultant general statement would only be a little less than inconclusive. A large number of valuable posts in the gift of the Executive tended to need legal training: and on the whole only a rather successful barrister could afford to enter Parliament. Those, then, who became members already had a fair *prima facie* claim to some post, which various actions on their part might do something to increase. Such a situation would operate to make men support the Liberals, the party that normally made appointments, in the long run, but would not have important short-run consequences. In any case, simply to be in Parliament enhanced and advertised a man's professional standing:

> Fitzjames stood for Harwich in the Liberal interest at the general election of 1865: but much more because he thought that a seat in Parliament would be useful in his profession, than from any keen interest in politics.[71]

Perhaps this was what expert testimony meant by saying: 'aspiring lawyers must enter it (Parliament), for it is the

[71] Leslie Stephen, *Life of Fitzjames Stephen*, 222.

avenue that leads most surely and directly to the highest prizes in the profession'.[72] For it is hard to trace a flow of lawyers from Parliament to lucrative Crown offices. Not more than two or three M.P.s were made Queen's Counsel between 1857 and 1868: though in 1869, out of fourteen Queen's Counsel appointed, four were in Parliament, and three of these were Liberals (Thomas Hughes, Henry James, and Osborne Morgan). Similarly, it is surprising to find none of the county court judges in 1870 had been in Parliament, though Disraeli gave a journalist friend to understand that such a post could be his for the asking.[73] Of the judges, some no doubt were partly appointed on political grounds. But of the judges in 1870 who were not part of the Ministry, thirteen had never been in Parliament at all, against only eleven who had. Of the eleven who had been M.P.s all but one could have been appointed by the party to which they belonged. (Since the month of appointment is not given in the Law List, this cannot be exactly determined in years when ministries changed.) One Conservative member was made a judge by Lord Westbury on grounds of merit. But there were signs that these appointments by merit were of recent origin. As early as 1857, when the new probate and divorce courts were set up, the Lord Chancellor 'refused to distribute any patronage under these acts, and gave the whole of it to Sir Cresswell Cresswell, the first judge in ordinary.'[74] Further, in 1863 we find Lord Westbury, the Lord Chancellor, writing to Palmerston: 'I wish the appointments of the puisne judges to be made exclusively on legal merits, as this principle affords the greatest inducement to exertion at the Bar.'[75] The wish, as the table of judges' appointments showed, was not entirely carried out, nor was it widely shared in the great party of progress: 'I have already got into great disgrace by disposing of my judicial patronage on the principle *detur digniori* [disappointed Whig counsel] . . . got me well abused in *The Times* and other newspapers . . .'[76] Besides legal patronage in general, there were three kinds of special patronage: that of

[72] *Law Magazine*, 1864, 254.
[73] T. E. Kebbel, *Lord Beaconsfield and Other Tory Memories* (1907), 63.
[74] *Dictionary of National Biography*, s.a. Rolfe, Lord Cranworth.
[75] *Life of Lord Westbury*, II, 63.   [76] *Life of Lord Campbell*, II, 372.

Dublin Castle, that used by Whips to pay off obligations, and that personal to the Lord Chancellor. To these we shall return. But having failed to show any striking direct connection between Parliamentary membership and the lucrative offices tabled in the Law List, it is necessary to point out two possibilities. M.P.s who may have taken nothing for themselves, may have done wonders in improving the prospects of dependants in the legal profession. Likewise M.P.s though not getting higher legal office, might have slipped into one of the abounding commissionerships and secretaryships reserved for lawyers. Certainly the smaller fry of politics found rewards at this level. The solicitor who gave unpaid assistance to the Tory Whip in managing the 1852 elections, received from the Tories a post worth £200 as solicitor to the India Board.[77] Samuel Lucas, a journalist on *The Times* who had helped arrange the coalition between Tories and Radicals against the Conspiracy to Murder Bill, was offered a distributorship of stamps at about £600 by the incoming ministry.[78] One Tory journalist was paid off with a factory inspectorship, while another declined an offer of that post,[79] one, incidentally, into which Sir James Graham had jobbed one of his own kin.[80] All such devious conduct had to be discreet, for public taste would no longer stand for declared and open manipulation, as the case of the dockyards showed. In 1847 a minute pronounced that all dockyard promotions (but not first appointments) should be by merit only. In 1852 the Tory Secretary to the Admiralty reversed this for reasons of party advantage, and though he appeared not to have used his revived powers, the ensuing hue and cry ended his political career.[81] Hence by the 1860's it is more practical to ask about the velocity of advancement for those with suitable affiliations, than about the precise way it came about. There was, for instance, an apparently political fluctuation in the number of Queen's Counsel appointed each year:[82]

[77] *Parl. P. 1852–3*, H.C. 243, Qq. 1795–1808.
[78] T. E. Kebbel, op. cit., 236.   [79] Ibid., 60.
[80] *Parl. P. 1852–3*, H.C. 243, Q. 1756.
[81] Whibley, *Lord John Manners and his Friends* (1925), II, 84–7.
[82] Coleridge said that his appointment as Q.C. without solicitation was unprecedented. (J. D. Coleridge to Yarnall, 1861, in *Forty Years of*

1856	0	1861	14	1866	28
1857	7	1862	7	1867	0
1858	11	1863	5	1868	21
1859	2	1864	4	1869	14
1860	0	1865	9		

On the face of it, at least, the Tories were very obliging, and taking the decade as a whole, it paid as well for a lawyer to be a Tory as to be a Liberal.[83] In this way, a short Tory ministry, even though a minority, could greatly help the morale of the party.

All the tables and statements should be taken to exclude Ireland. In Ireland legal patronage was definitely an important engine of the government at Dublin Castle. Mr J. H. Whyte has shown how the snares were laid for the Irish party in the 1850's by judicial office being offered their leaders.[84] In the 1860's the situation was much the same: an Irish county court judge wrote:

> Political feeling was at its lowest ebb in Ireland from 1850 to 1872 and as a result, lawyers found seats in Parliament . . . in rather larger numbers . . . these M.P.s accordingly engrossed the lion's share of professional rewards for what they had done at Westminster . . . political services counted for more than legal requirements at this period as a passport to the judicial office . . .[85]

The result was that the legal class, unlike the rest of the population, were considered loyal as Dublin Castle understood loyalty, and this was of some value to the administra-

---

Friendship, ed. C. Yarnall, 1911, 69.) But the solicitations would not necessarily have been political.

[83] An example of the expectations held occurs in the Wilson papers in Manchester; J. B. Torr to George Wilson, 13 January 1869: 'I hope we shall persuade Lord Hatherley that there sadly needs a reinforcement of Radicals among the Tory host of Q.C.'s.' A refusal followed from Hatherley: but the document illustrates the angle from which local party men might regard the matter.

[84] J. H. Whyte, *The Independent Irish Party* (London 1958), 58. Out of twenty-one Irish judges appointed between 1828 and 1852, fourteen had been M.P.s.

[85] O'Conor Morris, *Memories and Thoughts of a Life* (1895), 144.

tion.[86] Yet this engine of patronage was only effective on individuals once elected: it did not affect the elections themselves, and it played no part in the marked movements towards the Tories in 1857–9 and towards the Liberals in 1865–8.

In England, there is very clear evidence of a living tradition of genial disregard for merit in those appointments personal to the Lord Chancellor, combined with indications that this tradition, flourishing in 1860, was crushed by earnestness in the course of the decade. A change of generation and outlook which in general politics started with Peel, affected the highest legal offices only in the 1860's. Lord Chancellors Campbell, St Leonards, Chelmsford, Cranworth, Westbury, and Hatherley were of the pre-1832 generation, and lived in the almost purely legal world of the *ancien régime* lawyer. Only Hatherley, a High Church radical and an intimate of Dean Hook, was much affected by newer currents of thought; and with him, and with Selborne and Cairns, all three Sunday School teachers all their lives and strong Churchmen, moral earnestness made its appearance in the legal world, and behind each career lay the restoration of Oxford to a *universitas docens*.

A telling entry in Lord Campbell's diary relates that on his becoming Lord Chancellor in 1859, Brougham 'warmly congratulated me on my elevation, and condescended to ask me to appoint his nephew a Registrar in Bankruptcy, which I very readily promised to do, reminding him that he, when Chancellor, had given a similar appointment to a nephew of mine'.[87] Similarly, a writer in *Fraser's* asked, 'Nay, we will go further, and ask, was any Lord Chancellor—dead or living— ever known to depart from the time-honoured custom of regarding a particular portion of his patronage as the provision of his family . . . or of his dependents, flatterers, and friends?'[88]

Lord Westbury, though conscientious in general with patronage, did not quite depart from the time-honoured

---

[86] Kimberley to Clarendon, 27 November 1865: Lord E. Fitzmaurice, *Life of Granville*, I, 515.
[87] *Life of Lord Campbell*, II, 370.
[88] *Fraser's Magazine*, August 1865, 249.

practice, and his religious opinions, or lack of them, turned a scandal into something like an impeachment. After his resignation, little was heard of the time-honoured practices, though one case where collateral considerations had weight in an appointment may be mentioned. When Cairns took Lord Chelmsford's place on the woolsack in February 1868, without avoiding giving offence to him, Cairns to some extent appeased Lord Chelmsford by appointing his son, Sir Frederic Thesiger, to the bench.[89] Chelmsford himself, incidentally, had in his day been a genial man of the world about his patronage, writing in 1859:

> Apropos to Lunacy I understand there is a storm brewing about my appointment of Higgins to the Mastership. My answer is that he certainly would not have been appointed if he had not been my son-in-law, but that being my son-in-law he would not have been appointed if I hadn't considered him perfectly competent (after a little instruction) to the duties of the office.

The whole point, indeed, of the changing attitudes towards the legal patronage of the Lord Chancellor lay not in its actual political influence, even in its heyday, but in the way which, for a particular institution, it illustrated the dividing line between Georgian and Victorian administrative manners, and exhibited the social and intellectual sources of the pervasive Gladstonian rectitude which distinguished the nascent Liberalism of the 1860's from the ways of the old Whigs.

There was one further category of legal appointments, those which paid a party debt. The 'Colliery explosion', caused by the appointment of the Attorney-General to the Bench by a stratagem, was not one of these: but the debate upon the subject naturally provided an opportunity to rake up any such cases. Yet Lord Salisbury could only draw the attention of the House to two legal appointments which to him were unsound: those of Mr Beales, the old Etonian agitator, to a County Court judgeship, and of Homersham Cox to a Welsh legal office, and these were warmly defended by Lord Hatherley. Probably, then, everything was above board, and we hear no mention of the Whips.

[89] *Dictionary of National Biography*, s.a. Thesiger.

On the whole large question of the relation between Executive patronage and the legal profession, we can provide a certain amount of small patches of information, but, from printed sources at least, no general answer, except the certainty that there was no very striking one. The principles on which appointments to such small but valuable jobs as Revising Barristerships (which Beales held till dismissed for political reasons) and other miscellanea, never appear in discussion. Nevertheless, there was an atmosphere of search for private advantage about the lawyer M.P.s which distinguished them from other Parliamentary groups, however discreetly they gained their ends.

LIBERAL NATIONALISM: THE IRISH, SCOTS, AND WELSH

Within the English Liberal Party there were all the marks of painfully contrived coalition. The best part of Society joined hands with the grimmest Puritanism; masters and men, landlords and labourers, Matthew Arnold and the Manchester School, Samuel Morley and Clubland, all made up English Liberalism. On top, however, of this mountain of complication, was added the federal alliance of English with Scottish and Irish Liberals. On the whole, this aspect of party development induced little political schizophrenia and was the least of the Party leaders' worries. Palmerston, indeed, almost went out of his way to demoralize the Irish Liberals. Although the whole structure of the permanent Liberal majority depended on their standing start in Scotland and their opportunities in Ireland, rather than on the narrow limits of variation in the English electoral system, the private army with which the lesser kingdoms supplied the English Liberals, received only a tithe of the public attention given to the (structurally less important) English urban and industrial radicals. The private army remained a problem only at the Whips' office; softly, it tipped the scales decisively in the lobbies: and made no other mark on history beyond being the passive bulwark of the permanent Liberal majority of the great age.

Dr Hanham's diagnosis[90] of the position in the three smaller countries in the 1860's, as cases where genuine social and confessional radicalism[91] and national feeling were muted and nullified by traditional influences, and by the Lilliputian scale of constituency politics, appears to be fundamentally just. To his account of the quality, the issues, and the organization of politics in Scotland, Wales, and Ireland, there is nothing to add. But in corroboration of his general line of argument, some points concerning the social background of the Liberal M.P.s elected may be brought forward. Socially, the Irish and Scottish Liberals were rather more aristocratic and territorial than the English, while the Welsh Liberals were gentry almost to a man till 1868.

Though the constituencies might be radical enough in doctrine, in Scotland they liked a laird as much as they disliked landlordism: in Ireland the opportunism of the priests usually bound the elector who was free of Tory landlord influence, to vote for his Whig cousin. Of the seventy-one Liberal M.P.s sitting for Scotland between 1859 and 1874, twenty-one had military connections, three were patrons of livings, fifteen were related to the peerage, and forty-three were large landowners or their sons. What was involved at Parliamentary level, in Scottish Liberalism was not any kind of revolt,[92] but a cultural and intellectual phenomenon, the devastating inroads made upon the traditional holders of wealth, power, and land, the natural conservatives, by Liberal ideas. As also in the English counties, an upper class had to a considerable extent been converted by sheer weight of argument (especially the argument from experience).

[90] H. J. Hanham, 'Scotland, Wales and Ireland', in *Elections and Party Management* (1959), 155–91.

[91] In Scotland, the most striking symptom of a general radicalism was not any political demand, but chaste electoral behaviour. Bribery was almost unknown there, and Scottish tenants, unlike English, had been known to vote 'almost in a body' against their landlords, according to the Hartington Committee. See *Sess. Papers 1870*, H.C. 115, 55.

[92] In 1857, for instance, Palmerston's triumph was completest in Scotland: for though some twenty-five Radical opponents of the ministry were returned, none sat for a Scottish seat.—G. W. T. Omond, *The Lord Advocates of Scotland 1834–1880* (1914), 193.

The sixty-five Irish Liberals listed in *Dod* for 1870 were composed as follows:

Landowners and sons	42	Banker	1
Lawyers	10	Journalists	2
Physician	1	Merchants	5
Brewer	1	Other manufacturers	3

The proportion of landowners sitting as non-Conservative members for Ireland, had indeed risen since the Parliament of 1852–7, when the non-Conservative ranks had divided into twenty-eight professional and businessmen, against thirty-five landowners.[93]

It is easier to see what kind of people, socially speaking, these Liberal M.P.s were, than to place them in relation to the ecclesiastical intricacies which were the chief background of their manœuvres. An analysis of the voting of the ministers of religion in the four Scottish universities in 1868 showed how uniform denominational opinion was:[94]

	Conservative	Liberal
Established Church	1,221	67
Free Church	33	607
United Presbyterian	1	474
Episcopalians	78	4
Not classified	35	360
	1,368	1,512

The shifting relations between types of churchmanship and political behaviour in Scotland, Wales, and Ireland, form a subject that cannot simply be treated *en passant*, and must not be pursued here.

Before 1868, Scotland, Wales, and Ireland were electing M.P.s, mainly from the 'upper crust', who had no reason and no power to set the Thames on fire. Their *raison d'être* came chiefly from local matters, particularly religious matters which had no parallel in England. Hence the relations

[93] J. H. Whyte, *The Independent Irish Party* (1958), 90.
[94] G. W. T. Omond, *The Lord Advocates of Scotland 1834–1880* (1914), 245.

between the various national sections of the Liberal Party were of minimum intensity, sufficient only to enable English Liberals to win everything at a canter.

Ministers, and informed opinion generally, simply did not know, quantitatively and analytically, why they, and not the other side, were in power. Consequently, they could not, and did not, try to relate policy to the structure of their majorities. In that structure, the three lesser kingdoms were enormously important. Yet, because of their own want of importunity and because they did not embody a socially threatening myth, as 'Manchester' did, they were treated like an inconvenient West African colony. Even allowing for the uncalculating Ministerial innocence which was one root of this negligence, there was much that would have been ungracious even to nations thoroughly Tory.

For instance, Lord Advocate Moncreiff's sixth attempt to provide a national system of education for Scotland was shelved by the Lords on the last day of the 1869 session. The Bill on one occasion was held back by Gladstone in order to make room for another dealing with episcopal retirement, and three months elapsed before the second reading.[95] From such frustrations as this, the demand for a Scottish Secretary of State was building up by 1870: but the official Liberals did nothing to anticipate this demand.

But Gladstone was the first politician to behave more warmly to the three countries. He appointed the first Welsh-speaking bishop in three centuries in 1870. In 1873, his presidential speech at the Eisteddfod was an apology for his past ignorance and an official recognition of Welsh nationality. Gladstone's initiative in 1865–8 in Irish affairs, which ensured that Ireland did as much for the Liberal Party as the Liberal Party did for Ireland, came in the nick of time: whatever else it was, it was a stroke of electoral genius, and won about twenty seats between 1864 and 1869. Gladstone had few words of sympathy at home for Ireland before 1864; but when 'opportunists' like Palmerston and the Whip were in despair, his flow of sympathy saved the day. Palmerston hardly thought it worth trying to get on with the Catholics: 'Don't allow yourself to be led by O'Hagan to shower Patronage

[95] Omond, op. cit., 247.

down upon Catholics . . . we ought rather to draw off from
. . . and the turn of the scale be given to the Protestants.'[96]
The Whip, a very able politician, had no inkling of the way
Gladstone was to build the Irish Catholics into the party for
ten years, for he still regarded them as the wild animals of
Parliament:

> You are losing the support of the Irish Roman Catholics,
> the natural enemies of a Liberal Government. It is time
> you endeavoured to enlist support from Protestants, who
> ought to be the allies of a Liberal Government.
>   . . . In the South our prospects are very bad: and all that
> we can hope to do, is to save a few seats from the general
> wreck.[97]

An even greater misreading of the Irish situation led him to
think the Catholics 'were on principle Ultra Tory, although
they may occasionally, to serve their own or the Pope's purposes, join hands with a Liberal Government'.[98] The Palmerstonian policy was to treat the Irish Liberal Protestants—a
minority of a minority—as their true friends, and to ignore
the social and ecclesiastical issues which could turn the Irish
Catholics into 'true friends'.

In the later 1860's, the three countries were beginning to
be allowed a proportionate influence in the formation of
Liberal policy, partly due to the way Gladstone thought a
party should work, partly due to their own growing emancipation. Gladstonian leadership integrated the regional sections
of the party, on the same principles of solidarity, concord, and
co-operation, as it did the various classes within the party.
This was electorally fortunate, perhaps even necessary; but it
was not a policy arrived at by such calculations, nor did it
suggest or commend itself to 'realists' like Palmerston or
Brand. While Gladstone and the old Parliamentary hands
tried to win 'public opinion' by popular pre-election budgets,
they were gaining the clear majority they could never get
from England alone, in Ireland, Wales, and Scotland, with

[96] Palmerston to Carlisle, 9 February 1863: Palmerston Papers, 'Private Letter Book 1862'.
[97] Brand to Palmerston, 24 August 1862: Palmerston Papers, unsorted.
[98] Ibid.

very little overt electioneering, and for reasons to which they were indifferent or even hostile.

The following tables[99] show:

1. the geographical distribution of the Liberal majority in 1868;
2. the radicalization of Wales;
3. the steady Liberal ascendancy in Scotland;
4. the rise of successive Tory and Liberal majorities in Ireland.

THE GENERAL ELECTION OF 1868

	Liberal	Conservative
England	240	223
Wales	22	8
Scotland	52	8
Ireland	65	40

THE RADICALIZATION OF WALES

Year of election	Liberal	Conservative
1852	11	18
1857	15	14
1859	15	14
1865	18	11
1868	22	8
1874	19	11
1880	28	2

THE LIBERAL ASCENDANCY IN SCOTLAND[100]

Year of election	Liberal	Conservative
1857	38	15
1859	38	15
1865	41	12
1868	52	8

[99] These tables are compiled from the *Constitutional Yearbook* (1907), 223 ff.

[100] The Liberals won a majority in Scotland at every election from 1832 to 1895 inclusive.

FLUCTUATIONS IN IRELAND[101]

Year of election	Liberal	Conservative
1852	63	42
1857	55	50
1859	48	57
1865	55	50
1868	65	40

[101] In the case of Ireland, the left-hand column includes all non-Conservatives.

2 The Rank and File

The Rank and File

A word of introduction may be in place here to show that the following topics, diverse and far-ranging as they are, have not been arbitrarily chosen, but are indeed essential to the theme of the attachment of the rank and file to Parliamentary Liberalism and to Gladstone. The previous sections, having shown what kind of people the Parliamentary Liberals were, leave no doubt that with all their virtues, all groups were alike in failing to supply the energy and force required for political achievement. They failed to do this, above all, because they represented their own small *élites* and responded to their ideas. The multitude could not see them as extensions of itself and its aims. The next step in the argument is to see what kind of people this multitude was, what it read, how far it was formally organized, what it expected to gain in a worldly sense, and what popular Liberalism was like in an actual constituency. The following sections deal therefore with a sudden and striking change in the nature of the Press around 1860, and with the great increase in the political effectiveness of Dissent at this time. These provided for the Liberal Party a mass of militant support more enduring than that of the Reform agitation, and an unprecedented means for free propaganda. It is argued that these things altered the political landscape much more than did formal party organization, local or national, which is discussed at length. In the same way, it is suggested that the working class political movements, although they were new, and often remarkable pieces of political construction, were less important than something which had not altered and was not a matter of organization— that is, the ascendancy, social, political, and even possibly numerical, of the skilled manual workers over all other forms of labour. What was politically important was not the trade union movement, but the internal occupational structure of the world of labour. Certainly, the zest, momentum, and hope which the multitude perennially attached to the Liberal

Party, are easier explained by remembering such craftsmen of fiction as Felix Holt, Adam Bede, and Jude Fawley, than by thinking of the 'factory slave' of legend. All these lines of thought converge on the final topic, popular Liberalism in Rochdale, where it was perhaps at its best.

THE NEW PRESS

'If a man were permitted to make all the ballads, he need not care who should make the laws of a nation.' Before 1855, the press was dominated by, and took its tone from, the traditional holders of power who dominated Parliament. After 1861, the press was a chiefly popular institution, representative of classes with little weight in Parliament. This change, one of the most far-reaching in the history of propaganda, was pushed through quietly by a small group of clear-sighted men, and was the equivalent, in the field of opinion, of the change from the Whig Parliamentary Party to the Liberal National Party in the field of politics.

Eighteenth-century conditions of newspaper production persisted up to 1855. Despite Radical incursions, the press remained a class institution. Up to the repeal of the Stamp Duties, a Manchester writer remembered, few people bought newspapers for themselves, and the chief duty of many of the news vendors was to lend them out at a penny per hour.[1] The first great jolt to the newspaper world came from the Crimean War, but, without fiscal changes, the advantages of this went almost entirely to the old established journals and to the semi-scandalous weeklies. The table opposite sets out their increases in circulation between 1853 and the repeal of the stamp duty in June 1855.[2]

Under the old system, the extremes flourished, and the middle was almost non-existent. The effect of the repeal of the stamp and paper duties was to raise to first position a

[1] F. Leary, *The Manchester Press* (1897), 273: ms. in Manchester Central Library.
[2] B.M. Add. mss. 43,665, f. 328, printed, n.d.: based on Parliamentary returns.

INCREASE IN COPIES SOLD 1853–1855

DAILY		WEEKLY	
The Times	14,188	Ill. London News	51,000
Daily News	1,549	News of the World	44,000
Morning Chronicle	570	Reynolds Weekly	21,000
Globe	1,422	Weekly Times	15,000
Express	774	Leeds Mercury	4,000

quite new class of newspaper, democratic but not Radical, cheap but respectable,[3] interested more in politics as it affected circulation, less in being the oracle of aristocratic factions and politicians. In 1854 there were only five provincial dailies, with a total circulation of 10,000 copies. In 1864, the provinicial circulations, both of weeklies and dailies, exceeded those of the London press:

London weeklies:	2,263,000 copies per week
Provincial weeklies:	3,907,000 copies per week
London dailies:	248,000 per diem
Provincial dailies:	438,000 per diem

Out of a total annual circulation of the United Kingdom press of 546,000,000 copies in 1864, 340,000,000 copies were of provincial journals.[4] Leaving aside for a moment the question of the nature and content of the new provincial press, some of its merely collateral causes and consequences must be noticed. The new press depended on at least three branches of invention: the railway, the telegraph, and the steam press. Of these, the telegraph particularly acted in favour of the provincial newspaper, enabling it often to anticipate the London journals with important news. The new press had important consequences in the field of political method, too, some of which enhanced, others diminished the importance of politicians.

Pamphleteering and the cheap political print or broadsheet, which had depended on the dearth of cheap popular reading matter caused by the old press laws, were killed dead

[3] 'The vast stores of intellectual wealth which the daily and weekly press scatter abroad . . . is one of the most wondrous marvels of this marvellous age,' said the Mayor of Wolverhampton about 1865.—E. H. Fowler, *Life of Lord Wolverhampton* (1912), 49.

[4] These figures are from Edward Baines, ' *Speech of 11 May, 1864, on the Borough Franchise Bill*' (Pamphlet, 1864).

by the cheap newspaper. The old League and Chartist propaganda found an audience who had practically nothing else to read. Later political tracts could hardly compete for attention with the far wider attractions of the political newspaper, let alone with such purely pleasurable features of the new journalism as the *Family Paper*, with a circulation between 200,000 and 300,000 weekly.[5] Political education and proselytism became a press monopoly,[6] and such bodies as the Manchester Liberal Party completely abandoned the calling of public meetings and the dissemination of propaganda. On the other hand, the press virtually raised the great popular orators to national thrones. Bright normally drew about fifty reporters to his provincial meetings, and his Birmingham speech of 1858 was the first great public meeting which was really a press conference. In the League days, Bright had concentrated on whistle-stop speeches and the conversion of the local audience in front of him: from 1858, he placed the emphasis on the prepared speech and on the national audience who would read it. By 1861, the structure of the national press had become what it is now, the few 'good' papers being completely outnumbered by the organs of the populace:[7]

Reynolds Weekly	350,000
Telegraph	150,000
Standard	130,000
The Times	70,000
Daily News	6,000
Morning Post	4,500

Bright could be sure of being reported by a largely favourable press, instead of, as in the League days, having to carry on agitation in spite of it. The press, previously largely tied to privilege and class, had in a matter of years become the chief instrument and emblem of that solidarity and community of interest preached by Gladstone, and often accepted

[5] John Cassell to Edward Baines, March 1861, Baines papers.
[6] '. . . prolonged local controversies, carried on by means of the newspaper press, have kept alive a feeling which might otherwise have been evanescent.'—Minute of the Liberation Society, County Hall, London: 4 December 1868.
[7] Woodward, *Age of Reform* (1938), 601, n.1.

as the creed of the new journalism itself. The mission of the press, as the religious editor of the organ of the Licensed Victuallers' Association saw it,[8] was 'to Enlighten, to Civilise, and to Morally Transform the World': exactly the task to which the Liberal militant rank and file had dedicated themselves.

The main developments in the London press between 1855 and 1870 were the attrition of the eighteenth-century aristocratic prints, the conquest of the popular market by two papers representing the orthodox Parliamentary parties, and the capture of the Radical press by militant Gladstonians.

The *Morning Chronicle* (1770–1862), the former Peelite journal, was quietly absorbed by the Liberal *Daily Telegraph*. The *Morning Herald* and the *Morning Post* remained the organs of the country party and of the Palmerstonian aristocracy respectively, Borthwick, the editor of the *Post*, being a well-known factotum of Palmerston's. These papers, with other minor ones like the *Daily News, Globe, Standard,* and *Morning Advertiser,* remained the journals of small and exclusive interests because of their price. They at best only maintained their position, while the cream of the popular market went chiefly to the new *Daily Telegraph* (1855–), later joined by cheap versions of the *Standard* and the *Daily News.* The *Telegraph* served the Liberalism of convention, the *Daily News* the Liberalism of conviction, but both regarded themselves and their readers as at one with the Parliamentary Liberal Party. Both papers marked great steps forward in the conquest of previously unattached or hostile areas of opinion by Parliamentary party.

Conversely, the public turned away from the old independent Radicalism at the very time when it was first possible to start a Radical paper. That there was no demand for a paper unconnected with an official party, the history of the *Morning Star* (1855–68) showed. Though in the 1860's it was independent of the Manchester School: '. . . it is entirely independent, I never had a shilling of money in it, and I really think I know more about the proprietary of the *Daily News, Telegraph,* and *Times,* than of the Star,'[9] it seemed

[8] James Grant, *The Newspaper Press* (1871), I, vi.
[9] Cobden to T. B. Potter, 4 January 1864: Cobden Papers, Chichester.

to many to think every country right but England. Samuel
Morley, thinking that the *Daily News* took a more patriotic
line, enabled it to become a penny paper and to buy up the
Morning Star, but in return Morley exacted the price of party
loyalty: '. . . on more than one occasion he threatened, in the
event of a line of opposition to Mr Gladstone being persisted
in, that he would discontinue his connection with the
paper'.[10] Whatever their faults, and despite their partiality
for persons, the old aristocratic journals were not entirely
predictable party supporters. The new mass press, with the
complaisance of its readers, was more an instrument of party
than the old, though it had far less personal contact with
leading politicians.

The Times, stripped of its monopoly, remained a monument to the fundamental unity of educated opinion, and a
testimony to the superficiality of party divisions among those
actively engaged in the direction of the country. Palmerstonian, Adullamite, sceptical of Gladstone and Disraeli
alike, it adroitly wove its way from one side to another, never
becoming a party paper. Matthew Arnold saw in it:

> . . . a gigantic Sancho Panza, following by an attraction he
> cannot resist, that poor, mad, suffering, sublime enthusiast,
> the modern spirit; following it indeed, with constant grum-
> bling, expostulation, and opposition, with airs of protec-
> tion, of compassionate superiority, with an incessant
> by-play of nods, shrugs, and winks addressed to the spec-
> tators; following it, in short, with all the incurable recalci-
> trance of a lower nature, but still following it.[11]

The function of *The Times* was to make the opinions of
specialists in the administration, the clubs, the professions,
and the *Saturday Review*, into the orthodox generalities of
public opinion: this it did well, and political *parti pris* re-
manied secondary. But a great institution like *The Times*
had interests of its own to look to, and it was the defence of

---

[10] Hodder, *Life of Samuel Morley* (1887), 247. P. W. Clayden (1827–
1902), leader writer on the renovated *Daily News* for thirty years, had
been a Unitarian minister and secretary of the Free Church Union, see
D.N.B. s.a. Clayden.

[11] M. Arnold, *Friendship's Garland*, 159.

these interests that caused the most serious imputations on its honour.

A newspaper must bargain with the State: but was it true, as Bright thought, that *The Times* decided on its editorial policy 'in the hope of darkening Gladstone, who will not consent to sacrifice £200,000 of post office revenue, to carry the whole *Times* at the rate of 6 ozs. of printed matter for a penny'.[12] Probably not: half of society wished to darken Gladstone, with no thought of such matters behind it. But was it not more likely that *The Times* was sustained in its bellicosity between 1854 and 1861 by the knowledge that, as soon as a peace time rate of expenditure was restored, the paper duties would be relinquished, and *The Times* become only one paper among many? Before 1854, when the paper duties seemed secure, Delane was friendly to the Manchester School,[13] and they to him; after the duties had been marked for the axe, it was war to the knife. In 1855, Delane paid a special visit to Clarendon to urge a general election 'the better—he says that the Peelites and peace men will be powerful in debate and he thinks that several of them, e.g. Gladstone, Cobden, and Bright, will not be returned'.[14] Such was the impartiality of *The Times* at the height of its power. In 1861, too, *The Times* was notably active in the House of Commons lobbying against the removal of the paper duties. The biographers of Delane show he was certainly not the creature of a ministry or a man to be bought by patronage, as the Cobdenites alleged.[15] But equally certainly, his paper was for seven years placed in the position of advocating a line of national policy, one certain consequence of which was the continued monopoly of *The Times*.

The provincial press in 1850 contained many organs of Liberal opinions, ranging from old Whig papers like the *Manchester Guardian* to the campaigning *Western Times* with which the Exeter Radicals fought their Bishop.[16] Whatever

---

[12] Bright to Cobden, 20 May 1860: B.M. Add. mss. 43,384, f. 197.

[13] Bright to his wife, 1854: Bright mss., University College, London.

[14] Clarendon to Palmerston, 15 November 1855: Palmerston Papers, unsorted.

[15] See: *Revelations from Printing House Square* by W. Hargreaves (1864). Hargreaves was Cobden's mouthpiece.

[16] R. S. Lambert, *The Cobbett of the West* (1939).

their tone, very few could afford to buy them. As a result of the Crimean War, the peace radicals set out to sweep away all restrictions on the press. Cobden told Sturge that the greatest human instrument for forming public opinion in England would be the penny daily press, and said the best he and his friends could do, would be to establish everywhere papers professing the politics of the *Star* and the *Manchester Examiner*.[17] Cobden lived to see a great part of his dream realized:

> A few years ago, *The Times* possessed almost a monopoly of publicity. Four-fifths of the daily newspaper circulation issued from its press. *Now* it constitutes, probably, one-tenth of our diurnal journalism. . . .[18]

To have dethroned *The Times* was to have done something for peace, but it was the new provincial press, far more than the new London press, which brought forward hitherto inarticulate elements of opinion, and though far from pacifist, it provided a great source of strength for the anti-Turk agitation.

One need not look far for the connection between local Liberal politicians and the new local press, for it is everywhere openly acknowledged. The Liberal *Oldham Times*, for instance, was advertised as including in its proprietary the leading members of Oldham Town Council.[19] The owner of the *Leicester Mercury* was vice-president of the Leicester Liberal Association.[20] The Rev. T. W. Briggs, owner of the *Dover Chronicle* and a Unitarian minister, was one of Bernal Osborne's chief supporters in Dover.[21] On a larger scale were Joseph Cowen's *Newcastle Chronicle*, the leading daily paper

[17] Cobden to Parkes, 3 November 1856: B.M. Add. mss. 43,664, f. 55.

[18] Cobden to Delane, December 1863: Morley, *Cobden* (1881), II, 426.

[19] (Mitchell's) *Newspaper Press Directory*, 1861.

[20] H. Whorlow, *The Provincial Newspaper Society 1836–1886* (1886), 98.

[21] P. Bagenal, *Life of Ralph Bernal Osborne, M.P.* (1884). In Lancashire, where the parties were evenly matched electorally, the Press was strongly Liberal, with forty-one Liberal journals to twenty Conservative ones, with two Liberal-Conservative and thirty-one neutral (mostly advertising or specialized). These figures are compiled from *May's Press Guide*, 1874.

in the north east, the *Manchester Examiner*, which expressed the views of the Manchester School, the *Sheffield Independent*, which gave the Leader family a central position in Sheffield Liberalism, and the *Leeds Mercury*, which gave Leeds three M.P.s from the Baines dynasty. All these papers had marked principles and proselytizing aims, and their teaching led the provincial mind more and more away from ancestral English notions—as Cobden intended—and also away from the discussions and studies by which those notions were being revised and extended.

TABLES OF PRESS EXPANSION

I. No. of members of the Provincial Newspaper Society[22]

1837	23	1855	135	1865	166
1840	100	1859	139	1870	198
1850	113	1863	159	1873	201

II. Daily sales of the Manchester Daily Examiner and Times,[23] *an advanced Liberal paper*

1856	18,150	1859	32,130
1857	22,224	1860	36,201
1858	26,096	1861	39,163

III. Numbers of United Kingdom newspapers[24]

	Total No. of Papers in U.K.	Dailies	London	English Provincial	Wales	Scotland	Ireland
1824	266	?	31	135	?	58	33
1856	795	?	154	375	18	118	113
1871	1,450	120	261	851	53	131	138
1886	2,093	187	409	1,225	83	193	162

MILITANT DISSENT

In the long run, the Liberal Party, still overwhelmingly Anglican at the Parliamentary level in the 1860's, had to

[22] From H. Whorlow, *The Provincial Newspaper Society, 1836–1886* (1886), 36.

[23] (Mitchell's) *Newspaper Press Directory*, 1863, 145.

[24] From H. Whorlow, op. cit., 37.

become the party of the Nonconformist conscience, for the simple reason that almost half the church-going population of the country was Nonconformist, according to the religious census of 1851. But Dissent was far from homogeneous even in its political outlook, it was very unevenly distributed geographically, and, very important from a political point of view, its rich men were concentrated in a few industrial districts.

The districts where Dissent was numerically strong can be shown from two enquiries made in the 1850's. Both the 1851 census, which gave figures for church attendance, and the 1858 return of Sunday School attendances, showed that the only English counties, apart from Bedford and Huntingdon, where the Dissenters were in a majority, were industrial and mining ones—Cheshire, Cornwall, Derby, Durham, Lancashire, Leicester, Lincoln, Monmouth, Northumberland, Nottingham, Staffordshire, and Yorkshire.[25] For the first half of the century, Dissent had had the industrial frontier to itself, with such results as this laconic entry tells: '1841. Population of Dukinfield 10,000: cotton factories 11, church 1, chapels 7, Catholic 1. Scholars: Church 100, Dissenters, 1,700; Catholic 300.'[26] For three reasons, however, it will not do to represent the internal balance of Dissent in the later nineteenth century as corresponding to this distribution. The numerical hold of Dissent on the great towns fell off, and its power told more in the mining and agricultural districts.

Firstly, Dissent in Lancashire and Yorkshire was largely Wesleyan, and the Wesleyans retained an Anglican and Conservative outlook, their paper, the *Watchman*, being favourable to the principle of an established church. (In the 1930's, the ratio between the chapels of the United Methodist Church and the chapels of the other dissenting denominations in Lancashire, Yorkshire, and Cheshire was eight to one.[27]) Secondly, Anglicanism in the North after 1850, par-

[25] From F. Bealey and H. Pelling, *Labour and Politics 1900–1906* (1958), 3.

[26] Town guide in Dukinfield Public Library.

[27] Tillyard, 'The Distribution of the Free Churches in England', *Sociological Review*, January 1935.

ticularly in Lancashire, developed a fighting and a popular
quality which, backed by the deeper purse, rapidly eroded the
advantages of the Dissenters' early start. Thirdly, even when
the Dissenters had a majority among church-goers in the
industrial districts, those districts had a much larger proportion of people outside any church than elsewhere. Some con-
firmation of this may be seen in the fact that if the English
counties are arranged in order of the number of Dissenting
ministers per head of population in the 1930's Lancashire and
the West Riding come thirty-second and twenty-fifth respectively.[28] For all these reasons, it is impossible to tie the fortunes of industrial Liberalism as closely to Dissent as the
traditional picture of the Nonconformist conscience might
lead one to imagine. What Lancashire and Yorkshire did do
was provide a small class of wealthy and confident Radical
businessmen who took charge of national Dissent and of most
of the Radical agitations in the country. Lancashire had
leadership without numbers, the mining districts and the
Cromwellian counties had numbers without a politically
skilled local upper class of their own way of thinking: from
the cross-fertilization of the two areas came the political
Radicalism of the Nonconformist conscience. Although the
English Parliamentary Liberals were overwhelmingly Anglican, although the Irish Liberals were largely Catholic, and
although Gladstone's brand of churchmanship was idolatry
tempered by hypocrisy in the eyes of good Protestants, the
ordinary chapel-goer saw Liberalism in terms of the Lancashire Radicalism which dominated Nonconformist discussion
of public affairs, and drew a conclusion, then staringly wrong,
which, by his adoption of it, later became correct: '. . . the
Liberal Party is that natural political instrument for those
who wish to promote the interests and establish the principles that Primitive Methodists have at heart'.[29] In considering the great expansion of Nonconformist political activity

[28] Ibid. To take this as the situation in the 1860's would be quite un-
founded: but the broad point is that in Lancashire and Yorkshire in
1930, Dissent in general was weak, and Wesleyanism was an unusually
large part of Dissent. This had not come about in a day.
[29] Canon Wickham, *Church and People in an Industrial City* (1957),
132, quoting a connectional journal of the period.

after 1850, it must not be forgotten that all denominations were enjoying a striking religious revival. In London, the increase in sittings between 1851 and 1866 was formidable: [30]

Denomination	% Increase
Anglican	25
Congregationalist	30
Baptist	61
Wesleyan	19

Movement of such dimensions was bound to bring Church questions back into political life. The provincial religious revival touched Liberalism at many points: through trade unionism, through the temperance, peace, and anti-slavery movements, and through the Educational agitation, but below we study only the work of the Liberation Society, the most powerful and the most directly political of Nonconformist pressure groups.

The Liberation Society aimed at the disestablishment and partial disendowment of the Church of England, for whose ultimate welfare it professed the highest concern. Though its arguments were keenly logical, they do not concern us here, because what mattered in them was not their logical status but their power of expressing Dissenting animosities and preconceptions. Though the society was too ambitious in the main aim it set itself, it was extremely successful in making the Liberal Party feel the weight of Nonconformist views on questions of religious equality, and its small but cumulative victories on minor questions, gained through unrelenting but unsensational electoral and Parliamentary pressure, made it the epitome of rational agitation.

It was associated with no great man, Bright having declined to become its Parnell,[31] but it had the support of a host of powerful and wealthy men, who ran the society partly themselves, and partly through idealist ministers and journalists like Dr Foster and Edward Miall, the editor of the *Noncon-*

[30] Skeats and Miall, *History of the Free Churches* (1891), 584. The great contractor, Sir Morton Peto, and the preacher Spurgeon, account for Baptist activity.

[31] Bright was invited to lead the agitation in 1854: Minutes of the Liberation Society, County Hall, London, 11 October 1854.

formist. It was connected with other radical and middle-class political and religious bodies by a system of interlocking directorates. It co-operated with older Nonconformist bodies like the Dissenting Deputies.[32] Through Samuel Morley, it was connected with the Reform Movement, through White-hurst, another member of its executive, with the Ballot Society, through Henry Richard with the Peace Society, and most of its leading members were to be found on the side of the Northern States in the Civil War and of the Negroes in the Jamaica atrocities of 1865. Other points of its informal social creed were the abolition of capital punishment and the enfranchisement of women, though on these points there was more division of opinion. All advanced views tended to cluster round the group of practical men who ran the Liberation Society, and virtue itself acquired a bad name from keeping company with men who plotted religious revolution.

The Society had all the money it could reasonably need for propaganda purposes. Its accounts[33] for 1866–7 balanced at £8,281, and with such resources it was possible to produce 825,000 Irish Church pamphlets and 57,000 placards for the 1868 election.[34] (Like all other societies and party organizations of the period, its funds were quite inadequate for it to sponsor candidates directly at elections.) Its funds clearly came from a few industrialists rather than from the faithful in general. Samuel Courtauld[35] left the Society £2,500: and the big subscribers to the 1875 special fund were Lancashire textile magnates,[36] Lee and Watts of Manchester, James King of Rochdale, and Hugh Mason of Ashton, each giving £1,000. If the normal income of the Society was tabulated according to counties,[37] the most ardent were:

Lancashire	£572
Yorkshire	£385
Gloucestershire	£254
Essex	£128

On the other hand, in the same year 1859–60, the strongly

---

[32] Minutes, 16 February 1854.   [33] *Liberator,* May 1867.
[34] Minutes, 11 September 1868.
[35] Liberation Society Papers, County Hall, London, ref. A.LIB. 40.
[36] Ibid., A.LIB. 37.   [37] *Liberator,* August 1860.

Nonconformist counties of Bedfordshire and Cornwall each contributed under £10.

With one exception, denominational differences were not important within the Society. Caught up in the web of their own logic, Liberationists took pride in supporting Roman Catholics and appearing on platforms with the godless John Morley, and common allegiance to the principle of a free church diluted or replaced specifically denominational belief. Only the great Wesleyan body was not fully drawn into the movement. An analysis of Methodist petitions for the abolition of Church rates in 1860 showed how the most numerous branch of Methodism was proportionately the least active.[38]

Denomination	No. of petitions to Parliament 1860
Conference Wesleyans	135
New Connection	97
Free Methodists	164
Independent Methodists	1
Wesleyan Reformers	34
Wesleyan Association	3
Primitive Methodists	265
	699

The propaganda on which the Society spent its money was not likely, to say the least, to appeal to the unconverted. What was important was the subsequent stage in the work of the Society, the organization of the converted in the constituencies and in Parliament in support of a policy of electoral blackmail. 'We can hardly do less for Free Religion than the League did for Free Trade.'[39] Though the Society had been in existence since 1844, it did not discover its strength, or adopt a policy of 'thorough' in regard to permeation of the Liberal Party, till after the Crimean War. The revelation of the numerical strength of Dissent by the 1851 Census was very important in leading the Society to extend its ambitions, hitherto chiefly defensive. The years between 1856 and 1871 showed much successful work in Parliament and the constituencies, and may be told as a single narrative.

The constituency work of the Society involved the cen-

[38] *Liberator*, May 1860.   [39] Ibid., July 1855.

tralized collection and dissemination of information, the building up of a national system of agents and branches, interviewing and recommending candidates, bringing pressure to bear on the recalcitrant, and conducting a campaign for registration in Wales. Part of this work was planned on the grand scale by the new policies adopted in 1856 and 1863: part arose from empirical processes of administrative growth.

Of the latter kind was the development of a system of local agents and branches. In 1858 the Society had paid agents at Leeds and Bristol, in 1864 an electoral agent was engaged,[40] and in January 1866 the number of agents employed had grown to six, each with his district.[41] In 1868 their number had risen to eight,[42] and in 1871 it rose again to thirteen, five of whom were assigned to Wales.[43] The national parties themselves, it must be remembered, had no regional organizations whatever at this time, and the Society alone had an adequate machine for interfering in constituency politics. And interfere it did. Some of its interferences were relatively casual and isolated. The electoral agent was given a list of eighteen random boroughs, for instance, in 1864, told to stir them up,[44] and no more was heard of it. Similarly elusive were some activities recorded in 1856 of Mr Pryce: '. . . he had visited Devon and Cornwall, chiefly for electoral purposes'.[45] A few months later at the general election, there was a Liberal landslide in the south west, but there is no means of determining what, if anything, it owed to this visit:

Cornwall:	1852:	Liberal, 6	Conservative, 8
	1857:	Liberal, 11	Conservative, 3
Devon:	1852:	Liberal, 11	Conservative, 11
	1857:	Liberal, 15	Conservative, 7

But what was undeniable was the effect of a tour of Wales made by Miall, Henry Richard, and Carvell Williams in autumn 1866, which led to the foundation of the registration societies which looked after the business arrangements of Welsh popular Liberalism.[46]

---

[40] Minutes, 1862–7, 278.   [41] Minutes, 1862–7, 345.
[42] Minutes, 24 July 1868.   [43] Minutes, 22 May 1871.
[44] Minutes, 1862–7, 278.   [45] Minutes, 8 September 1856.
[46] See Minutes, 26 June 1868, and 15 July 1870, for grants of money to these societies by the Society.

When the Liberation Society intervened on a large scale, it did so with science and copious preparation almost unexampled in English politics. The elections of 1857 and 1865 were its field days, the 1859 election appearing to have taken it by surprise, and in 1868 the Society was superfluous:

> On the occurrence of former elections, the Society's electoral committee have had to discharge the important duty of assisting the Society's friends to obtain suitable candidates, or to secure suitable pledges . . . A marked characteristic of the recent election has been the small necessity for any such assistance; the energy of the Liberal party, local or central, having sufficed for the supply of candidates, and the readiness of such candidates to support Mr Gladstone's ecclesiastical policy having made any pressure on the part of the Society's supporters altogether needless.[47]

It is to 1857 and 1865 we must look, for an estimate of the Society's power. In 1857 the aim of the Society was to see advanced Liberals, or indeed Liberals of any hue, returned in the place of Tories. In 1865 its aim was to force the bulk of Anglican Liberal candidates to accept Nonconformist views on the church rates question. In both years, it succeeded beyond expectation.

The 1857 election has generally been considered as a vote of confidence in Palmerston and his conduct in the Crimean War and in China. So much is true, but it is not the whole story of the Liberal triumph of that year. Besides the wave of aristocratic enthusiasm for Palmerston, a very strong cross current, by no means friendly to Palmerston, was at work. The Society's plans were laid in 1856. Each county was examined in the light of its past history and of 'a continuous receipt of information, more or less confidential, dating back for more than a twelvemonth . . .' Ten county seats were selected, where it was felt it would be their own fault if they did not insert a congenial M.P.[48] Then their registration was attended to, partly by the sale of faggot votes, 'to pay 4% rental without risk or trouble',[49] partly by circularizing the Dissenting chapels with printed forms of qualification for the franchise,

[47] Minutes, 4 December 1868.   [48] *Liberator*, July 1856.
[49] Ibid., June 1856.

in the chosen constituencies. There was also an extensive correspondence carried on between Dissenting local notables and the head office, which took every opportunity to press home the importance of registration.

At the 1857 election the number of county seats held by Liberals rose from thirty to fifty-three. There were contests in twenty-seven counties, twenty of which were those operated on by the Society. 'With the exception of Berkshire, Dorset, and Herefordshire, all the gains have been made in our list.'[50] How far was the Society responsible? It did not even know itself:

> Now we do not mean to say that we have done much towards producing this result: but we certainly think the result proves the truth of what we have said. There is an electoral preponderance in the counties we have named on the side of the Liberal party.[51]

There was a Liberal landslide, and there was a uniquely vigorous electoral campaign by the Dissenters, but the connection between the two must remain an open question.

The problem facing the Society in 1861 was quite a different one. Measures embodying its views were systematically defeated by otherwise sound Liberals who voted with the Tories on church questions, and simply to increase Liberal representation in the Commons was no answer to this. Hence a plan of discipline was designed and adopted by a series of conferences,[52] in 1863 and 1864. Allegiance was demanded from Liberal candidates, not unconditionally, but in proportion to the electoral strength of Dissent in their constituencies. The penalty was desertion. Though many Liberal Anglicans would never have accepted any change without pressure, what the Society asked was moderate and sensible, and usually the threat was enough. Disciplinary action, as conceived by the plan of campaign of 1863, only had to be used in ten divisions in 1865, where it was successful in forcing the candidate to surrender in six cases.[53] A few sincere Churchmen lost their seats as the price of their and the Society's zeal, but in general, candidates changed policy

---

[50] Ibid., May 1857.   [51] Ibid., May 1857.
[52] C. S. Miall, *Life of Edward Miall*, 252.   [53] Minutes, 31 July 1865.

mechanically in proportion to the pressure applied. So swiftly and quietly was this conversion accomplished, that while the Parliament of 1859–65 had passed not a single law favourable to religious equality, it was possible to draw up a table of such measures passed by its successor: [54]

> 1866: Qualification for Offices Act
> 1867: Dublin Professorships Act
> Transubstantiation Declaration Act
> Offices and Oaths Act
> 1868: Compulsory Church Rates Abolition Act
> Irish Burials Act
> West Indies Ecclesiastical Grants Act

The Voluntaryist group in Parliament illustrates the processes of party evolution in an interesting way. In the 1830's and 1840's the original handful of dissidents, in this case the half dozen Nonconformist M.P.s, found that their lack of numbers prevented them effecting their objects through the party to which nominally they belonged. They therefore became a more consciously dissident group and sought to increase their numbers. Having increased their power as an independent body, which the Dissenters had done by 1857 as much as they needed, they could then enter negotiations with the main body of the party from a position of strength, reach an acceptable compromise, and disband their forces. The process was cyclical, and one cycle had been completed in 1868 when Gladstone wrote to the Society: [55]

> I must add that nothing could be more loyal and considerate than the conduct of the Abolitionists, in and out of Parliament, throughout the proceedings on this Bill from 1866 to the final close. And I have seen enough to know that no small share of this acknowledgement belongs to you.

A new cycle of dissidence and reconciliation began with the Education Act controversy of 1870: but always, the purpose of minority intransigence was an ultimately peaceful absorption in the main body of the party. Here, only two points need

[54] Minutes, 7 August 1868.
[55] Minutes, 14 September 1868, quoting from a letter from Gladstone to the Society, 14 August 1868.

be noticed in connection with the intransigent phase of
militant Dissent. The Liberation Society had its own Whip
in connection with Religious Equality Bills (until 1865 he
was Sir Charles Douglas): [56] and it may well, by secretly con-
certed action never then or since suspected, have brought
down the Palmerston ministry in 1857:

> The Chairman, Dr Foster, then brought under the notice
> of the Committee the fact that they had been opposed or
> hindered by the Government in all their proposals relative
> to Religious Freedom: instance, particularly the Church
> Rates Bill, in the case of which the Committee had accepted
> considerable responsibility in order to meet the views of the
> Government and had been defeated by Lord Palmerston's
> non-acceptance of the decisions of his own Cabinet: that
> though this Bill alone might not be a sufficient ground on
> which to take up an attitude of hostility to the Government
> generally, the fact was, it was the same with all measures of
> Reform . . . He thought it impossible that this state of
> things could long continue, and that a union now effected
> among a few M.P.s—from 10 to 20—for the purpose of
> acting together adversely to the Government on the next
> party vote, if avowed, would have the effect of altering the
> present policy of the Government on the above questions.
> He was preparing to do what in him lay towards effecting
> this union. . . . [57]

At this point, unfortunately, the Minutes were discontinued
for two years. But on the next party vote, a week or two later,
Government were defeated, and a General Election followed
at which the well prepared Liberationists gained largely.

Too much may be made of the Nonconformist contribution
to Liberalism, and in particular to its moral quality. The
concern of the administration for getting things right,
the disquiet learnt at university and from the reviews and
literature, and the quiet good sense of the Anglican country
gentlemen, gave counsel as clear as that of the Nonconformist
conscience. On some issues, notably those concerning Ireland,
the Catholics, and the working class, the Nonconformist

[56] Minutes 1862–7, 285.
[57] Minutes of the Parliamentary Committee, 16 February 1857.

conscience shone with a most faltering light: on others, like reform or foreign policy, it temporized or was swayed to a passionate excess in accordance with the mood of the day. What it brought to Liberalism was not conscience, which the party was already troubled with, but votes, given without reasonable hope of return. For the aims of militant Dissent, which would have been oppressive if carried out by a majority, could never be carried out by a permanent minority, and the Liberal Party would never destroy itself by introducing Liberationist measures. By astute lobbying, a series of concessions were won which removed the worst anomalies, leaving the Dissenters, of course, further than ever from their theoretical objectives, but with their votes bound hard by habit to the Liberal Party.

The Nonconformist assault on the Liberal Party entered a second phase in the 1880's, which culminated in 1905. Here an actual change in the personnel of the Parliamentary Liberals occurred, from Anglican to Nonconformist, on a large scale. But what ended Anglican control of the Parliamentary Liberal Party was not Nonconformist agitation as such, which could be contained, but a new line of division in politics, of which the axis of controversy was the place of property in a democracy.

THE WORKING-CLASS LIBERAL

Though there are many printed and manuscript items bearing on working-class politics, it is in the nature of the case that all such evidence must lead to a less than full, even to a misleading statement of the situation, unless tempered by general considerations. For the evidence, pre-selected by the mere fact of its existence, represents the active, the organized, the exceptional in working-class politics, the rare and exciting times when a few of 'the masses' broke away and behaved like orthodox politicians. Hence it is appropriate to offer here these general considerations in the light of which to approach further evidence.

Working-class support of Gladstonian Liberalism has astonished many. (When John Burns told a London mob that Bright was a silver-tongued old hypocrite, they tried to pitch him into the Serpentine.) Attempts to explain it away have stressed mainly either the flexibility and sleight of hand of the popular Parliamentary Liberals, or the institutional and financial inadequacies of working-class organization. The possibility that, propaganda apart, the working class was genuinely Liberal in the same way—and with the same complications from religious and social causes—as the middle class, has not been sufficiently considered.[58] Indeed, the attractiveness of Liberalism to both was much the same. The middle class lived under the shadow of personal economic disaster as much as did the working class: perhaps it was even more terrifying and irremediable for the middle class. Liberalism did nothing to solve the problem of personal security for these people; what it did, in a mild way, to add to the general prosperity of the country, affected the middle class and the working class alike. The canons of Peelite administration might as well have been applied to another planet for all the provinces knew of them. If people in Sheffield were affected at all by competitive examinations for the Civil Service or abolition of purchase in the army, it was through their sense of justice, not of interest. If, despite this, the urban middle class was on the whole strongly Liberal, there was no reason why the working class should not be also.

There is, however, at least one line of argument which suggests the contrary. There were separatist working class religious denominations, above all the Primitive Methodists, which were strong in organization, finance, and numbers. Should there not, then, barring some sinister influence, have been a similar class political organization?

We would argue in return that, though there was no real bar to a working-class party in politics corresponding to the Primitive Methodists in religion, this alternative was consciously rejected on understandable grounds. Great parts of

[58] It was chiefly the working-class voters who were likely to react resentfully to Tory coercion, e.g. 'If the screw is taken off the salt works at Droitwich [the Liberal] wins by 300: if not, [the Tory] will not be ten ahead of him,'—Glyn to Gladstone, 9 October 1868, B.M. Add. mss. 44,347, f. 193.

the electoral system were weighed hopelessly against democracy: other constituencies, like Halifax and Birmingham, that were potentially democratic, may have been 'worked' with deliberate malignity by Radical employers against the working man. But in a fair number of industrial boroughs after 1867, the opportunities were quite good, and were not taken. In Manchester in 1868, Ernest Jones, the former Chartist, polled ten thousand odd votes as a working-class candidate, but none of those ten thousand put up under the same colours after his death. The borough of Stafford in 1874 was induced to elect Alexander Macdonald, the Scottish miners' leader, as an independent working-man's candidate in 1874, and what happened in Stafford could have happened elsewhere; there were no miners in the borough.[59] If the working class had wished for political expression as it had done in the 1840's, it would have found many openings, though with no hope of a national majority, in the constituencies.

There was no question of want of organization holding it back. The big unions had plenty of funds and great managerial expertise. The Reform League at its height, with its hundreds of local branches, could get hundreds of thousands of people on to the streets with a drill and discipline unsurpassed in English history. At the very bottom of society, though dismissed as a race of slaves by the urban trade unionists, the village labourers showed considerable powers of corporate action in large areas of England from the 1870's onwards. The chapels and the temperance societies recruited and trained local leaders, and there was no need to look beyond the Old Testament for the ideology of the Radical smallholder. Again, if it is insisted that before the individual can be politically active he must be integrated in a group, there were always the pubs. England was urbanized more by the small workshop than by the factory: hence trade unionism, like the chapels, had little access to large sections of the manual or town workers. But the pub was ubiquitous, and had subsidiary functions, often since perished: that of employment exchange, committee and club room, small money-

[59] Henry Broadhurst, M.P., *The Story of His Life . . . told by Himself* (1901), 67.

lender and pawnbroker, reading room, and most universal unit in forming opinion. To consider the 1851 census of occupations, and the returns of the number of employees per unit of production, is to see that the manual working class was far more likely to be united by the leisure activities which it had in common than by its infinitely various occupational industrial experience. There was, too, among working men, still a significant number who were self-employed and owners of property. Many were rated for the relief of the poor: and so far as the aristocracy of labour entered into sympathy with the really destitute, it was by the same act of imagination that middle-class reformers did so. For differentials of income and barriers of caste were high. Thomas Wright, the journeyman engineer, thought it would be both immoral and dangerous for him, a man with a trade in his fingers, to take a job as an unskilled labourer in competition with untrained men.[60] What Lord Clarendon, looking on at the working-class celebrations in favour of Garibaldi, called 'that union and fusion of classes which constituted the real power of England',[61] was really the result of the elaborate craft stratification of pre-industrial town life which minimized conflict by simple separation. Popular Radicalism was the product of the leisure of Saturday night and Sunday morning, the pothouse and the chapel, not of the working week.

The richness of the rich was not taken as a great affront. The *Beehive*, even in the period when it was owned by the trade unions, never put forward generalities about property and wealth. Their complaints were that this inspector of mines favoured the masters, that this shipowner kept bad faith with a seaman, but there was no questioning of the doctrines of property and no sense of the essential injustice of the rich existing at all. There was more to this than simple want of Socialist doctrine, for in Ireland there were at least the symptoms of implacable resentment against the rich as such, and the Irish peasants were not Socialists. The events of the Paris Commune, too, revealed strength of class feeling

[60] Thomas Wright, *Some Habits and Customs of the Working Classes* (London 1867).

[61] Clarendon to Russell, 15 April 1864: Russell Papers, P.R.O. 30/22/26.

which had no equivalent in England, where it appears to have been absent not from suppression or propaganda or the partiality of the surviving evidence, but from the nature of circumstances. What the poor *saw* the rich do, was give and spend, rather than take. The poverty of the poor arose, often very noticeably, from the unproductiveness of their labours, and it was understandable that the poor should regard the rich as a national resource like coal, a bonus given by nature which radiated benefits without taking anything back. Though the debates on the Second Reform Bill revealed a fairly common opinion among the rich that it was their money that democracy was after, the general feeling of the country was that it was the rich who maintained, and whose duty it was to maintain the poor, not the poor who maintained the rich. Still less did any argue that the richness of the rich created the poverty of the poor. The experience of working-class life was all against such doctrine. What they could hope for from politics was not improvement of condition or satisfaction of antipathies, but a sense of their own audacity and shrewdness, a feeling of participation in a wider national life, the excitement of partisanship in a demonstrably superior cause, and the prospect of gradual improvements in living conditions and in the justice of social arrangements, improvements assuredly not unconnected with their own and their leaders' endeavours. This made the Gladstonian Liberal Party as suitable a party for the working men as for any other class.

What kind of people were the working-class electors? The section dealing with Rochdale gives the answer in one particular case, and sections on popular Liberalism in Whitby and Leeds, bear out what is said about Rochdale. Apart from this, however, it is possible to take the poll books of English boroughs—the heart of Liberalism—and show what kind of person the Liberal working-class elector was. His religious views and habits are obscure, but his occupation is not. He was a skilled craftsman, differing from the 'middle-class' shopkeeper or clerk not in his wealth so much as in the fact that he worked with his hands. Some craftsmen, like tailors and cobblers, obviously were often closely tied to a shop. In borough after borough, the main groups of the working men

are the same; tailors, shoemakers, building craftsmen, and
metal workers of various kinds. On this rock the Liberal
majority in the borough and in the nation was based. The
figures for Cambridge in the 1868 election were typical:

	Liberals	Tories
Leather and luxury work	25	14
Tailors	178	58
Painters	45	29
Furniture makers	42	25
Printers	46	17
Shoemakers	121	63
Metal workers	118	62
Building craftsmen	207	85
Coachbuilders	12	9
Bookbinders and minor crafts	15	24
Sweeps	0	7
	809	393

What was less important was unskilled labour:

	Liberals	Tories
Labourers	214	108
Railwaymen	75	15
Servants	65	120
College servants	25	115
	379	358

Before 1868, the 'intelligent artisan' employed in the immemorial crafts of old Europe far outnumbered the other
sections of the working class in the electorate. Servants, gardeners, and coachmen were never numerous, railwaymen and
textile workers were very rarely voters, even in the factory
towns. Before 1868, 'labour' in the sense of the political economists, 'labour' of the kind which Carlyle felt bound by the cash
nexus, had not arrived in the electorate: in many boroughs,
indeed, it had not arrived outside it either. Even after 1868,
'labour', with its own way of looking at things, only became a
dominant element in a handful of industrial constituencies.

In the county towns and market towns and cathedral towns, the key to the electorate was still the cobbler, the tailor, and the (probably related) corner-shop grocer. Liberalism was before all else the way these people looked at things, their domestic morality writ large. They belonged to a traditional town life that was passing away, devoured by clothing factories, shoe factories, and chain stores. As their relative importance declined, the kind of politics they had demanded disappeared.

PARTY ORGANIZATION

The massive development of party loyalties throughout the country preceded any corresponding full development of party organization by almost a generation. This section, therefore, is written in deprecation of any view that might take party machinery to be the leading thread and clue in the history of party. In the 1880's, party machinery became a matter of intense concern, because of its temporary identification with the careers of Chamberlain and Churchill. Their genius gave to mere machinery, a social force and meaning which it has lacked before and since, and which has rather stood in the way of proper appreciation of its nature.

Three governing axioms may be put forward. There was considerable advance in the forms of organization; but, owing to the growth of the electorate and changes in electoral conditions, the electorate in general never became any more organized. The organizational leviathan of 1880 might have less grip than the pothouse committee of 1832. Secondly, the juggernaut theory of organization does not take due regard of cyclical ineffectiveness. London head offices might maintain a consistent level of administrative activity year in year out, but provincial and voluntary organizations could not do this. The cultural and social climate in which party machinery had to operate, was one in which the impersonal and ruthless bureaucracy of the State could not be imitated. Thirdly, to the credit of human nature, the electorate in the boroughs reacted violently to the thought of being dragooned, and some of the more prominent early attempts to organize the boroughs ended in fiasco.

Again, one can consider the various phenomena of Liberal politics in turn, and enquire where party organization touched them. The propaganda of the party was carried on by the new Press, not by party organs proper; and the great standing armies which bound men to serve under the Liberal flag, were those not of the Liberal Associations, but of militant Dissent and the labour aristocracy. Still less, of course, did the Liberal hold on Society, the aristocracy, and the mind of England, involve the creation of even the smallest party organization—apart from the great Whig clubs. Among the leaders, Whigs and Radicals alike left questions of machinery to the solicitors. Palmerston left no string unpulled,[62] but his methods were essentially those of Monarch and Court. Gladstone, Mill, and Bright (and the later Cobden) regarded the local managers as relics of the old electoral system, slightly corrupted by their vested interests. They certainly did not look on them as models for the future. Indeed, the idea of using party machinery to gain ends which would otherwise be smothered, had fallen away considerably by the 1860's. In the 1840's and 1850's, it had played a large part in Radical wish-fulfilment:

> . . . how to work this popular power? Create opinion—direct it—concentrate it. Needful for financial or Parliamentary reform. Register. Qualify. Boroughs and Counties. Associations—committees—co-operate—40 shillings *Tindal*—populous counties all to be gained. Thus by moral means shall steadily advance to good and honest government.[63]

But when Bright in the 1860's came to create and direct opinion, he ignored the question of getting that opinion organized and on the register. Bright was no innocent in

[62] 'The strength of the Government consists not simply in the Balance of Votes in our Favour in the House of Commons, but mainly in favourable Public Opinion, and in the Division of Sentiments in the Conservative Party.'—Palmerston to Brand, 14 August 1863, Palmerston mss. Gladstone paid far more attention to the Whips than did Palmerston.

[63] Bright's notes for speech, 10 January 1849: B.M. Add. mss. 43,392.

matters of machinery, having played a leading part in the
formation of a very effective Liberal Association at Rochdale
in the 1830's, but with a democratic Press behind him, he
was probably right in thinking he could abandon the concentration on machinery as belonging to a more plutocratic
phase of agitation.

Any description of party organization before the 1880's
must turn chiefly on the expedients adopted in the English
borough, where the machinery had some connection with the
social balance of a town. Solid local organization was a necessary preliminary to a national chain of command. But in the
1860's, though there was no chain of command, there were
already two levels of political activity besides that of the
borough managers. Very little can here be said of either,
beyond indicating some future lines of research which might
throw light on these very dark places.

These were the club movements in the wards, and central
party organization. Both date from the 1860's. The Liberal
Registration Association, founded by the Whips and party
leaders in 1860, with its office in London, carried out much
of the normal work of a party headquarters from the start,
in interviewing candidates, organizing voters who for some
reason were inaccessible to local parties, and stirring up
dormant constituencies. Unconnected with policy or any
great career, and not lavishly provided with money, it was at
least as much the prototype of the modern national organization as was the National Liberal Federation. Like that body,
it sought to federate the local Liberal parties, though in terms
of expediency only, and without the democratic rhetoric of
Chamberlain. There is no reason to doubt that in its time it
was a considerable advance on a preceding anarchy, and that
it did effective liaison work for the party. Unfortunately,
though the office in Victoria Street has been continuously
active since 1860, all its early archives are said to have been
lost about 1920. Barring some stroke of good fortune, then,
the office has effectively covered its traces, and one can best
learn of its work through the papers of the Liberal Whips
who guided it.

The prospectus issued on the foundation of the Liberal
Registration Association in 1860, showed how humbly party

organization, national as well as local, was bound to electoral registration:

> Every day's experience shows, that the main reliable source of success in Electioneering, is a careful supervision of . . . the Register. In many of the principal constituencies, care is taken of this most important matter by local societies, with which (when properly managed) it is not proposed to interfere. There are, however, a vast number of constituencies where no organized plan of Registration is adopted, and where attention to the Register is either altogether neglected, or is dependent on individual efforts inadequate to the task. To constituencies such as these a Liberal Registration Association would afford much valuable assistance. . . . The Members would not be limited in number, or restricted to members of the House, and every effort would be made to include in the Association representatives of all shades of Liberal political opinion.[64]

The extended personal membership was meant as a first step to the confederation of the Liberal societies, as well as a way of raising money: 'We also much desire to have the countenance of Chairmen of local Liberal Associations and I hope you will be able to induce the Chairman of your Association to join.'[65]

In 1868 the secretary was writing to George Wilson in Manchester, in an attempt to win Cheshire for the Liberals:

> Our Committee were asking me about Cheshire among other places this week . . . I did not know to whom to look for reliable information. It appears to me that if the registrations of the two divisions were thoroughly attended to, we ought to return two Liberals for North, and one for mid-Cheshire.[66]

The conception of its work as advice, support, and encouragement, which was taken by the Liberal head office, was a

[64] B.M. Add. mss. 44,193, f. 12, about 1860.
[65] Liberal Registration Association to B. Wrigley, 19 March 1861: Melly Papers III, 733, in Liverpool Central Library.
[66] T. N. Roberts to Wilson, 6 March 1868: Wilson Papers, Manchester Central Library.

sound one. But a managing clerk, however good, whose powers were virtually limited to correspondence, could have no real *locus standi* with local managers: still less could his office form the basis of a national chain of command. The central office was further overshadowed by the tendency of the Whips and the party leaders, particularly at election times, to organize the local parties through their massive private correspondence. Thus in 1868, while the Whips handled the candidatures themselves, they delegated the routine work to the office:

> We have an office in London with a secretary, etc. in communication with all the local agents, giving them advice, supplying them with all forms of claims, etc., also doing most important work at an election, in looking up the out-voters. This is supposed to be kept alive by annual subscription but I find £300 a year is all I get towards an expense of £1,500. I have kept this up this year as it would have been most foolish to lose all this perfect machinery (the only basis of organisation which we have) upon the eve of a General Election. Hayter says it costs more than it is worth: Mr. Brand has been a strong advocate for it, and I certainly *now* find it most necessary. I am sure we have saved thousands of votes, by the information and instructions sent to local agents from our headquarters.[67]

The central organization which developed in the 1860's involved no attempt to create a bureaucratic party or a chain of command. The humdrum tasks which it did perform successfully were of little moment electorally; and there was no attempt to carry on propaganda through strictly party organs. The three essentials of political patronage, the promotion of candidatures, and the control of funds, were not institutionalized in the central party organization, but remained with the Whips. There was no institution which at all corresponded to the impalpable national party.

At the lowest social level of explicit party politics was the movement which created working-class clubs in the wards. These clubs had nothing to do with the provincial political

[67] Glyn to Gladstone, 7 December 1869: B.M. Add mss. 44,347, f. 161.

clubs, tied to the local Exchange, which were founded in emulation of the London Carlton and Reform Clubs, and of which the Manchester Reform Club was the most imposing example. These businessmen's clubs are relatively well documented: but the existence, let alone the meaning, of the working-class clubs has barely found record in print. Even the date when such clubs were first organized, cannot be given, though the system of ward clubs probably went back to the 1860's. The first sources which mention them—political almanacks and town guides of the 1880's—suggest that the clubs in the northern industrial towns had grown to maturity over the previous generation, and that by 1890 there was no room for any more. As regards the earlier limit, no working-class political clubs can be traced before 1860, except, of course, those which represented some agitation in violent dissent from the Parliamentary parties. In 1887, Stockport was described as having more than a dozen local Liberal clubs:[68] in Manchester in 1894, there were twenty-eight Conservative and thirty Liberal ward clubs.[69] One of these, the Chorlton-on-Medlock Liberal Club, we know to have been founded in 1870, because George Wilson, the Anti-Corn Law League chairman, sent it a donation of twenty pounds.[70] The Liberal clubs movement is still strong in the Northern industrial working-class districts,[71] but it would be expecting much to hope to obtain any tradition of its origins from its present leaders, and in view of the silence of the printed records on the subject, the history of these clubs must be written from the imagination. That imagination must surely see in them one of the most striking emblems of the attachment of working-class opinion to the Parliamentary parties, for whatever help they may have received from party managers, their successful continuance must have depended on working-class support, and that support must have been freely given from the 1860's onwards to justify so great an investment in bricks

[68] *Liberal and Radical Yearbook*, 1887.

[69] W. A. Shaw, *Manchester Old and New* (1894), III, 59.

[70] Chorlton-on-Medlock Liberal Club to George Wilson, 25 October 1870: Wilson Papers.

[71] Huddersfield, which still has a Liberal newspaper and long had a Liberal M.P., has as many as twenty-five local Liberal clubs.

and mortar. Party politics, as much as seaside excursions or commercial football, was one of the first activities which the town artisans turned to as their conditions improved, but one can trace no formal link between the clubs and the official middle-class borough managers. The papers of such city bosses as Wilson, Cowen, Baines, and Rathbone, show only dealings with men of their own social standing; transactions between these so-called 'wirepullers' and the politically organized groups in the wards must have been either done orally or through intermediaries, and there was a greater gulf between the top and bottom of political life within the constituency, than between the local party heads and the national leadership.

The local notables, organized at constituency level, therefore had the field to themselves, with little pressure from above or from below. Very few contested their right to propose and to dispose, and they were therefore under no necessity to develop elaborate institutional disguises. There were fashions in nomenclature, changes in the size of the ostensible sovereign body, and absorption of foreign bodies arising from agitation, by some kind of treaty, but the vertebra remained a matter of families, firms, and estates. The registration societies, which were normally exclusive, Whig, and in imperfect control of the constituency, were perhaps the most honest embodiment of this state of affairs. When a constituency ceased to be manageable by private negotiation or by influence, a few leading gentlemen clubbed together to hire political bailiffs to manage it for them, without any pretence of democracy. As the expenses of registration were heavy and borne by only a few, this system had the merit of testing sincerity, but a chief disadvantage was that the real work all fell to only one of the many Liberal factions, which then used it as an engine of intrigue against their fellow-Liberals. In West Derby hundred,

> . . . the Whigs have the management of the County Registration, and I have no doubt the Tories have beaten them, as they have done, on previous occasions, on the Register. I believe that no good will be done until they are displaced and fresh hands employed.[72]

[72] Robertson Gladstone to Wilson, 15 May 1863: Wilson Papers.

Whig control of the registration in the West Riding meant in a similar way that the party moved at the pace of its slowest man, Earl Fitzwilliam. The contrary process occurred in south east Lancashire, where the faggot voting techniques of the Manchester School, designed to enforce extreme Radicalism on a moderate constituency, succeeded in turning it Tory.

Registration Societies might even create majorities by their labours for candidates they disowned. Colville, elected for South Derbyshire in 1865 as an independent Liberal, wrote to the local caucus:

> I presume the Liberal Registration Society does not consist of more than one or two hundred members. I shall appeal to the constituency at large, and not as the nominee of any committee or society and I shall stand to win or lose single handed and alone.[73]

The Registration Societies were well suited to the work of combining a moderate number of family influences in a central agency for the purpose of working a county seat; but, incorporating no element of agitation, too obviously reliant on money power, and without any democratic claim to legitimate authority, the new formal registration associations that had appeared in the boroughs had become anachronistic by 1870, or even by 1860.

The general pattern of the 1860's in the open constituencies, both county and borough, was for the Liberal Registration Association to become the expression of the Palmerstonian and anti-democratic sections of the party, while some parallel local organization arose among Radicals who had hitherto been smothered by the notables. By 1868 the Palmerstonians would have given way and remodelled the Registration Association as a broad-bottomed Liberal Association which they almost inevitably came to dominate. Only in the special case of Wales was registration not a bulwark of the Liberal right, for there the Liberal registration

[73] C. E. Hogarth, *Parliamentary Elections in Derby and Derbyshire 1832–1865*: (thesis, 1957, in Arts Library, Manchester University), 145 et seq.

societies were from the beginning entirely in the hands of militant Dissent.[74]

Before turning to those boroughs which had organizations more sophisticated than the registration associations, we should consider those boroughs which had no formal organization at all. At the very bottom of the scale came towns like Cockermouth, cut off from all political life by its sheer unimportance, and not even vitalized by the patronage of a great family:

> . . . Since the death of General Wyndham, Tory influence here has subsided, and we could return 2 Liberals. Mr. Steel opposes an extension of the franchise. He is 75 and only a Solicitor here, and I fancy has never spent £20 in his election, and if you wish to enter Parliament you could be readily returned, for Dissent can turn the scale here, and if you drop a note to Rev. Mr. Hale, Independent, or Mr. Jos. Brown, Harris, and Son, Spinners, or John Pearson, Esq., manufacturer, you would find a ready response, as they are puzzled who to invite.[75]

In such a town—and there were many of them till 1885—only men made decisions, not committees or societies. In slightly larger towns, the electoral arrangements were jolted out of stagnation by the increase in the electorate. At Macclesfield, in 1865, the Brocklehurst family ran their own candidate and their own committee, saying 'They had never coalesced, and they never would.'[76] But in 1868, they had almost turned right round:

> The Brocklehursts, who have furnished one member since 1832, are the greatest employers of labour in the town, and are in possession of the Whig influence, but hither to the present election, they have previously chosen to run single-handed for their chance—this has worked to the loss of the Liberal party . . . They still profess at the present juncture to run alone—but the tacit understanding is a coalition

[74] *Liberator*, December 1866, 204: August 1867, 154.
[75] Anon. to G. Wilson, 15 May 1865: Wilson Papers.
[76] *Macclesfield Courier*, 8 July 1865.

between him and Chadwick—the second Liberal in the
field . . . There is but one single committee, acting nominally for Chadwick, in reality canvassing and working for a
united return.[77]

Only in the narrow band of boroughs where a consciously
modern business class was faced with stiff Tory opposition did
the party organization really develop. In places like Macclesfield and Cockermouth merely personal and proprietary influences retarded development, while, contrarily, the very
large seats also encouraged political primitivism, since they
were only manageable by very rich men, or by distinguished
men whose candidature was in the hands of the very rich.
In the very large seats, where a Liberal of some colour was
normally returned as a matter of course, there was no reason
to abandon the most extreme individualism in the 1860's.
School board elections and the rise of middle-class Toryism
were the background to the movement towards unity in the
1870's.

Thus in Glasgow the Liberals won all three seats without
creating a representative association; in the city of Derby, the
Liberals returned their men through a General Liberal Election Committee, apparently self-appointed: '. . . I called on
a number of Liberals in the county town . . . the Liberals are
strong here . . . ; but there is really no organization and I
expect there will be no stir until the election.'[78] Such important towns as Sheffield and Newcastle had not got beyond
the committee stage in the 1860's, the Mundella-Roebuck
contest at Sheffield in 1868 being fought out by candidates'
ad hoc committees. In London there were probably no representative associations till the 1880's: 'Political life in London
was almost non-existent, except under special circumstances,
as at Chelsea, where they had an association connected with
the working classes, and another with the middle classes.'[79]
London had its Radical organizers, but they could not afford

[77] Election Reports, Howell Collection, Bishopsgate Institute.
[78] National Reform Union agent to Wilson, 25 April 1865: Wilson
Papers.
[79] Statement by a Mr Firth of London in *Proceedings Attending the
Formation of the National Federation of Liberal Associations* (Birmingham 1877), 38.

to take advantage of their opportunities. The trade unionist Cremer, chairman of the Marylebone Electoral Reform Association, said his society had spent £300 at the 1868 election to get 5,400 lodgers on the register:

> It was done through our association: through the instrumentality of the working men there, but of course not with the working men's funds. We had to appeal to friends outside, which we were very sorry for, but which is almost a necessity now.[80]

Experienced working-class politicians had no liking either for the caucus system or for the unorganized large popular constituencies, regarding both with much justification as plutocratic.[81]

In the 1860's there was political life everywhere, adequate political organization in very few places. From 1860 onwards, the ward clubs and the national headquarters were adding their mites to the total of political activity in each constituency. In most boroughs, too, there would be at least one society for Parliamentary reform, one group of temperance reformers, and another political organization representing the Liberationists. There might be organized trades union or Irish blocs. Hence the party managers had to broaden their arrangements or simply become one faction among many. Nothing fundamental being at issue, the 1860's and 1870's were marked by the formation of representative constituency parties in the boroughs. Chronological and other evidence shows this trend to organization was rarely in emulation of Birmingham, but was a parallel development all over the country under the stress of circumstances.

The Birmingham caucus was founded in 1865 and reorganized for the general election of 1868. The following table indicates the gap between the towns which developed early on their own lines and those which were modelled on the Birmingham pattern under the influence of the anti-Turk

[80] Report of Select Committee on Registration, H.C. 78 (1868-9), VII, 86-7.

[81] e.g. G. Howell in the *New Quarterly Magazine*, X, 1878, 579-90, G. J. Holyoake, *Working Class Representation* (Birmingham 1868).

agitation: the Lancashire boroughs are listed as a convenient sample:[82]

Ashton	1873	Burnley	1878
Birkenhead	1862	Bury	1877
Blackburn	1878	Rochdale	1834
Bolton	1870	Stockport	1850
Bootle	1873	Wigan	1860

The Manchester United Liberal Party was founded in 1862, the Liverpool party was being built up by Rathbone about 1860, and the Newcastle Liberal Association was founded on a hint from Bright in 1873, the organizers having even then no knowledge of the Birmingham system. 'Our Association was modelled on that of Rochdale.'[83] So may that of Birmingham itself have been: certainly at Rochdale and Stockport in the 1850's and 1860's, inner-party democracy, policy discussions, and caucus discipline over the candidate and electors, had reached the fully modern stage.[84] The Leeds Liberals were also probably the authors of their own salvation:

> The difficulty of keeping a large constituency in hand, is very great, but some means must be found for this. I have been thinking of perfecting our system of ward representation on the Committee of the Liberal Association, so as to have feelers in the different districts of the Borough—but this is only one step. Be assured I will not let the subject drop . . .[85]

The absence of any reference to Birmingham is at least curious, and was paralleled in the discussions which led to the formation of a Liberal Association at Scarborough in 1876. There the association was formed by the coalescence of the traditional patron, Sir Harcourt Johnstone, with a committee of advanced Liberals, each to put forward one

[82] From *Liberal and Radical Yearbook*, 1887.
[83] R. Spence Watson, *The National Liberal Federation* (1907), 3.
[84] See B.M. Add. mss. 43,388, f. 156, for a letter by the M.P. for Stockport recording a stormy debate on national policy in the Stockport Reform Association.
[85] T. Marshall to Edward Baines, 17 February 1874: Baines Papers, Leeds election bundle.

Parliamentary candidate. In 1878 the Association had 1,110 members, of whom 965 were voters, and it spent £968 at the 1880 election. Throughout its proceedings there was no mention of an outside model.[86]

Where the Liberal association of the 1860's and 1870's marked a real change was in the degree of dilution the managing oligarchy was forced to concede. What was conceded was not democracy within the party, either really or in form, but a broadening of participation by the many, in decisions necessarily taken as before, by the few. If oligarchy remained beneath the surface, the old oligarchy which sought monopoly and displayed its pride had been made impossible by the electorate itself by about 1860. The new associations were generally a compromise between Tammany and chaos made by men reacting against both. Their object was to distribute power wide within the constituency, while retaining the authority to ensure stable Parliamentary representation. In Stoke, for instance, the chairman of the Liberal Council held an open meeting in 1868 'to ratify the decision of the Liberal Council, which had been elected in the most fair and open manner, as representative of the great body of electors, and as authorized by them to select the candidates for the representation'.[87]

The power of the cry against 'dictation' at elections had been shown chiefly in Manchester, Nottingham, and Chester. At Manchester it was the local machinery of the Anti-Corn Law League which was objected to: at Nottingham it was a caucus of town councillors—'the wealthy Whig party'[88]—called 'Number Thirty': and at Chester, the seat which was not controlled by the Grosvenors was in the hands of about six men whose power came from their monopoly of access to the rates collectors' books.[89] In all three cases, the electorate took pleasure in inflicting crushing and final defeats on their masters in the period 1857–62.

Another writer has made a detailed study of Manchester

[86] A complete set of the Minute Books exists running from 24 January 1876 to the present.

[87] *Staffordshire Advertiser*, 14 November 1868.

[88] P. H. Bagenal, *Life of Ralph Bernal Osborne, M.P.* (1884), 246.

[89] Mass Observation, *Browns of Chester*, 144.

Liberalism,[90] excellent both in its choice of subject and in its execution. For in Manchester more than anywhere else, all the logical possibilities of organization were explored, in militant isolation from outside influences. In the beginning, each candidate had his own committee. By the end of the 1830's, the Liberal candidates were running in harness, but there was no standing Liberal organization, the want of which was supplied by the Anti-Corn Law League and its successor organizations between 1847 and 1857. The defeat of the League party in 1857 left a vacuum which was first filled by a Reform agitation under survivors of the League. This led on to reconciliation and the foundation of the United Liberal Committee on a broad basis:

> It is well known that the United Liberal Committee which is the only representative committee of the Liberal Party, has no connection with any political organisation whatever, but consists of about 500 of the most active politicians from every ward of the city.

In 1873, by adding an apparatus of constitutions and committees, this informal body was turned into the Manchester Liberal Association, which lasted till 1885, when the division of the constituency brought about another reorganization.

The same leading families, the same economic and confessional groups, the same attitude of mind, and the same iron law of oligarchy, were the real material of party organization in Manchester throughout this period, and the machinery was their shadow. And so it was elsewhere; the broadening of the basis of town politics and the formation of permanent organizations in the 1860's, usually raised the tone of municipal life without creating a sinister predominance of any one group, but the democratic expectations with which Chamberlain decorated this arrangement were quite out of place. For rank within the party corresponded very closely to rank on the Exchange and in society: and the various agitations which

[90] P. Whitaker, *The Growth of Liberal Organisation in Manchester from the 1860's to 1903* (1956), a thesis in the Arts Library of Manchester University, on which the following summary is based.

swept over the Liberal Party locally, always found adequate leadership in the large businessmen whom everyone looked to to manage party business.

The roots of party organization were in electoral registration and electioneering on the one hand, and in political agitation on the other, the normal state of both being dormancy. Combined in the more advanced constituencies to form something like modern party organization, though without the modern national chain of command, they nevertheless amounted to no more than a marginal influence in that penetration of the national mind with the notion of supporting, or being a member of one of the Parliamentary parties, which occurred in the generation before Chamberlain.

POPULAR LIBERALISM: ROCHDALE

In the nineteenth century Rochdale was one of the most alert and socially creative towns in England. Thanks to this, and to its excellent library, it is possible to reconstruct Rochdale politics in unusual detail.

Two pamphlets in Rochdale Public Library, entitled *Copy of the Poll, 1 July 1841 . . . Published by Order and Under the Direction of the Non-Electors' Committee,* and *Copy of the Poll, 30 March 1857 . . . Published by Order of the Non-Electors' Committee, Rochdale, 1857,* classify the electorate according to party and occupation. They therefore provide data for relating political opinion to social class in a precise way. Tables summarizing these poll books are printed at the end of this section. The results of the two elections discussed here were as follows:

1841	Crawford, Radical	399
	Fenton, Tory	335
1857	Ramsay, Tory	529
	Miall, Liberal	487

The following suggestions, to be developed later, may be made on the basis of the poll books. The drink trade emerges as clearly the most important organized interest, though its influence was sometimes dormant. Less important was the favour apparently given by the middle-class franchise of 1832 to owners of property, particularly owners of industrial property. The non-electors—meaning those legally excluded from the electoral register—were better placed to exercise influence than the factory owners. The influence of both as classes at elections was perhaps less than that of certain individuals skilled in intrigue and organization.

The fact that both parties were well represented in most occupations and at most social levels indicates that some of the most important political divisions were not matters of class and occupation.

Though Rochdale was a factory town if anywhere was, the social structure of the electorate was such as to prevent conflicts of capital and labour from becoming a political issue. The great majority of electors had both the cares of property and the feelings of the poor, and had no direct concern with factory production. The pre-industrial tone of politics was therefore electorally rational. An aspect of this situation was that though trades unions existed and many of their members were voters, neither the unions, nor the fear of them, played a discernible part in town politics.

While the social structure of the electorate kept it free from dictation from above and open to influence from below, the social structure of the local party organizations expressed much more accurately the deference accorded to the permanent *élites* in the town. The notables controlled the town through their ascendancy in party cabals as working politicians, not as employers through the factory.

Events, in Parliament and in the churches, occurring at a national level, really made a mark on the politics of even so self-absorbed a town as Rochdale. Nevertheless, this—the explicit content of politics as set forth in contemporary speeches and the Press—was of secondary importance.

Finally, an analysis of the voting can also be used to show how a skeletal Tory party survived throughout sixty years of eclipse, thanks to being solidly based on family tradition, social prestige, beer, corruption, and the Church.

Drink was by far the most active of the interests in 1857.

At that election the social structure of the electorate, reckoned as part of the 1,020 electors who voted, and ignoring the 235 who abstained, was as follows:

Capitalists	9%
Craftsmen	23%
Drink interest	14%
Respectables and dependents	18%
Retailers	26½%
Others	9½%

But of these sections, only the drink interest acted as a unit. Its component sections and their affiliations were as follows:

	Liberal	*Conservative*
Beersellers	16	63
Publicans	10	46
Wine dealers	1	5
Spirits dealer	0	1
Maltster	0	1
Hop merchant	0	1
Brewer	0	1
Cooper	1	0
	28	118

This result was no accident. First, an advertisement asked the beersellers to reserve their votes till a general meeting of the trade could be held.[91] The sitting member, Edward Miall, an extreme Liberal who had entered politics from the Congregational ministry, attended this meeting, and was sharply attacked for 'leaving the House when Henry Berkeley's Bill came on' that Bill being well regarded by the trade. However, his attackers were in a double sense not disinterested, for of the two persons described as secretaries of the Beersellers' Association, one, Peter Johnson, was believed to be attending to the electoral register for the Tories at £100 a year, and the other, Thomas Bamford, beerseller, warper, and bellringer at the Parish Church, must have been against Miall on Church grounds.[92]

What was new, and fatal to Miall in 1857, was the union

[91] *Rochdale Standard*, 14 March 1857.
[92] Report of Committee on Rochdale Election Petition, *Parl. Papers* 1857, session 2, H.C. 128, QQ. 1999–2015.

of the publicans and beersellers to form a single interest. Previously the two sections had been naturally distinct, in legal and social status and in politics. The publicans were traditionally Tory in Rochdale. The beersellers, probably recruited from the radical milieu of the small shopkeepers, had hitherto split their votes half and half. The apparent influence of this class division in the trade may be shown by an analysis of voting at Stockport[93] in 1847:

	Cobden, Liberal	Kershaw, Liberal	Heald, Conservative
Beersellers	24	29	18
Publicans	42	30	52

Similarly in Rochdale in 1841 the divisions were:

	Liberal	Conservative
Beersellers	28	24
Publicans	14	31

(According to a town directory of 1845, there were ninety-eight beersellers and eighty-six publicans in Rochdale, so that about half of each section of the trade had the vote.) In 1852 the beersellers were nearly equally divided for and against Miall; in 1857 they went four to one against him.[94]

The instance of a single election proves no more than that the drink vote was volatile and effective, whenever the Liberal candidate incurred guilt by association with temperance men, or failed to canvass trade interests in Parliament. (Lowe, at Kidderminster, where the trade was supposed to have 150 votes out of 495, had the same difficulties over the same obscure Beer Bill.[95]) But before the liquor legislation of 1869–72 it was only the rare Liberal candidate who fell foul of the trade, not the Liberal Party as a whole who incurred displeasure. However, the Rochdale election of 1857 was a presage of how formidable that displeasure was to be later in the century.[96]

[93] From a poll book in Stockport Public Library.
[94] Committee on Rochdale Election, *P.P.* 1857, sess. 2, H.C. 128, Q. 2098.
[95] A. P. Martin, *Life and Letters of the Right Honourable Robert Lowe, Viscount Sherbrooke* (1893), II, 112, 156.
[96] See J. Rowntree and A. Sherwell, *The Temperance Problem and Social Reform* (9th edition, 1900), 680–95, for the electoral effects in the 1890's.

Poll books for other towns show no marked pattern in the voting of the liquor trade at this period:

VOTING OF PUBLICANS AND BEERSELLERS

	Tory	Liberal
Ashton, 1841	43	24
Bedford, 1841	15	13
Bedford, 1857	21	22
Cambridge, 1866	38	30
Cambridge, 1868	40	41
Shrewsbury, 1857	32	53
Stockport, 1847	74	66 (for Cobden)
Warrington, 1847	40	29

The non-electors had a powerful interest in the system which excluded them, having perhaps more influence without the vote than if they had had it. Their influence, of course, like that of everybody else, needed to be 'properly worked' to make itself felt, but there were certainly signs that it was properly worked. In 1857 the non-electors were felt to be an immemorial institution: [97]

> Has it been the custom to hold meetings of non-electors?
> —Always.
> Has that been for the purpose of giving them an opportunity of discussing political questions, and the merits of each candidate?—Yes, for canvassing the merits of those they thought desirable . . .[98]

But the detailed piece of electoral analysis brought out by the non-electors in 1841 showed that they were a committee as well as a meeting, and that they were no mere pot-house agitators. There were no permanent newspapers in Rochdale before 1856, so the operations of the Non-Electors' Committee are hard to trace. But their analyses of the poll were published at each election (though only two now survive), indicating the continuity of working-class militant radicalism. In 1859 they formed a Non-Electors' Reform Association and held a meet-

[97] Comm. on Rochdale Election, *P.P.* 1857, sess. 2, H.C. 128, QQ. 2016–17.

[98] For similar proceedings in Yorkshire, see Guttsmann, 'The General Election of 1859 in the Cities of Yorkshire', *International Review of Social History* (1957), 251.

ing of 1,500 people to quiz the Tory candidate on Reform.
The earliest surviving minutes of the Rochdale Reform Association show good relations between the two bodies:

> The Secretary reported that the Non-Electors had
> applied to him to express their strong wish to have a recep-
> tion demonstration to Mr. Cobden on his entrance into the
> town . . . That this Committee heartily approved of the
> object of the Non-Electors.[99]

The strength of the non-electors was in their numbers.
(There is no direct evidence as to the politics of the non-
electors as a whole, as opposed to the Radical militants
amongst them. But in 1865 the show of hands, in a crowd
of 15,000, was said to be twenty to one in favour of the
Liberal.[100]) A very large part of the retailers and a fair part of
the craftsmen would be working mainly for working-class
custom. The intention behind the poll analyses was clearly to
boycott Tory shops: 'The Non-Electors will read, mark and
learn who have supported their claim to the suffrage, and
who have not recognized that right, and will not fail to bring
all legitimate influences to bear upon the latter.'[101] The
Radicals worked a similar system of exclusive dealing in
Stockport in 1837:

> . . . those publicans and shopkeepers who voted for the
> Major now find their counters deserted. The consequence
> is . . . the butchers and greengrocers in the market place
> cry out from their stalls, Cobden beef, Cobden pototoes,
> etc.[102]

In an industrial town, the carriage trade was of little importance to most shopkeepers, and the boycotting system gave
Demos a greater leverage than the employers, so far as he
cared to use it. In Rochdale the system was worked forcefully:

> The reason why the [Tory] Sick and Burial Society was
> formed was that the Radical party had printed a book of

[99] Minute Book, Rochdale Reform Association, November 1864.
[100] *Rochdale Observer*, 15 April 1865.
[101] Rochdale Poll Book, 1857.
[102] Letter by Cobden, quoted Morley, *Cobden* (1881), I, 116.

both sides of voters, showing that they were determined to support no other but their own party. This exclusive dealing . . . was carried on to a great extent at the time . . .[103]

The unfortunate writer, a Tory shoemaker, was twice ruined by this system:

> I had once more worked up a good connection when another election took place. I again took a prominent part. [After the 1841 election] . . . The Radicals sent into Yorkshire for Mr. Simpson, shoemaker, now Alderman Simpson, who came to lodge and work next door to me. They also induced another shoemaker to commence business in opposition to me on the opposite side of the street . . . my work fell off, I was again ruined, and forced to remove.[104]

In Warrington, similarly, in 1841, the Radicals did all they possibly could to prevent the Tories from getting a living.

> Many would remember . . . the printed list of black sheep, issued by their opponents . . . Perhaps they would also remember that tickets were stuck up on public-houses, beershops, toffey-sellers' shops; and when a party was seen going into any one of these places, he was told: 'You must not go in there: he is a Tory: you must not deal with him.'[105]

The list of black sheep may be found in its very comprehensive second edition in Warrington Public Library.[106] Again, it was alleged that at Ashton in 1868 customers chose shopkeepers for their political opinions, without much regard to the price and quality of their goods, and that there was more exclusive dealing in 1868 than ever before.[107] This practice was not confined to Lancashire. The Morpeth miners settled their differences with the Liberal shopkeepers of the town by

---

[103] *Autobiography of Hamlet Nicholson* (Rochdale 1892), 82.
[104] Ibid., 41.
[105] *Report of Conservative Meeting in Public Hall, Warrington, 31 July 1868*, pamphlet, Warrington Public Library.
[106] *The Black List*, Second Edition, Anon. n.d. Ref. S. 10,121.
[107] Report of Hartington Committee, *P.P.* 1869, H.C. 352, QQ. 2770–82.

an economic boycott in 1873.[108] Working-class economic pressure won a Stoke election in 1852:

> In many streets the publicans were the only electors, but the working men were enthusiastic for free trade, and won the election for us by threatening the publicans and shopkeepers to withdraw their custom unless they promised to vote for us.[109]

It is claimed, therefore, that the working class in the larger boroughs, far from being excluded from all voice in government by the franchise of 1832, actually benefited by being saved from bribery and coercion from above, while remaining free to practise much the same things from below. The working-class non-elector could intervene effectively where he had the wit to do so: the working-class elector could not.[110] The spirit behind it is best conveyed by an anonymous Huddersfield poem of 1852:

Non-Electors Can Vote On A Saturday Night

Although we are rabble, an immoral mob,
Unworthy the notice of Tea-selling snob,
And cannot with wealthier neighbours have right,
We're registered ready for Saturday night.

And when our friend Willans again does appear,
He'll find opposition is banished from here,
For none can withstand the terrible might,
Of Working Men's Votes on a Saturday Night.[111]

Even the processes of justice might incur a democratic check. In one case, the chief magistrate of a Lancashire borough during a protracted strike was a tradesman. Many offenders were charged with intimidating, and the Bench had

---

[108] W. E. Adams, *Memoirs of a Social Atom* (1903), II, 543.

[109] F. Leveson-Gower, *Bygone Years* (1905), 239.

[110] When Gladstone sat for Newark, 1,200 of the 1,600 electors were working men. But, as he naïvely pointed out, they 'never thought of acting together as a class, or of setting up a separate interest'.—Scrutator, *Mr Gladstone and Oxford* (1856), 26. They were, in fact, powerless compared with the Rochdale non-electors.

[111] Among ephemera in Huddersfield Public Library. Saturday night was the great shopping night.

to be rather severe. When it was all over, the tradesman was boycotted, his business went away, and he was obliged to leave the town. He was singled out, and none of the other Justices was so treated.[112]

Trades unions, the fear of which dominated educated discussion of reform, existed in Rochdale, but were below the political horizon, as the Co-operative Movement was not. In 1861 there were thirteen unions in the town, all but two meeting in public houses. Six were not industrial unions at all —the Boot-makers, Joiners, Cabinet-makers, Smiths, Masons, and Tailors. The industrial unions, apart from the Cotton-carders and Wool-sorters, were confined to engineering, viz. the Boiler-makers, Engineers, Engine-builders, and Iron-moulders.[113] Apparently the bulk of textile labour remained unorganized. The trades that were organized were fairly well represented in the electorate under the 1832 franchise. Indeed, the Second Reform Bill may well have reduced the proportion of trade unionists in the electorate. But neither contemporary comment nor the statistics of voting show any sign that the organized artisans formed a political unit as the drink interest so obviously did. Trades unionism, which men like Palmerston were so chary of admitting within the Constitution, had long been taken for granted in Rochdale, as a thing of no importance, for it no more represented a proletarian threat to society than did the working-class friendly societies.

The 1832 franchise, which paradoxically put great influence in the hands of the non-electors,[114] also curtailed the power of employers by excluding most of their employees. In towns where pre-1832 freemen were numerous, this might not be so; but Rochdale was not such a town. Before 1867 Rochdale employers, as such, had almost no direct influence; after 1872 their coercive, as distinct from their persuasive, power

[112] William Chadwick, *Reminiscences of a Chief Constable* (Manchester and London, n.d.), 142.

[113] Based on *United Kingdom First Annual Trades Union Directory, 1861*, a rare pamphlet in Birmingham Public Library.

[114] Democratic feeling was so strong in the town that Rochdale managed somehow to avoid the anti-popular provisions of the Municipal Corporations Act and secured a lower municipal franchise than any other large town in the country.

was annulled by the ballot. The 1868 election was therefore
the only one which might be called an employers' election.
Even so, given the character of the people, it is doubtful
whether factory hands ever voted *en bloc* as the tenantry of
large estates did. For instance, in the comparable town of
Macclesfield, it was said:

> The Weavers as a class show much independence, wages
> being low, and their Work precarious. They are nearly as
> well off at play as at work, which renders them very careless
> of their masters. They will be guided much by their feel-
> ings how they vote. Extraneous influence will not percep-
> tibly touch them.[115]

As shown in Rochdale in 1857 craftsmen formed twenty-three
per cent of those voting, a proportion comparable to the
national return of 1866 which found that twenty-six per cent
of borough voters were working men.[116] (These twenty-six per
cent, on enquiry, were found to include a large number of
'urban peasants'—self-employed men and small capitalists in
overalls.) But a breakdown of the general category reveals
how misleading it would be to think of this group, in its
chaotic variety, as in any way 'proletarian':

	Liberal	*Conservative*
Blacksmiths	3	3
Boiler-makers	3	1
Boot and shoe makers	13	5
Brass and iron founders	6	5
Bricksetters	3	1
Brush-makers	1	2
Cabinet-makers	8	3
Card-makers	2	0
Cloggers	4	9
Coachbuilders	6	9
Curriers	4	1
Doffing plate makers	3	0
Engineers	9	7
Joiners	11	7
Machine-makers	11	4

[115] Report on Macclesfield 1868: Howell Collection, Bishopsgate Institute, London.
[116] *P.P.* 1866, vol. LVII, 747.

	Liberal	Conservative
Mechanics	5	1
Painters	5	3
Plumbers	1	5
Reed-makers	4	2
Ropers	1	1
Saddlers	0	3
Shuttle-makers	3	0
Spindle-makers	0	2
Stone masons	0	3
Tailors	11	6
Tinners	2	3
Watch-makers	3	2
Weavers	3	5
Wool-sorters	8	2
	133	95

It will be seen that this kind of working-class voter was not a factory hand[117] but a craftsman in a traditional skill, possibly a proprietor of a small workshop, more probably self-employed, and certainly able to aspire to a proprietary position. The poll analysis, realistically enough, did not distinguish masters from employees in these crafts. Apart from the important group of small engineering shops serving the textile industry, a great many of these voters looked to a retail outlet or to small commissions for their livelihood. Such people were certainly very exposed to miscellaneous influences, but they were not, by mere fact of occupation, under the thumbs of an employing oligarchy.

Throughout the period 1832–67 the Rochdale electorate was more sharply divided within each class and trade than between different classes and trades. There is the strongest evidence that 'lateral' divisions on a basis of principle, pride, and religious denomination were the essence of the town's politics. The drink interest, so unequally Tory in 1857, was the only real exception, and even then, only a partial one. Even the Radical Non-Electors were paralleled by the Conservative Workingmen's Benefit Society.

There is every reason to suppose the fundamental division was denominational,[118] but this cannot be shown quantitatively.

| | 1841 | | 1857 | |
	Liberal	Conservative	Liberal	Conservative
Commercial and Professional	47	99	88	106
Craftsmen	44	28	133	95
Drink	47	59	28	118
Capitalists	—	—	34	54
Retailers	154	73	167	102
Textile interest	102	65	—	—

The electorate was perhaps the most democratic that could have been devised under a system of open voting. Nevertheless, an oligarchy of notables kept a tight grip on town affairs through their control of the Reform Association, the Press, and the Town Council. The eleven original proprietors of the town's only paper were leading tradespeople and lesser manufacturers, all of them on the council of the Reform Association: they included a draper, a chemist, a solicitor, a painter, a carpet designer, a flannel dealer, a currier, an ironmonger, a woollen manufacturer, a hatter, and a woolstapler, the sole ownership eventually coming into the hands of W. A. Scott, the chemist, who bought the paper in 1865.

It is possible at least to estimate the social character of the Rochdale Reform Association (founded 1834) on the basis of the classified lists of voters given in the 1857 poll book. These lists enable us to identify the occupation of most of the members of the Council of the Reform Association in 1865, the first year for which a list of the Council is available: [119]

Large manufacturers and bankers[120]	44
Agents	3
Drapers	2
Grocers	2

[117] There were no railwaymen electors listed as such in 1857.

[118] 'Generally speaking, there were two shops of each trade: one which was patronized by the Church and Tories, and another by the Dissenters and Whigs. The inhabitants were divided into two distinct camps—of the Church and Tory camp the other camp knew nothing.'—*The Autobiography of Mark Rutherford* (14th edition), 26.

[119] From Minute Book, 10 April 1865. This, the only extant Minute Book of the period, runs from 20 October 1864 to 6 January 1876. This committee was endorsed by acclamation at an electors' meeting as fit to transact all Liberal business: how it was chosen we are not told.

[120] Including John Bright, M.P.

Ironmongers	1
Textile merchants	2
Timber merchants	2
Publican	1
Currier and printer	1
Smallware dealer	1
Hatter	1
Painter	1
Chemist	1
Chemist and newspaper owner	1
Solicitor	1
	64

This table is certainly accurate in principle, but some of its details, because of the largeness of families and the duplication of certain common names, cannot be sworn to. It is highly probable that this charmed circle of grandees put up most of the money going into the support of Liberal politics. Certainly Edward Miall, the Liberal candidate in 1857, 'paid no part of his election expenses',[121] and Cobden's electoral expenses[122] were on so extraordinarily small a scale as to suggest that others were bearing the real burden. Beside the fighting of elections, the Reform Association also maintained a Registration Agent, John Butterworth (from 1861 to 1875), at a salary of £100 a year, raised to £150 on 20 April 1868.[123]

The group of manufacturers who dominated the party organization played the chief part in relating Rochdale politics to the wider national life, their natural area of activity, as businessmen, being the whole region which centred on Manchester Exchange.

The Brights[124]—owners of the second largest business in

[121] *Rochdale Standard*, 28 March 1857.

[122] See W. W. Bean, *Parliamentary Representation of the Six Northern Counties of England* (Hull 1890).

[123] One unlikely source of income was profits on meetings. For Cobden's last speech at Rochdale in November 1864, 1,500 tickets at one shilling were rapidly disposed of, raising £75.

[124] John Bright and his father were founder-members of the Reform Association, his brothers Thomas and Jacob were both Treasurers for some years. The education of the Liberal *élite* stopped at fifteen: that of the professional men and of the Tory gentlemen continued three to eight years longer, widening a gulf into a chasm.

Rochdale—and the Ashworths were Miall's chief backers in 1852 and 1857: it was a cooling-off by some of the 'flannel lords' towards him which expert politicians thought really fatal to his chances. The correspondence of the time at least suggests that the really important initiatives within the Reform Association came from the real grandees, those who were magistrates[125] as well as great businessmen—the Kemps, Kelsalls, Ashworths, Fentons, Hoyles, and Tathams. Cobden wrote:

> The fact is that Miall is not rich enough for the Rochdale flannel lords. They would have tolerated Hadfield with precisely the same principles—but then Hadfield has £200,000. . . . Indeed I doubt whether he would not find many better seats in the South of England than in any of the rich manufacturing districts, where the wealthy dissenters are terribly snobbish.[126]

Whatever the real channels of power, the Reform Association (which was reconstituted after the Second Reform Bill on a more democratic basis) maintained the outward forms of inner-party democracy. In 1865 the whole council of sixty-three, in two ballots, voted on the selection of a Liberal candidate on Cobden's death: the first vote was as follows:[127]

T. B. Potter	26
Leatham, M.P.	9
Stansfeld	3
William Fenton of Rochdale	12
Samuel Morley	13

The Council of sixty-three was also the election-fighting body. It met as soon as it was known that Parliament was to dissolve.[128] It used the same methods that were described by Bright in 1841, 'nine Central canvass districts being adopted for the whole Borough, with a Chairman and Secretary to

[125] There were at least seven magistrates on the Council of the Reform Association. Peto, the great contractor, married a Kelsall, the daughter of one of them.

[126] Cobden to Henry Richard, 23 June 1857, B.B. Add. mss. 43,658, ff. 353–5.

[127] Minute Book, 3 April 1865. John Bright had earlier been unanimously invited to stand.

[128] Comm. on Rochdale Election, *P.P.* 1857, sess. 2, H.C. 128, Q. 1987.

each, responsible for the working of the canvass in their own districts . . .'[129]

Standing out above all these details emerges a general picture of the domination of Rochdale politics by a narrow class of Nonconformist businessmen, itself dominated by half a dozen great firms and families. This small group, however, ruled not by a crude exercise of naked power—except, to some extent, in so far as they paid the bills—but rather by general consent and by being able and willing to undertake a wide variety of public and political work: that is, they were a responsible *élite* rather than a ruling class.

The traditional Dickensian picture of this Liberal *élite* is an unjust one in this case. They were a party of expenditure, not of economy—the Tories represented the ratepayers' cry for parsimony. They built magnificently, and worked municipal socialism successfully twenty years before Chamberlain. Contrary to the myth popular then and now, their administration of the Poor Law was more lenient than elsewhere:

> Mr. Sotheron Estcourt said to us, 'Oh, but yours are not workhouses, you know, they are almshouses.' 'Yes,' I replied, 'that is exactly the word: they are almshouses, and they are not intended to be workhouses in your sense of the word. They are intended as homes for the homeless poor.'[130]

The practice of democratic Liberalism proved better than its principles.

Rochdale people knew perfectly well what was going on in the great world outside, and they had strong views on it. Their organ, the *Rochdale Observer*, which represented the shopkeeping rather than the manufacturing Liberals, reached an extraordinarily high standard, as a general as well as a local newspaper. But well-informed though they were, the explicit content of national politics made little stir in Roch-

---

[129] Minute Book, 8 April 1865. This minute book was consulted by courtesy of the Rochdale Reform Association, 144 Drake Street, Rochdale. For the organization of the Reform Association in 1841, see H. J. Hanham, 'The First Constituency Party?', *Political Studies*, 1961, 188–9.

[130] Alderman Livsey in 1858 on a deputation to the Poor Law Board: Holyoake, *History of the Rochdale Pioneers* (3rd edition, 1900), 172.

dale at election times. The one great exception was Church issues.

Miall had opposed the Crimean War and voted against Palmerston on Cobden's Chinese motion. Rochdale was not very interested in such things: 'And also I believe there was a good deal of difference about his vote on China?'—'Yes, some disapproved of it . . . Some few left him on that, but they would be very few, I think . . .'[131] There was almost no mention of the Crimean War in the election campaign, nor in the post-mortems afterwards. None the less, there was strong party feeling in Rochdale, stronger perhaps than in Parliament:

> Do parties run high upon a good many questions in Rochdale?—They do.
> Do you think there is a wide difference between what they call the Liberals and the Conservatives?—There is.
> Rochdale is a place where party spirit has evinced itself very strongly?—It has strongly.[132]

This strong feeling arose almost always—except in the case of the liquor trade—with reference to Church questions. Miall and his predecessor, W. S. Crawford (M.P. Rochdale, 1841–52), represented a Radical interest composed of three sections, the militant Dissenters, the Chartists and political Reformers, and the Free Traders. These sections of course overlapped considerably, but the decline of Chartism and the acceptance of Free Trade in the 1850's brought Church questions to the centre of practical politics. The change from social Radicalism to confessional militancy was probably damaging electorally for the Liberals in Rochdale and in Lancashire generally. Too many good Liberals were Anglican, too many Dissenters were not attracted by Liberationism, and the militant Dissenters had always voted Liberal anyway: 'There were many Churchmen voted for him [Miall], and he had Dissenters vote against him: a considerable section.'[133]

---

131 Comm. on Rochdale Election, *P.P.* 1857, sess. 2, H.C. 128, QQ. 2105–6: evidence of Alderman Tom Livsey, leader of the working-class Liberals in Rochdale.

132 Ibid., QQ. 1943–5: evidence of J. W. Lawton, master printer.

133 Alderman Livsey, referring to 1852. Ibid., Q. 2091.

Miall's rather unexpected attack on the Irish Church in 1856 served to detach his Anglican supporters, and the Vicar of Rochdale correctly concluded that it would prevent Miall ever sitting again. Miall's successor as Liberal member in 1859, Richard Cobden, was an Anglican who was very guarded in his support of Dissenting demands. The political appeal of Miall's opponent, in national terms, in 1857 lay chiefly in his identification with the Church, rather than in his party colours, since Ramsay was a Tory who was committed to the support of Palmerston. Disraeli was never mentioned.

The Rochdale Liberals, besides being a series of overlapping militant Radical groups, were also simply representative of all the classes in the town whose chief interest in life was 'making Rochdale what it is'. It was a quasi-municipal body, a collection of people who transacted public business, as much as a sectional group. The nucleus of the Tories, on the other hand, was a collection of sharply defined special interests, attached to which was a genuine Toryism of opinion, not derived from social position, much of which probably originated in Liberals who found their party getting too extreme for them. The Tories of 1857 were divided into four great groups—the Drink interest (118 votes), the Respectable interest (160 votes), the lower middle-class Tories (197 votes), and the Tory working men who had no votes. The control of the party was vested beyond dispute in a sort of social Stonehenge of pillars of pre-1832 society, still impressive but in a backwater from the main life of the town: the Entwisles of Foxholes, representing the old Lancashire squires, the Royds family,[134] Tory bankers, and the Molesworths, the head of which family acquired a leading position in the town for his sons and grandsons during his forty years as vicar. Throughout the nineteenth century this group—socially superior to any in the town—retired into the well-furnished institutional fortresses of the Parish Church, the Flying Horse Inn, the Grammar School,[135] and the local military.

---

[134] Whose rivals, Fenton's Bank (1819–78), occupied the corresponding position on the Whig side, providing several Whig and one Tory candidates.

[135] In 1857 '. . . we Grammar School boys were all Tories . . .', Henry Brierley, *Reminiscences of Rochdale* (Rochdale 1923), 111.

Cutting across the vertical structure of the Tory Party, was the Orange Institution. Very little is known about this: but its existence in Rochdale is shown in a parliamentary enquiry of 1835. In that year there were twelve Orange Lodges in Rochdale, with 339 members.[136] It was publicly and generally known that the military belonged to the Orange Associations of the town.[137] At the Rochdale election of 1835, members of the Lodges who voted Liberal were expelled,[138] as was to be expected, for the sitting Tory member, Entwisle, was widely understood to be an Orangeman.[139] Thereafter, a silence descends upon the workings of Orangeism in Rochdale. But clearly Orangeism did not make Tories: it combined some of the existing Tory nexus in a slightly different way, absurd or sinister or convivial as opportunity demanded.

Most of what vitality and electoral success the Tories had was due, however, to free-lance action by individuals from the three lower-class groups, working independently of the hereditary chiefs of the party. Such were Peter Johnson, who won the 1857 election by sending fifty of Miall's pledged supporters free of expense to Liverpool and Southport on polling day,[140] afterwards going into hiding to escape arrest for abducting witnesses; Hamlet Nicholson, the shoemaker, who organized the Tory benefit society[141] among the working men, and the beersellers' leaders who organized their own bloc vote so efficiently. They belonged to the type of 'card' celebrated by Arnold Bennett, and they had much in common with the 'gentlemen'. The trade union leader Howell pointed this out: 'The Liberal party are losing ground much, for many reasons. Some of their Economics are considered harsh and partial:—everywhere there is less of geniality and bonhomie in the treatment of the working classes by the Liberals than by the Conservatives.'[142] The Tory gentlemen stood for a less narrow, more robust world than any of the Liberals.

[136] *P.P.* 1835, XVII, 341.   [137] Ibid., XXIII.   [138] Ibid., XIX.
[139] Ibid., Q. 3294.
[140] A. Miall, *Life of Edward Miall* (1884), 216.
[141] With 700 working-men members in 1892.
[142] Diary of W. Rathbone, n.d. 1870: Rathbone Papers, Liverpool University Library, IX, 5, 2–3.

Most of the Tory candidates and all the Tory M.P.s for Rochdale came from the Entwisle-Royds connection, the two families having been linked by a double marriage in the 1820's. John Entwisle, M.P. (1832–5), and candidate in 1835, was the father-in-law of Sir Alexander Ramsay, M.P. (1857–1859), and candidate in 1852 and 1859; Clement Royds, the Tory candidate in 1837, was the grandfather of Colonel Clement Royds, C.B., M.P. (1895–1905), candidate in 1892, who was chairman of the Rochdale Canal Company and of William Deacon's Bank, as well as Colonel commanding the Duke of Lancaster's Own Yeomanry.[143] In 1841 the Tories ran a renegade Whig, Fenton; in 1847 there was no contest. In 1865 and 1874 they ran carpet-bagging lawyers.[144] It is clear whenever the Tory chiefs had a good chance of winning, they regarded the seat as a family possession. The only Rochdale man outside the family compact who was permitted to run was W. W. Scholefield, squire of Buckley Hall, a flannel manufacturer of the Countess of Huntingdon's connection, who stood in 1868; his deep purse had kept the Tory benefit society solvent during the Cotton Famine, and he had a gentry background.

The only real rivalry came from the Parish Church. The plebeian Tories had no wish to challenge the hereditary chiefs; the Molesworth family had its way to make in the world, and its head, the vicar, became involved with High Church or Ritualist groups in his congregation. The vicar was a political force in his own right[145]—as one of the wealthiest men in Rochdale, as organizer of the Church Defence Association in the district, and as head of an important

[143] Janet H. Robb, *The Primrose League 1883–1906* (New York 1942), 236.

[144] 'Our Tory leaders were practically kept prisoners in the Lyceum until they produced a candidate which by the aid of the telegraph they did . . .' He was R. W. Gamble, Q.C., an Irish lawyer (Brierley, *Reminiscences* (1923), 111).

[145] The vicar (who was the stepfather of Robert Bridges, the Poet Laureate) was related to the Entwisles through the Scottish family of Mackinnon of Mackinnon, the 33rd chief of which had a sister who married Molesworth (1815) and a son (M. P. Rye, 1865–8) who married the daughter of John Entwisle, M.P. in 1832. No Rochdale Liberal had 'national' connections of this kind.

family. One son became the vicar of another church in Rochdale; three others went into and took over a firm of Rochdale solicitors, one becoming Coroner and Agent for the Ecclesiastical Commissioners, another becoming Deputy Coroner. This strength turned to weakness when the great revolution of feeling in the Church of England began to shake Rochdale as it had done Oxford. The vicar's Churchwarden built an Anglican nunnery in the town; Hamlet Nicholson, the Tory cobbler, published a study of the Inquisition. The heads of the gentry were Evangelical: 'Puseyism . . . divided the Churchmen of the town, some going over to Dissent and others becoming apathetic . . .' and the division between the gentry and the Parish Church would have prevented the Evangelical Ramsay coming forward, had it not been for strong pressure by the working-men Tories. There was probably a Thucydidean truth in the story that Ramsay lost his seat by making an eloquent little speech about throwing the Ritualists out of the Church by the scruff of the neck: 'When the cheering had subsided, one of the leading Puseyites came up to me and said "Mark! Ramsay will never be M.P. for Rochdale any more . . ."' [146]

The motivation of the other sections of the Tory Party, below the respectable class, is obscure. The Sick and Burial Society certainly was an active electioneering body, no doubt on a *quid pro quo* basis; the activity of the beersellers was self-explanatory. The great capitalists would fairly naturally tend to throw up an anti-popular wing [147] which events would align with the old Tory gentry. The commercial and professional men, one step down from the capitalists, but not to be confused with retailers, had a fairly natural tendency to be drawn, via the Grammar School and Church, into relations of social deference with the Tory leaders. All groups would draw after them the ones and twos they could influence, servants, gardeners, bailiffs, sextons, carters, masons, and a few shopkeepers and employees. But allowing for all this and for

[146] H. Nicholson, *Autobiography* (1892), 86.
[147] The majority of large employers were Tory in 1857. A fair proportion were Tory in 1841. This, I think, novel information, clears the Rochdale Liberals of the cruder charges of 'economic Liberalism'. The essence of Liberalism in Rochdale was popular politics, not business.

corruption too,[148] the lower middle-class vote (102 retailers, 95 craftsmen) for the Tories in 1857 was no merely marginal phenomenon. The only piece of electoral logic applicable is the probable conflict between (Radical, proletarian, ex-Chartist) Co-operators and the private shopkeepers, on a business level. Cobden provoked some shopkeeping opposition by identifying himself with the Co-operative interest, but that was in 1864, when times were desperately hard for shopkeepers. There is no evidence that it was of major importance.[149]

By 1857 the Rochdale Tories included a large part of each class. Since their principle, however, was to ignore this remarkable fact and simply go on supporting the gentry, the Tory party remained, in its explicit content and its final purpose, a re-enactment of the days when the local honorific hierarchies really had coercive political power.

TABLES COMPILED FROM THE ROCHDALE POLL BOOKS

1841 Election	*Liberal*	*Conservative*
Drink interest	47	59
Textile interest, total	102	65
Cotton masters and manufacturers	46	30
Wool sorters and staplers	19	10
Machinery makers	7	3
Overlookers	1	5
Weavers	24	9
Dyers	5	1
Shoddy dealers, fustian dressers	0	7
Craftsmen, total	44	28

[148] The Liberals organized but did not corrupt—in Rochdale.

[149] Since the artisans and small masters voted Tory in the same proportions. But in one election (1865?) this poster appeared:

Look OUT

Are the shopkeepers aware that the chief supporters of the Bright-and-Cobdenite faction are also leading members of the Co-operative stores? ... There is but one sane course for them, and that is to vote for Ramsay, Liberty, and Justice, and not for Cobden and Livsey's pet *bastille*.

A SHOPKEEPER

—Holyoake, *History of the Rochdale Pioneers* (3rd edition, 1900), 97.

1841 Election	Liberal	Conservative
Blacksmiths	3	3
Bricklayers	2	1
Engineers, wheelwrights, etc.	15	3
Ironfounders	6	5
Masons	0	3
Plumbers	3	4
Printers	3	2
Tinplate workers	5	2
Other craftsmen	7	5
Retailers, total	154	73
Barbers	6	3
Shoemakers and cloggers	15	5
Butchers	14	11
Drapers, hatters, etc.	28	6
Druggists	4	4
Grocers	58	22
Tailors	9	6
Other retailers	20	16
Respectables and dependants, total	47	99
Auctioneers, surveyors, agents	5	7
Bailiffs, farmers	1	12
Bankers	0	4
Clerks, travellers	6	8
Gentlemen	7	24
Organist, Parish clerk, sextons	0	4
Schoolmasters	5	3
Solicitors	5	14
Surgeons	3	4
Servants, gardeners, etc.	3	11
Wholesalers, small businessmen, etc.	12	8

1857 Election	Liberal	Conservative
Drink interest	28	118
Capitalists, total	34	54
Bankers	0	3
Corn-millers	1	2
Cotton-spinners	12	26
Dyers	3	1
Woollen manufacturers	18	22
Craftsmen, total	133	95
Retailers, total	167	102
Barbers	7	7
Butchers	16	25
Drapers, hatters, etc.	40	9
Druggists	3	7

1857 Election	Liberal	Conservative
Grocers	71	37
Other retailers	30	17
Respectables and dependants, total	88	106
Auctioneers, surveyors, agents	32	35
Farmers	0	4
Schoolmasters	2	4
Solicitors	2	13
Surgeons, dentists	4	11
Wholesalers, small businessmen, etc.	35	34
Clergymen, ministers	13	5
Miscellaneous	36	54

POPULAR LIBERALISM: WHITBY

Neither Rochdale, nor Whitby, nor any other town, can be regarded as a 'typical parliamentary borough', Rochdale, for instance, having a very different electoral history from that of the other cotton towns, Whitby, too, having an unusual feature in its whaling industry. However, both towns were broadly representative of a central category of the most important type of constituency between 1832 and 1885. There were about 170 English borough constituencies, and the great majority of these were neither great towns, nor parts thereof, nor were they nomination boroughs. About a third of the House of Commons, and a still higher proportion of the Liberal Party was returned by these intimate and independent communities. Bearing in mind that the detail and weight of local feelings differed in every town, some record of the small beer of politics in Whitby and Rochdale still helps to suggest how, from many unrelated sets of idiosyncrasies in each borough, a general Liberal idiom and pattern emerged.

In Rochdale, political opinion can be located exactly in relation to its social background. Yet, despite the fullness of the information, it is a kind of dumb show. All the performers are clearly seen, yet the sound is almost switched off, save for a little of the opaque language of official politics. Whitby, under a different microscope, supplies the need to 'hear people talking'.

The political life of Whitby cannot be reconstructed by rule, line, and number, as that of Rochdale can;[150] yet it has left some traces of real vernacular politics which are, imaginatively, of equal value. The collection of election squibs and ephemera from 1780 to 1890 in the Pannett Park Museum at Whitby, on which this chapter is based, is perhaps unique of its kind, and no other kind of evidence could give the same impression of the pungency and vivacity of street politics, in a period of nominal party differences at Westminster. (There is no reason to suppose that Whitby was at all unusual in bringing out a hundred or so flysheets at each election, though these have not survived elsewhere in any quantity.)

Whitby elections were alive with social and economic content: in 1868, there was the denominational issue as well. There were two main lines of fissure: between the (generally Tory) shipping interest, and the (generally Liberal) railway interest, and another, equally important between Whitby and the outside world. The existence of a 'menu peuple' of shipwrights, fishermen, and workers of jet, with a class-conscious outlook,[151] was only a latent source of conflict in this period, since they and their Reform League co-operated at elections with the middle-class Liberals.

Whitby was Tory from 1832 to 1859. This was due not so much to the local Tory gentry, as to the temporary conjunction of the (generally) protectionist shipping interest,[152] with the personal Toryism of Robert Stephenson,[153] who brought the railway to Whitby and therefore had a kind of Messianic status in the town. Robert Stephenson epitomized the working-man Tory:[154] behind him stood the industrial empire

---

[150] *Sylvia's Lovers*, by Mrs Gaskell, a novel similar in subject and period to *The Trumpet-Major*, and set in Whitby, supplies a generous amount of social detail.

[151] There was a lockout of unionists in the shipyards in 1856. v. Squibs, D. 26.

[152] v. Squibs, D. 1, n.d., for complaint of ruin of coastal stone trade by foreign competition, *c.* 1855.

[153] M.P. for Whitby 1847–59. His predecessor (1832–47) was a London shipowner.

[154] 'It is all nonsense Lord John preaching and preaching education to the working classes,'—Stephenson to the Royal Society, 1859, quoted J. C. Jeaffreson, *Life of Robert Stephenson* (1864), II, 144.

building of his friend Hudson, the railway king. Whitby was
not the only example of a small borough controlled by an
industrial patron and not the only case where Toryism was
unconnected with the landed interest. Tynemouth similarly
remained Tory so long as the shipping interest remained
protectionist;[155] Middlesbrough, Sunderland, Barrow and
Birkenhead were industrial pocket boroughs. Joseph Locke,
the engineer who brought the railway to Honiton, was conscientiously returned by that borough for many years.[156] The
small boroughs did to a considerable extent register the industrialization of England.

In 1859, however, the railway fell into Liberal hands, and
Whitby had to reconsider its best interests: 'Let us have
Thompson[157] and Railways for the future Prosperity of
Whitby: We don't want a man who has neither money nor
influence. . . .'[158] The shipping party could not produce a man
with local claim:

> BROTHER CHIPS:
> Have you ever assisted to Repair or Build a Ship for Mr.
> Chapman? If not, what claim has he to our sympathy or
> support?
>
> —A Shipwright.[159]

Some Liberal administrator had also made a shrewd move:
'. . . it was t'Tories, they wouldn't hev owt for nevvy but
Welsh cooals. But when t'Liberals come in, they said it was
wrong: and now they divide it between Welsh cooal and
North Country cooal.'[160] In such terms, the railway interest
easily won the 1859 election. But their enjoyment of victory
was quickly spoilt by the emergence of conflict between
Whitby and the world within the railway interest. The land-
ladies were appalled by the lack of cheap tourist tickets to
Whitby; local business could not withstand big business
methods: '. . . That Company (the North Eastern) has always
been the determined enemy of the Shipping of this port. To

---

[155] G. M. Trevelyan, *Sir G. O. Trevelyan. A Memoir* (1932), 72.
[156] J. Devey, *Life of Joseph Locke* (1862), 247.
[157] H. S. Thompson, M.P. for Whitby 1859-65, chairman of the N.E.
Railway.
[158] Squibs, G. 46.   [159] Squibs, G. 29.   [160] Squibs, D. 107.

run off the small colliers of Whitby . . . (it sold coals at Whitby below cost till they were ruined).'[161] By the 1860's it began to be realized that the control of the town by the railway might not be entirely beneficial; the railway rates controversy of the 1880's was developing. Whitby desperately wanted to become another Middlesbrough, or at least a Scarborough, and for this purpose the railway company was inadequate. In these straits it turned in 1865 to Hudson, the railway king, who had an estate on the West Cliff, and who promised a great programme of development. Hudson would almost certainly have been returned in 1865, had not his enemies on the railway company had him arrested for debt forty-eight hours before the poll, and imprisoned in York for the duration of the election.[162] Nevertheless, a substitute Tory candidate was found, and the railway Liberal defeated. Even in 1868 a strong stigma was attached to the railway party:

Who is Mr. Gladstone?[163] I answer—the nominee of the North Eastern Railway Company. The object of that Company in fitting North Eastern boroughs with their own creatures I hesitate not to be a foul conspiracy against the trade of this district, for the purpose of bolstering up the exclusive power of that Company, by shutting out all opposing lines of Railway.[164]

The Liberals were returned in 1859, and defeated in 1865, principally because of their railway connections. In 1868, and for a generation afterwards, they succeeded as a popular, even a class, party, acting in alliance with the old denominational and commercial Liberal interests. On these terms, Whitby remained Liberal from 1868–85. The equation of Gladstone and democracy, made concrete and visible by the Tory use of social power in electioneering, was the key to the smooth and sudden acceptance by Whitby people of national politics as the main claim on their interest at election times. The

[161] Squibs, D. 101.

[162] v. R. S. Lambert, *The Railway King* (1934), 296–7.

[163] W. H. Gladstone, M.P. Whitby 1868–80, the Premier's eldest son.

[164] Squibs, D. 101. 'What we want', said Mellows . . . 'what we want is a Branch.'—*The Uncommercial Traveller*, chapter XXII.

assumed obligation resting on all working men of goodwill
to vote Liberal is well put here:

ANOTHER TURN OF THE SCREW.

On Saturday last, a well-known respectable gardener, who
had occupied the position for 46 years, left his place in
consequence of an altercation with his master, C. Bagnall,
Sneaton Castle, our late M.P., who knew him to be opposed
to him in political matters, and who refused to vote pink.[165]
Working Men of Whitby—
Will You For Ever Be Slaves to the Will of Tory Masters?
Vote for Gladstone and Independence.
And prove to all that neither Situations, Money,
Blankets, or Coals, will hinder you from exercising
your privilege to—
Vote For The Man of Your Choice.[166]

All these questions are from anonymous, *ex parte* statements,
whose scientific value lies entirely in the atmosphere they
suggest, not in their factual information. A few remarks may
be made about this atmosphere. First, elections were the chief
means of working out real conflicts of everyday life, both
within Whitby, and between Whitby and national government[167] and business. Second, the quality of the tone of
deference which ran through these squibs was important. It
was a self-assertive, demanding deference of which wealth and
influence was the collusive victim. It was deference based on
rational consideration of the benefits to be derived from
deference. It was not too humble to change sides as suited it.
To think of these people as politically in a state of nature,
depending pathetically on their betters and looking up to
them for 'leadership', would be quite against the conventions
suggested by the squibs, and a waste of sympathy. They did
vote with their betters, but the process was much more re-
ciprocal, the bargaining keener, the insight clearer, than a

[165] Pink was Tory in Whitby.
[166] Squibs, E. 9. Bank employees also canvassed customers for the
Tories in a sinister way—v. Case 11/1, Pannett Park Museum, Whitby.
[167] Another bone of contention was Lowe's Bill on Shipping Dues
(1857), which tried to abolish passing tolls levied by Whitby as a harbour
of refuge: A. P. Martin, *Life of Viscount Sherbrooke*, II, 149.

bald statement of the existence of a politics of deference usually indicates.

On the other hand, deference with a coercive element, that took advantage of a man's weakness, was quite unacceptable to street ethics, whatever happened in practice. That the Tories, being a minority party whose best chances lay in sailing near the wind, were so associated with brow-beating and 'rat-catching' practices, was a fatal memory for them with the post-1868 electorate.

Thirdly, the alfresco debates of the wall sheets appealed to rational considerations and a high level of (mainly local) information and experience. There was no question of ignor-ant provincials having to take the official political conven-tions, in all their prudery, at their face value. The people of Whitby needed no political scientists, and what they liked on a poster was a solid argument founded on solid and preferably disreputable information. Their Liberal Party had germin-ated under the force of local interests and the local situation; but it did not flourish till it drew strength from a nation-wide popular radicalism identified with Mr Gladstone, the first national politician whom the fly-sheets use as a vote-winner:

> him who stands first in that array of glorious names by whom the battles of freedom have been fought and won— W. E. Gladstone.[168]

> He stands forth as the archetype of all that is wise and statesmanlike in the conduct of our national affairs.[169]

The role of Gladstone in changing the popular notion of the content of politics from a local to a national one could not be more clearly illustrated. This idiom is far removed from that of 'cooals for nevvy'. What the old and new styles of politics had in common, however, was the purposeful use of the political system by the Whitby voter.

[168] *Whitby Blue Banner*, 3 August 1868: Museum Case 11/1.
[169] Ibid., 17 August 1868.

POPULAR LIBERALISM: LEEDS, 1874

The accounts already given of Whitby and Rochdale show the successful and cumulative combination of various different motives and sections, as parts of a national political party. To emphasize the difficulty of such an operation, we now take an example where this crystallization failed to occur. The Leeds Liberal Party had been formed by a union[170] of the Whig Registration Association with the local branch of the Reform League in 1867–9. Like a badly set limb, this arrangement had to be broken in the early 1870's, to be re-set in the late 1870's, under the influence of the Birmingham caucus and of the Eastern Question agitation. It took the Midlothian crusade and a centralized election-fighting machine to impose party discipline on the sophisticated and wilful public opinion of Leeds. The following letter of Edward Baines (M.P. for Leeds 1859–74), shows how far from a foregone conclusion was that 'conquest of public opinion by the Parliamentary parties'[171] that has since distinguished English from French constituency politics. The letter shows how the same random elements which had fused together so smoothly in Rochdale and Whitby, had failed to achieve even moderate co-operation in Leeds. One of a very small collection of papers in the hands of the Baines family,[172] it was written by Edward Baines to his brother-in-law in Australia on 13 March 1874. After referring to family matters, it went on to list the causes of his recent defeat as follows:

1. The immense power of the publicans and brewers, put forth under the influence of resentment for the Licensing Bill, and the still greater threatened restrictions of the Permissive Bill.

2. The intolerant folly of the Permissive Bill party, who, presuming on a strength, which they did not possess,

[170] For the details of this union, see 'Minute Book of the Proceedings of the Leeds Reform Committee, 1866–1870', in Leeds Central Library.

[171] The phrase is quoted from Derek Beales, *Cambridge Review*, 5 March 1960.

[172] The family owned the *Leeds Mercury* throughout the century. Edward Baines was an ardent Congregationalist, teetotaller, Voluntaryist, supporter of education, and Gladstonian.

withdrew their votes even from friends of temperance who could not support the Permissive Bill, and thus actually played the game of the Publicans.

3. The Irish Catholics and Home Rulers who under the direct influence of their priests voted against even their old Liberal friends who would not promise to support Home Rule. Of these, there are from 2,000 to 2,500 electors in Leeds, most of whom formerly voted for Liberal candidates, and now only for Radical Home Rulers.

4. The Trade Unionists, most of whom also supported the Radical ultra candidates—the latter having promised to vote for the repeal of all the laws that punish coercion and intimidation, and withheld their votes from candidates who could only promise to do equal justice between master and man.

5. A great number of retail dealers, offended by the Adulteration Act—which, however, was not a Government Act, though ignorantly resented upon the Government— their friends. Every milkman and every grocer in Leeds (I was told) voted against me—though I was as innocent of the Act as you.

6. The demands of workmen of every class for increased wages: and their insubordinate conduct to their employers which not only offended, but alarmed the latter: and also frightened a great number of the middle classes because evidencing a growth of intolerant democracy.

7. The fears of the Clergy and the Church, excited first by the disestablishment of the Irish Church, second by the demands of the Liberationists for the separation of Church and State, and third by the hostility of the Nonconformists and the Education League to any kind of religious teaching in the Board Schools which threatened an attack on the whole mass of Church schools.

8. The offence taken by the Nonconformists at the Elementary Education Act, and especially at clause 25: and their determination to vote against all candidates who supported Forster or his policy.

9. The fears of the landed interest, that the principles of land tenure in Ireland would also be introduced in England; that the agricultural labourers were getting the

upper hand of their employers: and that the extension of the suffrage to householders in the counties would still further increase the powers of the labourers.

10. Gladstone's promise to repeal the Income Tax which offended the monied interest, more than it propitiated the payers of the tax.
11. The threatened reform of the Corporation of London.
12. The reform of the Endowed Schools and Charities.
13. The abolition of purchase in the army: the reduction of the Dockyard Labourers: and the retrenchment in the Civil Services.

. . . In my own case, I lost many of the Permissive Bill men, all the Home Rulers and Catholics, two thirds of the Trade Unionists, a few of the middle class masters, a considerable number of retail dealers, many of the bitter ultra Radicals, etc., besides having provoked the strong hostility of the publicans and brewers. My Radical colleague, Carter, got the votes of all the Ultras because he was favourable to their demands: and he also got nearly all the moderate Liberals, because I used my utmost influence to induce my friends to vote for him. Dr. Lees, a Permissive Bill Lecturer, and an Ultra of every Radical section, got from 5,000–6,000 votes: which being taken from the general strength of the Liberal party, and from me, the moderate Liberal, left me in the minority you have seen.

I don't deny that the Government committed some errors, chiefly under the urgency of their Radical supporters. But I maintain there never was a Government that was more truly Liberal, just, and patriotic, or cherished higher and nobler aims.

THE SPOILS OF THE GAME: MAGISTRACIES

Because Victorian public administration was so respectable compared with that of the previous period, it has been overlooked that rewards and incentives remained a systematic part of political life throughout the nineteenth century,

and were not much affected by the elimination of formal
patronage and the spring-cleaning of the State by Peel and
Gladstone. In the public man who lives by his wits, in the
fatherly M.P. fishing for his constituents, and in the impor-
tunate claimers of local honour, we have, not an anachronistic
survival of aristocratic abuses, but one essential element of
modern politics—the irreducible need to consult the personal
advantage of the small minority of persons actively engaged
in politics. The peculiar position of the host of lawyers who
sat in Parliament, perhaps the most striking instance of the
quiet and decent pursuit of private advantage under the
guise of political activity, is a question in itself, and, as in the
case of the back-bench Radicalism which was so often placated
by the acceptance of office, it is a subject on which conclusive
details are hard to find. What can be stressed here, however,
is the variety of personal rewards located at all levels of the
political system, and the creative function they performed, at
the level of magisterial appointments in particular, in induc-
ing local notables to tether themselves to one of the Parliamentary parties. There are some sub-plots, too, such as the
different ideas of public morality existing at different levels
of society, and the much greater importance of the serious
aristocracy than of the Radicals in creating the chaste State.
A more general conclusion is what a dearth of other satisfactions there must have been for the pursuit of a 'little brief
authority', or even more illusory honours, to become so strong
a motive. The search for local power and prestige was the
opposite side of the coin to the absence of any socially approved life of pleasure, and to holidays at Ben Rhydding and
Buxton.

What is fairly well known is the change in public morality
at the top. The published letters of Peel, the Queen, and of
Gladstone refer often to the disposal of honours, the Garter in
particular, and for them it was clearly a chore regulated by
precedent. Palmerston's practice as usual belied his House of
Commons manner, for he applied the strictest standards of all:

I am adverse to making Privy Councillors except in virtue
and by Reason of official position. If Privy Councillorships
were to be scattered Broadcast among applicants for

Favour, there would be no end to the list, and no meaning to the thing.[173]

During Palmerston's administrations, the number of peers actually fell appreciably, and his policy was typical of that of the official Whigs. Sir George Grey, when Chancellor of the Duchy of Lancaster, expressed the feelings of most Liberal holders of that office when he wrote: 'I am most anxious not to make the appointment of Magistrates a political or party question. Nothing . . . can tend more to degrade the Bench . . .'[174]

The awkward point of political ethics that confronted the Whigs lay not in turning down the claims of supporters, which they found easy to do, but in considering their public position apart from their private fortunes. For the temptations of official salaries were very great. The nostalgic idea of great noblemen undertaking office in a spirit of *noblesse oblige* is quite without foundation, for probably at least half the Liberal Cabinet ministers earned more from their official incomes than from their private ones. In addition, Gladstone, Bright, Newcastle, Clarendon, Russell, and Hartington had money worries which must have been appreciably relieved by the profits of office. But, professionals though they were, any tendency to rapacity was annihilated by an absolute and peremptory code of honour. At the top of politics, the great personal rewards to be found there played no part.

Very striking rewards, then, did not act at all on the people at the top, because of the prevailing morality there; nor did the people at the top much wish to create a system of rewards for those below them. Naturally, too, the mass of the electorate could not be influenced by these means. But in the middle level of politics, at the point of contact between the M.P. and the leading notables, the joint system of honours and patronage came into its own. Government patronage continued to be very useful in the 1860's in binding civic leaders to the Cabinet, and in raising the authority of those civic leaders locally.

[173] Palmerston to Brand, 1 November 1862: Palmerston mss., unsorted.
[174] Grey to Ewart, 11 August 1860: Duchy of Lancaster Papers, Liverpool file.

What jobs were available were used rather for clients of M.P.s and of regional party leaders, than for nominees of ministers. The pattern of patronage within the ministry was decentralized and departmental. Palmerston found it convenient to explain that diplomatic and consular patronage rested entirely with the Foreign Secretary, and that he never interfered in the patronage of other ministers.[175] Colonial appointments were in the hands of the governors. The pattern shifted over time, too. In the Tory ministry of 1858, the Postmaster-General asked Cairns to recommend names for London postmen, while in the 1860's postal patronage is found flowing from the Treasury. Within the Treasury, the seat of power also varied, for while Ward Hunt in 1867 could say 'I have no voice in the distribution of patronage',[176] that being reserved to the Whip, Gladstone used Treasury and postal patronage as a means of keeping in touch with his following among provincial civic notables:

> The Chancellor of the Exchequer desires me to ask you whether he may refer the appointments of Rural Post Offices, Post Messengers, etc., in the Salford Hundred to you for information and opinion: or if not, whether you would be so kind as to point out any one to whom they could be referred as the organ of the party.—
>
> Mr. Wm. Rathbone junior has undertaken to perform this office for West Derby Hundred.[177]

Similarly, Disraeli, hopeful of winning over Roebuck, offered him two nominations to Post Office jobs in his Sheffield constituency.[178] In all departments of business life, too, instances might be found where solicitations led to politically inspired appointments. No doubt in many of the cases in the Wilson papers, politics were a pretext for help given on purely charitable grounds, but it is clear that the Liberal big

[175] Palmerston to Sheridan, 25 July 1862: Palmerston mss., Letter Book 1862.

[176] Ward Hunt to Roebuck, 7 December 1867: Hunt Papers, Northampton Record Office.

[177] R. B. Gurdon, Gladstone's secretary, to George Wilson, 28 December 1865: Wilson mss., Manchester Central Library.

[178] Treasury to Roebuck, 6 June 1867: Leader Collection, 187, No. 349: Sheffield University Library.

businessmen around Manchester often wrote to each other pointing out the merits of some stationmaster or workman or teacher—who, of course, was always a strong Liberal. The Liberal Lancashire and Yorkshire Railway Company, moreover, was accused of awarding its contracts chiefly on political grounds.[179]

However miraculous to the recipient, these favours were trivial in that they did not bear on the central function of patronage—the enhancement of the prestige of local party notables.

This was done chiefly by magisterial appointments, because there were so many of them, and because other forms of patronage were decreasing. Honours naturally took the place of the old salaried patronage:

> My position in the Treasury as Patronage Secretary is gone . . . It alone is organised and distributed upon a System . . . I will only say that I lose, without notice and at once, the great advantages of the daily correspondence and communication with members of the party which the ordinary dispensing of the Treasury patronage gave me, to say nothing of the power which it placed in my hands.[180]

Though the magistracy was only one rung in a ladder which passed down from the Garter through the Lord-Lieutenantcies, with a collateral branch in the Church, it was the centre of the system of political reward, because it was the only honour within reach of the local businessman, and because the other honours depended on being limited in number to be effective; as Brand, the Liberal Whip, wrote:

> My voice is for postponing this and all similar applications for honours, whether for Peers, Privy Councillors, Baronets, or Knights, until after the General Election. The expectation of favours to come is a strong motive, while a favour conferred generally makes one man ungrateful and ten disgusted.[181]

The higher branches of the honours system were far from

[179] Wilson Papers for 1870, *passim*.
[180] Glyn, the Liberal Whip, to Gladstone, 7 December 1869.
[181] Brand to Palmerston, 3 December 1864: Palmerston mss., unsorted.

unpolitical, but they principally affected the landed gentry, and therefore the county seats, while the area where patronage was really needed to play a creative role, was in organizing the leaders of the borough electorate behind the Parliamentary parties.

Many of the landed gentry, however, were as unreformed in their political appetite for titles as the borough Radicals were unrefined in their greed for magistracies. The conventional decorum of Victorian public morality can be recognized for what it was—a discipline imposed by the front bench on worldly surroundings, by the very few on the many. Average sensible country gentlemen wrote to the Prime Minister or the Whip about their claims, enclosing details of pedigree and fortune, without a fig-leaf of modesty. At the time of the Prince of Wales' marriage in 1862, the following gentlemen wrote to Palmerston for a political peerage or a promotion: F. Beamish, R. S. Adair, Sir W. R. Clayton, Sir H. L. Bulwer, Sir R. Levinge, Erskine Wemyss, Sir Henry Mildmay and Lord Oranmore.[182] A Kentish gentleman, Dering, told the Whip, 'Promise me a peerage, and I will carry the County.'[183] After the 1868 election, a Mr Lloyd of Llandysail wrote to the Liberal Whip claiming a peerage for political services.[184] Even such a relic as the Vice-Admiralty of Yorkshire had its attractions: 'The office has neither duties nor salary attached to it, it is merely titular, but Lord Londesborough is very desirous of holding it.'[185] But such attempts could rarely succeed, or hierarchy would have lost its magic as an incentive. At a lower level, it was easier to oblige: 'Have seen Glyn [the Liberal Whip]. He will write to Lord Sefton about Blacklock if you send him a letter recommending him to a Deputy Lieutenancy and procure one also from Grenfell if possible.'[186] Magistracies, lower still, were so widely held among country gentlemen and urban businessmen that it was almost invidious not to hold one. The upper reaches of the

[182] 'Private Letter-Book, 1862': in Palmerston mss., unsorted.

[183] Brand to Palmerston, 5 December 1862: ibid.

[184] Glyn to Gladstone, 25 November 1868: B.M. Add. mss., 44,347, f. 258.

[185] Palmerston to the Queen, 25 February 1860, in the Royal Archives RA. A. 28. 35.

[186] C. Macdonald to Wilson, 21 December 1868: Wilson mss.

system, however, where rewards were usually withheld, nevertheless belonged as much to a general system of personal rewards as did the rather freely granted magistracies.

It was far more the party character than the class character of the Bench which was really in dispute. Poachers, Primitive Methodists, trade unionists and Matthew Arnold might grumble about the ignorance and class viewpoint of magistrates, but these things were a foregone conclusion and were not created or even affected by the political flavour of the method of appointment. It is the political flavour of appointments, its ubiquity, and its revelation of the expectations of local *élites*, that is chiefly discussed below, but a few remarks on the relation between social class and the magistracy are in place first.

The Bench belonged to the gentry in the counties; to the gentry and the manufacturers in the industrial counties; and to the leading tradespeople and councillors in the boroughs. Until 1873, when Gladstone made a complaint, there were no Dissenters on the Bench in Huntingdonshire, a highly nonconformist county,[187] and G. O. Trevelyan, appointing the first working-class magistrates in 1884, was greatly shocked at his daring.[188]

Only in Lancashire, where by 1863 there were 400 manufacturers on the Bench against only 200 landowners,[189] and a few other industrial districts, was there much dispute over the social character of the bench, and even here it was only a case of one aristocracy against another. What can be seen in such documents as the one below is the reality of the social prejudice between trade and land, just as described in *Coningsby*. The question at issue was the appointment of a Unitarian wholesale grocer to the Rochdale bench:[190]

> I have just heard from Mr. Ellice respecting Mr. Benjamin Heape. He consulted two gentlemen, one a strong Tory, the other a strong Radical:

[187] *Hansard*, vol. 259, col. 372, 18 June 1880.
[188] See *G. O. Trevelyan. A Memoir*, by G. M. Trevelyan (1932), 116: and the autobiography of Henry Broadhurst.
[189] Wilson Patten in *Hansard*, vol. 171, col. 1171, 19 June 1863.
[190] Danvers to Clarendon, 3 April 1841: Clarendon Deposit, Bodleian, 'Duchy' box.

Habits of Society Tory.—'No meaning of word in Rochdale: all there spend their leisure in public houses.'

Radical.—'Rather of a better order than the public house men of Rochdale: his habits for *Rochdale* are very respectable.'

Even Lord Holland, a very liberal Whig, made it his rule never to appoint a person 'actually engaged in manufacturing trade', where others could be met with.[191] Here was a profound social gulf between economic equals; but the actual struggle for magistracies was fought out in terms of party and personal advantage, rather than as a struggle between classes.

There was no period between 1832 and 1886 in which magisterial appointments did not fan the flames of party. A curious document of 1834 from Leeds,[192] which gives, among other particulars, the number of votes obtained by candidates for election to the municipal bench, establishes that there the Whig Party at least used a prepared party list. There was always a flurry just before a ministry resigned, or just after a party returned from a spell in the wilderness. Thus in 1841 an acute observer wrote of the swamping of the Bench by Graham and Lyndhurst with victorious Tories.[193]

After 1886, a new phase began with the Bench overwhelmingly Tory.[194] Before 1886, however, the Liberals had a fair fight in the counties, and more than that in the towns. The municipal bench reflected the choice of the Home Secretary in consultation with the local council and the local M.P.s; the county bench was in practice chosen by the Lord Lieutenant, subject to the approval of the Lord Chancellor. Hence much turned on the appointments to Lord-Lieutenancies. At the beginning of 1886, of the forty-two Lords-Lieutenant,

[191] Danvers to Clarendon, 23 December 1840: Clarendon mss., Bodleian, 'Duchy' box.

[192] *Leeds Municipal Pollbook for 1834*, in the Library of the Society of Genealogists.

[193] Jessie K. Buckley, *Joseph Parkes of Birmingham* (1926), 178.

[194] See J. M. Lee, 'Parliament and the Appointment of Magistrates', in *Parliamentary Affairs*, XIII, No. 1.

twenty-six were Liberal, and sixteen Conservative;[195] this Liberal ascendancy, going back to Palmerston's time, was self-extending. Disraeli spoke very frankly to that effect:

> Walked with Mr. Disraeli. He said that the wonder was how the Conservative party had kept together in spite of the want of patronage . . . 'But what I regret more than anything is the Lord-Lieutenancies. For they influence the County gentlemen to a great extent. For instance, suppose a gentleman wishes to be on the Commission of the Peace, he makes up to the Lord-Lieutenant by exerting himself for his party. Now we have hardly any Lords-Lieutenant.'[196]

The magistracy acted therefore as a Trojan horse for the Liberals amongst the generally Tory country gentlemen.

The easiest source to use is evidence about Lancashire, where appointments were under the general responsibility of the Duchy of Lancaster. The tone was much sharper there than in other counties. Bright said that the moment there was a change of government, letters and deputations began to flow from the boroughs, leading to a general scramble which placed many unfit and many unnecessary men on the Bench.[197] Though Bright deplored the system, he played a typical part in it. In 1854 he helped Granville choose the Rochdale magistrates;[198] in 1865 two nominees of his were placed on the Bench by Clarendon;[199] in 1869 he played postman between the Manchester Liberals and Lord Dufferin, who held the Duchy of Lancaster: 'The Tories have no scruples as to this use of patronage—but Lord Dufferin is too conscientious to follow this example. I hope your friends will be content to wait awhile . . .'[200] But the rank and file, even when they were austere Radicals in general politics, could not understand the frigid public spirit which held that political appointments to the Bench degraded it. The highly respected

[195] J. M. Lee, op. cit., 88.

[196] Rosebery's diary, 5 September 1865: *Lord Rosebery*, by the Marquess of Crewe (1931), I, 31.

[197] *Hansard*, vol. 159, cols. 260–273, 7 August 1858.

[198] *Bright's Diaries*, ed. Walling (1931), 176.

[199] Clarendon to Bright, 25 January 1865.

[200] Bright to Wilson, 3 August 1869: Wilson Papers.

millionaire shipowner who sat for South Lancashire complained that the Chancellor of the Duchy 'did not seem as disposed as he ought to be, to appoint magistrates recommended by the Liberal party'.[201] The leading Radical millionaire in Bolton even went so far as to regard magistrates as party functionaries: 'Our leading Whigs here are very lukewarm about the Reform Bill. Will not the Government take some means to spur their own magistracy to support them?'[202] In a crisis, even a hardened official Whig like Lord Granville could press the Lord-Lieutenant to create more Liberal J.P.s in Lancashire.[203] The Rochdale Reform Association recorded its pleasure at the appointment of three additional Liberal magistrates in the town in the frankest way.[204] A firm of Manchester solicitors canvassed a magistracy for their client on the ground that: 'Mr. Spencer is in politics a thorough Liberal and is one of the Vice-Presidents of the Reform Union . . .'[205] The more realistic candidates were anxious to make party use of the magistracy. When George Melly was nursing Preston, he wrote to the then Chancellor of the Duchy:

> With respect to Mr. Smith (the chairman of Melly's committee) . . . if he is omitted, it will be a bitter disappointment, both to me and to the now perfectly united Liberal party at Preston, and will most seriously affect my now excellent prospects at the General Election . . .[206]

An anonymous memorandum viewed the Bolton Bench with the same end in view:

> Richard Stockdale, Is Mayor of Bolton 1864, 1865. Is a retired Draper. A Liberal in politics . . . It is also considered that his appointment would be a most politic one, inasmuch as there is a wide breach in this borough between the Whig party (to which the present Mayor belongs) and the

[201] Wm. Brown to Wilson, 17 December 1857: Wilson Papers.
[202] Thomas Thomasson to George Wilson, 1866: Wilson Papers.
[203] Ramm, *Pol. Corr. of Gladstone and Granville, 1876–1886*, II, 232.
[204] Minutes of Rochdale Reform Association, 30 November 1864.
[205] Wilson Papers, 1869, no date.
[206] Melly to Cardwell, 19 March 1863. Duchy Office papers, Preston bundle.

Extreme Radicals, and as the former almost openly supported the Conservatives at the last general election, the appointment would be regarded as a most conciliatory one.[207]

The Liberal Whip lent his support to this type of solicitation: 'Mr. Woods the member for Wigan is most anxious to see you with reference to the magistracy of Wigan. Pray hear what he has to say. He is a trustworthy man.'[208] A man described as the largest employer of labour in a Manchester ward was recommended by the Manchester Liberal M.P.s a month after the General Election.[209] A request for a magistracy for a Warrington Liberal was cheerfully complied with by Mr Gladstone himself.[210] And so on: but the total effect may be statistically illustrated, at least for the Duchy of Lancaster, as follows:

Ministry	No. of Appointments[211]
8 Jan., 1859–10 June, 1859	32
November, 1859–October, 1865	132
October, 1865–June, 1866	21
June, 1866–December, 1868	161
1868–1874	204
1874–1880	125

The Tories openly expected their Chancellors of the Duchy to gratify their appetites. They claimed to be represented in proportion to their strength on the Town Council, or in the electorate, or simply to have half the Bench. As the statistics above showed, they succeeded, and the Liberals coming back in 1868 were forced to redress the balance. Walpole in 1858 declared his new appointments were all Tories, made with a view to bringing the parties into equality on the Bench.[212] Disraeli wrote consolingly to Derby: 'You

---

[207] Anon., October 1866: Duchy Office Papers, Bolton bundle.

[208] Brand to Clarendon, 1 December 1864: Duchy Office papers, Wigan bundle.

[209] Duchy Office Papers. Recommendations Book, 20 January 1869.

[210] Gladstone to Rylands, 31 December 1868: *Speeches of P. Rylands M.P.* (1890) I, 47.

[211] Based on the Parliamentary Return of Lancashire Magistrates 1859–1869, 30 June 1869, and the Recommendations Book (in the Duchy Office papers) 1869–80.

[212] *Hansard*, vol. 150, cols. 260–273, 7 August 1858.

have done very well for your friends, 3 Garters, 4 Bishoprics, 8 Lord Lieutenancies, and almost the whole Bench in the three Kingdoms.'[213] As in other fields of action, the Tories could only keep up with the Liberals by sailing close to the wind: in doing so, they unintentionally enhanced the attractiveness of the Liberals as the party of pure and just administration. On the Liberal side, the question of magistracies illustrated the social distance between the Executive and the unreformed, unself-conscious (even if Radical) provincial notables, the blindfold impact of different political moralities within the one party, and the difference between middle-class jealousy of aristocratic privilege and aristocratic zeal for chaste administration.

More than this, though, magistracies formed the small change in which debts between the notables and the national party were adjusted. By this means men were led to undertake by no means illustrious work in the local levels of a national party in exchange for local power and social eminence, and the clay of merely casual ambition was worked into the higher form of the national party. Unlike the corruption of the eighteenth century, when political power was used to extract personal profit from the State, the Victorian mixed system of patronage and honours worked to the benefit of the State and Party. The country gentleman or urban businessman handed over to the national Parliamentary party—who might not be 'his kind of person' at all—all the realities of his local influence, wealth, and political toil, and received in return for his substance and independence, the shadow of social position.

This section, based on Lancashire sources for reasons of convenience, cannot claim to prove that magistracies were political appointments. But certainly the local *élites*, particularly in the towns, wished them to be so; and whether they were so or not—and the question is essentially one of degree—what was more important was that they were widely regarded as such. The moral aura surrounding them, as sketched above, was that of the spoils system. Whether the donkey got the carrot in the end is a secondary matter.

[213] Disraeli to Derby, 1 January 1868: quoted in W. D. Jones, *Lord Derby and Victorian Conservatism* (Oxford 1956), 336.

The kind of induction by simple enumeration used above is necessarily fallible, but the impression which the documents cited give is of a secondary political culture, parasitic upon national Parliamentary politics, and of no great interest to the electorate at large, which had a public morality and interest of its own. This public morality of the middle stratum of politics clashed strongly in theory with the attitudes of Whig ministers, but was reconcilable in practice because of the triviality of the rewards demanded. This distinctive milieu of the local notables did not affect the course of national policy, nor did it affect whether a man was Tory or Liberal. But, once a man had got his money and formed his opinions, the question of whether he went forward into politics or not was much affected by the rewards system as sketched above, and at this level the secondary political culture, and its relation to the provincial culture in which the choice of satisfactions was thus biased in favour of choosing power, must be taken into account, without disrespect to the view that social conflict and political passion were the great and general business of politics in Victorian England.

3 Leadership

Leadership

The mid-nineteenth century was the first period of English history when great political careers were made outside Parliament. The paradoxical consequence of these careers, however, was not to diminish or undermine the leaders of the Parliamentary parties, but to place them more firmly in the saddle and to give them new means of control. For the men concerned, Cobden, Bright, Mill, Miall, and Chamberlain, built up the goodwill for which Gladstone lived to be the universal legatee. They built up, informally, bodies of people who responded in a disciplined way to the great Liberal tenets. When these tribunes of the people had done their work, it was easy for Gladstone to appear on the scene and use these same tenets as the Open Sesame to his listeners' confidence.

This group of tribunes and agitators, working outside Parliament, was not at all a challenge to it or to Parliamentary leadership. Their very success out of doors depended on their having a credible Parliamentary purpose to put before the public. They all tried to make the House of Commons one of their platforms. Their words were directed as much to the official mind and to educated opinion, whose views they valued, as to the populace. They rejoiced more in the 'conversion' of Peel or Gladstone than in the support of the Radical man in the street. They could become loyal subordinates, as Bright was to Gladstone. The tribunes all derived their stature from their attempt to influence Parliament, because that was where people expected things to happen. Agitators equally competent in sowing disaffection, like Ernest Jones or Odger, who were really outside the Parliamentary framework, met with little response.

What the tribunes did do, was to assist in the conquest of public opinion by the Parliamentary parties. The ordinary M.P. could not do this well: he simply gave the picture of a very rich man addressing poor men on subjects not of burning interest to either side. The Whigs would not do it, though they could have done. Palmerston and Russell, with their acceptable convictions on English nationalism and Reform respectively, could have gained a far more authoritative position in Parliament by doing a little of what Gladstone did —and Gladstone himself did little enough public speaking in the 1860's. As it was, many of their convictions never became policies, and it was therefore left to the 'tribunes' and to Gladstone to bring new constellations of opinion within the Parliamentary system. Palmerston, Russell, and Gladstone differed, it is argued, not so much in their convictions, as in the amount of political energy they could deploy to carry them out.

Each leader had his own political formula. Cobden's leadership was based on the manufacturing interest. Bright's was based on the working-class demand for Reform. Miall's was based on confession, Chamberlain's shifted uneasily from class to confession, from organization to Radical doctrine. Mill's position was based on an unparalleled intellectual ascendancy. Not all these figures are discussed below, for Chamberlain and Cobden fall outside the period of this book while Miall, gifted propagandist though he was, was not more than one among many leaders of Dissent. Of those left, Palmerston and Russell (like Disraeli) show one side of the argument: the difficulty of controlling a Parliamentary party on the basis of Parliamentary support alone. Mill and Bright, on the other hand, show the antithesis, that pervasive mental influence and grandiose agitation, exerted outside the normal seats of power, could not galvanize the Parliamentary Liberals. Gladstone made a synthesis by using his standing with the electorate to control and guide the Parliamentary party from inside. More emphasis has been given to Bright than to Gladstone, however, for in the 1860's Gladstone was only slowly moving towards the position of tribune of the people, and his forays into the provinces occupied very little of his time or attention. Bright, however, expended his energies, in an act that consumed him, in a narrow block of time, and with much greater immediate effect. He undertook the dangerous work, which Gladstone shunned, of connecting to the Parliamentary Liberals a powerful Radical and working-class movement. In the winter of 1866–7 when feelings ran highest, Gladstone went to Rome for a long holiday, but

Bright stumped the great cities, making the Reformers temperate and Reform irresistible. Because Bright did so little afterwards, it is easy to forget how much he was the centre of attention. His momentary and hard-earned ascendancy has therefore been more fully treated than Gladstone's leisurely progress towards popularity.

PALMERSTON AND RUSSELL

The position of Palmerston and Russell in the creation of the Liberal Party is clear, despite some incompleteness in the evidence available. Russell's family papers are said to have been destroyed, while his official papers deposited at the Public Record Office give little indication of the part he played in general domestic politics after 1859. An enormous mass of Palmerston's papers has only lately become accessible to students. These papers may yet substantiate in detail the traditional assertions made about Palmerston's skill in controlling 'public opinion'—that is, the Upper Ten Thousand and the high-priced London newspapers—by rather devious means. They may also throw more light on his handling of provincial notables and back-benchers, and of his interest in party organization. But such day-to-day techniques of management and manipulation are small beer, affecting only a tiny fraction of society, and any 'revelations' of such practices would not be inconsistent with the view here offered of the basis of the traditional Whig leadership.

That leadership was based on Parliamentary support, administrative pre-eminence, social prestige, and the approval of a very narrowly limited 'public opinion'. It may or may not have had popular support, but it did not make that support operational in politics. This, it is argued, was the essential difference between the old Whig leadership and that of Gladstone, and not a difference of opinion as to policies. On many important matters, the opinions of the Whigs were as advanced as those of Gladstone: sometimes, indeed, more so. Gladstone did not think so differently from the Whigs as his enthusiastic provincial audiences thought: the novelty consisting chiefly in the nature of the audiences to whom he addressed himself. Circumstance assisted this bifurcation; for Gladstone's absorption in Treasury work led him towards 'the people' as naturally as Palmerston's and Russell's preoccupation with foreign affairs took them away. Further, Palmerston had enough on his hands keeping his Parliamentary flock in one fold. Yet, however great its justification, the Whigs' implicit acceptance of the limitation of political life to those circles in which birth had placed them, threw on to Gladstone as an individual, a popularity much of which was properly due to public men in general for their progress in rationality, disinterestedness, and generosity of feeling.

Among official men, Russell stood out for his insight and for his real accord with certain popular demands.[1] Yet his thirty years' tenure of advanced opinions left less mark than Gladstone's vigour in making similar opinions prevail, when he had only barely arrived at them himself.

Russell was notably honest on the question of Reform. He would accept no trumpery substitute for a substantial admission of working men into the borough constituency. But he never agitated the subject out of doors. Similarly, he was sound enough at heart on the main social questions demanding legislation. In the 1830's he adopted a view of the Irish Church question which came fairly close to that eventually adopted in 1869. In the 1840's he concluded that security of tenure and compensation for improvements were necessary in Ireland. In English education he combined the credit for the inception of the system in his youth, with the honour of being one of the first official Liberals to state its inadequacy in his old age. This he did, in a series of resolutions[2] before the House of Lords in the autumn of 1867, before Mr Gladstone had shown any interest in national education. Russell, in short, had many of the notions for which Mr Gladstone was so largely praised, arriving at them earlier, and holding them with more consistency.

All this was quite vitiated by lack of the right kind of

[1] When his son, Lord Amberley, entered a radical phase, Russell bore this with admirable good humour.

[2] 'Gladstone is very angry about his resolutions.' *Life of Granville*, I, 517: Granville to Argyll, 22 November 1867.

public with whom to make contact. Russell was the prisoner of his family, his years, his pocket, his shyness, his period, and his colleagues. Living essentially a private life, his popularity was great far beyond his seeking of it. Unfortunately, the circles he did frequent easily, were the last to bring out his genuine sympathies in domestic affairs, and the first to assist his growing absorption in foreign affairs. He was quite unfit to take up the social role once played by his hero Fox in aristocratic society, which influenced him without receiving any impulse from him in return. The atmosphere at his home, Pembroke Lodge, has been described as 'timid, shrinking, that of a snail withdrawing into its shell, full of high principle and religious feeling . . .'[3] From this world Russell rarely emerged. In the whole of the 1860's his public engagements were as follows:

1861 Banquet at Newcastle: two speeches
1863 At Dundee and Blairgowrie: two speeches
1866 Address at Tavistock Town Hall
1867 Tour in Ireland: apparently no speeches.[4]

Till 1861, Lord John was a younger brother on an allowance too frugal for him to entertain politically: after 1861, a necessarily absentee landlord of 5,000 Irish acres, he performed the social duties falling on him as chief of the party, but without in any way creating a focus for advanced aristocratic opinion. Another indication of the extent to which Lord John was sunk in private life, is the entire absence of surviving political communication between him and anyone outside a narrow circle of Whigs and officials.

Cut off from all external support, Lord John's genuine Liberalism was readily contained by less genuine Liberals, some of whom very much feared his breaking loose as a Radical leader.[5] The Parliamentary Liberals could not be brought to rally behind a leader who did not give his genuinely popular sympathies the authority of massive popular support. Lord John brought to the birth of the Liberal

---

[3] *My Life and Adventures*, 2nd Earl Russell (1923), 10.
[4] Based on information in Spencer Walpole's *Life*. In 1867 his health broke down for good.—*Life of Granville*, I, 517.
[5] v. Argyll, *Memoirs*, II, 134.

Party, not ingenuity of Parliamentary management, not favour of outdoor support, but a great name, and a traditional and hereditary support from particular quarters like the Three Denominations, the Jews,[6] and the City of London, and from those, numerous everywhere, whose Liberalism consisted chiefly in admiration of their past achievements, and who found in Lord John's historic career an embodiment of their self-approval. To have this was much; but Lord John could have had something much greater, he could have had that devotion and hope which were later laid solely at Gladstone's feet:

> John's reception at Sheffield equalled anything of the kind I had ever seen in our high and palmy days. So little had we expected *any* reception, when . . . we saw the crowds on the platform I could not think what was the matter . . . From the station we had to drive all through the town to Alderman Hoole's villa: it was one loud and long triumph.[7]

Whether Russell so conceived it or not, his failure to rest his cause upon the adoration of the provinces was one of the great refusals of English party history.

Palmerston occupied a larger place in political life, but the pattern was the same. On the one side, he was serious, intellectual, even theoretical: militantly progressive and humane; scientific and modern, to an extent rarely realized. He 'got up all the sanitary questions and *believes* in them',[8] and was court of confidential appeal for Florence Nightingale. Further, though Palmerston's method of Parliamentary management involved crude belligerence abroad and class fear at home, the man looked on his method with complete detachment, and himself escaped that flight from intelligence he tended to produce in others. As with Russell, much that was good in him was never effectively brought into play, for lack

[6] 'Lord John it is said will come in for London as all the power and wealth of the Rothschilds will be at his service.'—Clarendon to Cowley, 17 March 1857: Clarendon mss., C. 138, Bodleian.

[7] Lady Russell to Lord Minto, 27 September 1857: *Lady John Russell. A Memoir*, by D. MacCarthy and A. Russell (1926), 171.

[8] G. C. Lewis to Hayward, 28 October 1858: *Mr Hayward's Letters*, ed. H. E. Carlisle (1886), II, 10.

of any vitalizing connection with the groups and classes who had some interest in sending folly about its business—the latter certainly being Palmerston's conception of his work at the Home Office. But no one knew better than Palmerston the difficulties of Parliamentary action, and this force of a man was brought to a policy of *quieta non movere*. Gladstone used to say that Palmerston 'had the appearance and reputation of courage without the reality':[9] but to say so was to make no allowance for Palmerston's isolation in the midst of supporters going in a different direction. Acts of courage alone would have been of little use. Like Russell, Palmerston succeeded where he touched the traditional prejudices and antipathies of the gentry class, while his ardour and business sense received little appreciation. The still current glorification of Palmerston's last years as a prolonged *dies non* may be a true stricture on the Parliamentary class as a whole, but it sadly undervalues the burden of work taken up by Palmerston. He was not the lion in the path of all reform that Bright saw: he was not the masterly architect of a policy of supineness: he was himself mastered by the supineness of the institutions and circumstances of the time.

The testimony of another writer to Palmerston's genuine concern to pass a reasonable Reform Bill is conclusive and need not be added to here.[10] Since Palmerston believed the lower classes were 'under the control of a small clique of socialist agitators',[11] and that they would be 'under absolute command as to their votes at Elections'[12] by the trades unions, and that any real reform would 'virtually disfranchise the middle classes'[13] his intrepidity in taking the question up in good faith as a normal matter of business witnessed the extent he sacrificed his personal beliefs to keep intact the party. What tripped him up was the predominance of other

[9] Lord Kilbracken, *Reminiscences* (1931), 134.
[10] See H. C. Bell, 'Palmerston and Parliamentary Representation', in *Journal of Modern History*, IV (1932).
[11] Palmerston to Russell, 27 December 1860: Russell Papers, P.R.O. 30/22/20.
[12] Palmerston to Russell, 31 March 1861: Russell Papers, P.R.O. 30/22/21.
[13] Palmerston to Russell, 27 December 1860: Russell Papers, P.R.O. 30/22/20.

business, both in 1860 and 1861, the absence of outside support and concealed opposition in his own party.

Beneath the light-minded landowner anxious to maintain class privileges, lay a character more Gladstonian in its moral earnestness—the Palmerston who exhorted the labourers at Romsey to austerity and virtue, who laboured almost single-handedly against the slave trade of the world with unmistakable zeal, who tried 'to compel the tall chimneys to burn their own smoke' and who, with desperate quixotism, seriously wished to abolish the beerhouse on moral grounds.[14] This Palmerston had learnt something from Shaftesbury, something from Chadwick, and no intellectual obstacle or defect of will remained to prevent his working wonders. As Home Secretary in 1852–4 he did work some sanitary wonders: as Prime Minister, he made no start on the work the age demanded. Though his attitude to education, for instance, was typically Liberal and generous: 'We have had the full value in the improved intelligence and good conduct of those [the lower] classes. It is natural that the amount should be greatly increasing . . .'[15] he yet took it for granted that 'where a district is very poor and cannot subscribe, no Public grants can be made. There is no help for this.'[16] If there were any signs that Palmerston did not see clearly what was desirable in social matters, the blank defect of achievement of his years of power would be less perplexing. It can only be suggested that Palmerston saw clearly, as we cannot, the resistances operating in the Parliamentary system he knew, and felt them to be too much for him.

Whether he had at his back real and substantial popular support must, in the nature of the case, remain an open question. Some contemporaries spoke of his influence as confined to clubs, cliques, and corridors: others supposed him to have touched the hearts of the people, to have become, as Bright said, the Feargus O'Connor of the middle classes. Certainly his appeal was not to the working class: certainly his influence was strong in clubs and cliques. To be Palmerstonian was to

[14] To William Cowper, 3 April 1853: Ashley, *Life of Palmerston* (1876), II, 10.
[15] Memo on Revised Code: 9 January 1862: Russell Papers, 30/22/27.
[16] Ibid.

be smart. In the great cities, Palmerston made his appeal, not to Demos, but to the flunkeyism of the new mayors, knights, and captains of industry. His visits to Leeds (1860), Manchester (1857), and Bradford (1864) were thus entirely different in spirit from those of Mr Gladstone,[17] being based on social emulation rather than on the manifestations of social solidarity promoted by Gladstone. Yet, for all his easy success out of doors, Palmerston remained essentially a House of Commons man, though speaking extraordinarily often for a man of his age at small public engagements up and down the country.[18] Friend and enemy alike bore witness to his mastery over Parliament in his second ministry, and there lay his real achievement. Not a moment too late, his tact and judgment bound together, by habit if not by affection, the jarring atoms of the Liberal sections in Parliament, thus providing the organized social forces growing up in the country with a means and a hope of getting at least their due weight in Parliament. What Gladstone did for the Liberal Party as a whole, Palmerston did for the Parliamentary party: he got all the birds accustomed to feed from his hand. Given the sources at present available, how Palmerston did this cannot yet be described in detail.

MILL

Behind the inconsequential policies of the 1840's and 1850's, some massive social changes were taking place, affecting each class in a particular way. The educated class received a new education, the middle class a new Press, and the working class, new institutions. In each case, the innovation looked towards Liberalism. The first and third of these changes

[17] 'Just now Leeds is basking in the sunshine of a Prime Minister's visit. They rush to do honour to the man who despises and insults them . . .' B.M. Add. mss. 43,384, f. 229: Bright to Cobden, 25 October 1860.

[18] Besides speaking often at his home, Romsey, he made two speeches in 1860 (both at Leeds), four in 1863 (Glasgow, Greenock, Edinburgh, and Leith) and six in 1864 (Hereford, Tiverton, Bradford, Wilton, Towcester, and the Guildhall).

belonged to a world to which John Stuart Mill, more than any other single man, gave a personal tone and common voice. From Mill, the 'thinking men' in all classes could learn a liberalism far more agreeable to their feelings than that taught by men of property in the Great Towns. Mill made it possible for young Oxford and for the labour aristocracy to be liberal without injury to their class feelings, and indeed with some flattery to them.

Mill was a frequent and effective speaker in Parliament; but what he said there could have been said by a much lesser man than Mill. His short career there simply afforded no chance for a general application of his teachings to politics: nor was he capable of so doing, had the opportunity offered. Least of all did he give expression to any of his Socialist leanings. As will be shown, his years in Parliament were in the nature of an excursion from his serious career as political instructor to the nation, for he had his real effect above and below the Parliamentary level: like the other great Liberals, he had a considered aversion for the middle class and a patrician disdain for its interests. As a young Radical, his connections were with gently-born Reformers like Molesworth and Buller: in the 1840's, he took no part in the Free Trade agitation: in the 1850's he was austerely scornful of the Administrative Reformers' crusade against aristocratic inefficiency: [19] and throughout his later books ran a tone of reproach against the low-minded worldliness of merely economic liberalism.[20] Mill's tentative suggestions for the protection of infant industries were regarded by the Manchester School as rank treason, outweighing all other good in the man. Finally, events abroad, and especially the American Civil War, revealed to Mill, so he thought, a degree of rottenness in England he had never suspected during his official career: and caused him, at least relatively, to exalt the morality of the humble,[21] and to place himself at their service

[19] Mill's *Letters*, ed. Hugh S. R. Elliott (1910), I, 186: to W. Holworthy, 11 July 1855.

[20] Particularly the ostentatious relegation of economic liberty to a mere question of expediency in the *On Liberty*.

[21] In his *Autobiography* (World's Classics edition, 228), he wrote that till the Civil War 'I had never felt so keenly how little permanent

as instructor and servant. There is a parallel between the way Mill organized his channels of instruction, and the way Gladstone ordered his bases of support. Both acted with a view to eventual realization of their aims by a Parliamentary party, but both chose to act only indirectly on the basically recalcitrant M.P.s, in all but the final stages by-passing them in favour of an appeal, on the one hand, to whatever was expert, disinterested, scientific, and open-minded in society: on the other hand, by drawing on the support of classes and institutions which still carried little weight in Parliament. By such a strategy, it was possible to maintain Liberal ministries well to the left of the average of their Parliamentary parties, and to circumvent the weight given by the electoral system to property and position.

* * *

Mill's influence upon the educated world coincided with something of a fresh start in that quarter. Pattison in a famous passage has related how Oxford cleansed its mind of Newman by embracing Mill's *Logic*, and it has frequently been remarked how superfluous the fight over subscriptions for an Anglican university was, when Mill had penetrated the very syllabus. In the 1860's, when Mill's influence stood highest, the universities expanded very quickly,[22] and a distinct public interested in ideas emerged. The *Fortnightly Review*, the typical creation of the dry, higher journalism which looked to Mill as rabbi, rose from a circulation of 1,400 in 1867 to 25,000 in 1872, figures which imply the existence of an intelligentsia of a kind which had not existed in the days when the *Westminster Review* obscurely struggled to keep alive. Some notes are therefore called for on the large part played by Mill in shaping the new intelligentsia, and on the capacity of that intelligentsia to take up the political role which the Liberal Party's assumed alignment with open-minded rationality demanded.

---

improvement had reached the minds of our influential classes, and of what small value were the Liberal opinions they had got into the habit of professing.'

[22] Admissions to Oxford and Cambridge stood at about 300–400 p.a. between 1825 and 1860, rising then to 800 p.a. by 1880.

Mill brought, in the first place, a wide and philosophic historical outlook to the problems of his day, and was able, for instance, to turn a humdrum Malt Tax debate into an occasion for discussing the whole future of English history: and on land questions, to disarm with massive information the parochial unbelief of Englishmen in what the Duke of Argyll called 'this peasant nonsense'.[23] But his historical outlook, based on an intimate acquaintance with the disturbed affairs of Greece, France, and India, countries teaching no lazy acquiescence in democracy, had to suffice where a knowledge of the social arrangements of contemporary England was more needful. Consequently, his politics were bodyless and hypothetical, and, not knowing what needed to be done, contained as much fear as hope. To two cardinal points of doctrine he lent his prestige. The first was the demythologization of the People. The second was that very important development of the 1860's, the shifting of stress away from the right of property to govern towards the claim of education to govern—though the beneficiaries of each doctrine were in practice congruent.

As regards the People, Mill can find nothing better to say of them, than that their superiors are even worse. Their idea of social reform, he found, was simply higher wages and less work, 'for the sake of mere sensual indulgence'.[24] If they once became the ascendant power, they would do so only to fall prey to a 'class of base adventurers in the character of professional politicians'.[25] Some of his utterances smack of trying to ride the chariot of reform only to apply the brakes:

It is an uphill race, and a race against time, for if the American form of Democracy overtakes us first, the majority will no more relax their despotism than a single despot would. But our only chance is to come forward as Liberals, carrying out the democratic idea, not as Conservatives, resisting it.[26]

[23] '. . . Ireland is in the main stream of human existence . . . it is England that is in one of the lateral channels.' *Hansard*, vol. 183, col. 1088, 17 May 1866.

[24] To Rev. H. W. Carr, 7 January 1852, *Letters*, ed. Elliott.

[25] To J. S. Kinnear, 25 September 1865, ibid.

[26] Packe, *Life of Mill* (1954), 418: Mill to Fawcett.

Mill had a far more vivid sense of the possibility of injustice being committed by the poor against the rich, than of the reverse process: and though he looked upon the general moral state of the educated classes as 'essentially low and mean',[27] he saw this lowness as operating principally in the direction of aiding the wicked and condoning English atrocities abroad, and of not adopting his own captious notions of Reform, rather than as acting against the interests of the poor. Nothing Mill said or wrote could lead anyone to gather that, while the question of the ascendancy of the poor was ripening, there were urgent social matters of a less hypothetical nature waiting in plenty, such as the agricultural gang system, or the hardships caused by metropolitan railway building, or coffin ships. And what was true of Mill was also true of many other of the best lights of his age: writers like Bagehot,[28] and George Eliot[29] and Leslie Stephen, for all their excellence, firmly fixed their political attention on crying over the unspilt milk of the future, exhausting on apprehension energies needed for investigation, producing in the end an intelligentsia unpolitical apparently through disinterestedness, but actually made so because of its lack of relevant social information.[30] At the time the preference of the Almighty for university men was being made, in many different books, part of the political creed of the educated world, their posture of apprehension, derived from abstract considerations rather than the actual workings of things, belied that supposition of superior knowledge on which they based their claim. 'Their knowledge was ignorance to the succeeding generation.'[31] So central was Mill in the instruction of this generation, that his very

[27] To Oscar Browning, 26 October 1867: *Letters*, ed. Elliott, II, 91.

[28] 'I am exceedingly afraid of the ignorant multitude of the new constituencies.'—Bagehot, *The English Constitution* (1872 edition), xxvii.

[29] As in the *Address to Working Men* by Felix Holt.

[30] In the Preface to the 1852 edition of the *Political Economy*, Mill wrote of the extreme unfitness of the labouring classes 'for any order of things which would make any considerable demand on either their virtue or their intellect'; taking no account of the Rochdale Pioneers or the A.E.U., which measured up well enough to any standard of disinterested administration.

[31] Henry Adams in *The Education of Henry Adams*: referring to the fine flower of English Liberal Society.

merit of conscientiousness in the kind of questions he was interested in[32] contributed to ensure the neglect of the topics of which he was ignorant. Just as Gladstone strained every nerve to relieve the middle-class income-tax payer while sincerely stating that the welfare of the working class was his chief concern, so Mill was precisely most successful when drawing attention to problems which, though of general relevance to any society, had little relevance to the particular needs of the urban poor, needs to which Mill was himself impressively awake. Though he was almost pathetically anxious to advance material progress as conceived by Chadwick,[33] the general effect of his influence—particularly through the *On Liberty*, which has as many readings as readers—was towards a departure from the practical to the metaphysical and over-scrupulous. Not a humbug himself, he was a source of humbug in his disciples. The failure of the Liberal Party to ally iself, as a matter of politics, with the progressive *élites* of the professions—which has been already illustrated in the case of the legal profession—and the power shown by Mill in making doctrine do the work of information and experience, led to a great deal of that apparent insincerity regarding social questions so often charged to class selfishness.

In the particular department of foreign policy, the failure of the Liberal intellectuals to make a fruitful relation between thought and politics, to replace casual judgments by systematic ones—as they did for instance on the land question—was grave. Two great theories of foreign policy existed, that of the ministerial class, based on national power, and that of the Manchester School, based on national happiness. Both existed only in an implicit and imperfect form, yet both deserved explicit and classical exposition. Yet the intelligentsia failed even to comprehend both these theories, and foreign policy remained an area of shadow on the intellectual map. Mill himself, so far as one can judge from his isolated deliverances on foreign relations, never felt required by his

[32] The political question on which he wrote most fully and passionately in the 1860's was on 'keeping the priests out' of the Irish system of national education. Here Mill was as clergymanish as any provincial reverend.

[33] Mill urged Florence Nightingale to become a politician.

role as a Radical critic of society to examine with detachment
the assumptions behind foreign policy, nor did he see in this
field probable grounds of separation between the Radicals and
the rest. His opinions had the rude health of the retired
Indian administrator. He believed in the maintenance of the
prestige of the British Empire,[34] the importance of military
drill in schools,[35] non-intervention except where liberty was
jeopardized,[36] that England was bound to protect Belgium;[37]
and he gave a regular donation to the Blackheath Volunteers.[38]

* * *

Mill was part of the intellectual landscape of the self-educated
from the 1840's onward. As early as 1854 his chapters on the
future of the labouring classes were reprinted separately for
circulation among the working people.[39] In the 1860's his
main works were published in people's editions, and there
was a brisk demand from the Mechanics' Institutes, then in
their heyday, for free copies of his works. The young heroes of
Thomas Hardy, out on the perimeter of the thinking world,
felt Mill's pull: similarly, in the 1850's a young Primitive
Methodist miner was reading 'Shakespeare, Milton, Scott,
Burns, John Stuart Mill,' at Seaton Delaval.[40]

His writings, fitting invaluably into a great popular movement for adult education, gave him an influence he for long
did not suspect, in quarters of which he long remained quite
ignorant. In 1860 he would have liked to help Fawcett in a
by-election at Southwark, 'but I have no power of helping any-
body with electors'.[41] In the 1850's his letters show he was very
imperfectly informed on the state of Co-operation in England,[42] although he came to be regarded as its peculiar patron:

[34] Mill to Cairnes, 15 June 1862: Mill Papers, vol. LV, f. 18.
[35] Letter of 29 December 1866, in *Letters*, ed. Elliott (1910).
[36] *Fraser's*, December 1859.
[37] Mill to Fawcett, 26 July 1870, *Letters*, II, 267.
[38] Mill Papers, Box IX.
[39] Mill to Furnivale, 13 February 1854, in *Letters*, ed. Elliott (1910).
[40] G. J. Holyoake, *Thomas Burt M.P.* (1895), 7.
[41] Mill papers, vol. III, f. 20: Mill to Fawcett, 24 December 1860.
[42] *Letters*, ed. Elliott (1910), to Professor Rau, 7 July 1852: to J.
Holmes of Leeds, 19 January 1858.

But it was Mr. John Stuart Mill who as an authority in political economy, extended to co-operation scientific recognition, and subsequently promoted, befriended, and advised all who worked for it and were at trouble to serve it.[43]

His candidature in 1865 revealed for the first time that he was one of the very few political figures of his day who could command national support. Holyoake wrote: 'In Rochdale as much interest was expressed as for Mr. Potter's election when I was there . . .'[44] But Mill did not show the same interest in the working men that they showed in him. The great sympathy he drew towards him, remained largely latent, though he made more and better platform speeches than is usually realized: while his action on the understandings of men was not so unrequited.

Mill's work in mellowing the orthodox political economy had five aspects. It reassured those already opposed to the old economics.[45] It set free those persons of good will who had been forced into necessitarian beliefs by the demands of their understanding. It gave scientific recognition—and more—to Co-operation. (Mill informed a correspondent that Co-operation, with the emancipation of women, were the two great changes that would regenerate society.)[46] It gave the approval of the most unimpeachable libertarian of the age, to those tendencies towards collectivism released by the Second Reform Bill. Finally, he developed a most powerful attack against those whose use of necessitarian economics coincided too closely with their private interests and preconceptions.[47] Indeed, Mill's socialism consisted much more of cogent denunciations of the errors of his former selves, than of the assertion of new principles.

[43] G. J. Holyoake, *John Stuart Mill as Some of the Working Classes Knew Him* (1873). This pamphlet was reprinted from the *Newcastle Chronicle*, a paper owned by Cowen, a Liberal Party boss and also the chief mover behind Co-operation in the north-east. Holyoake had received money from Mill and Grote in 1856 when in great straits.

[44] Mill Papers, Vol. IX, f. 198: Holyoake to Mill, 21 May 1865.

[45] See R. V. Clements, 'British Trade Unions and Popular Political Economy 1850–1875', in *Economic History Review*, August 1961.

[46] Mill, *Letters*, ed. Elliott (1910): to Parke Godwin, 1 January 1869.

[47] Especially against Lowe: see *Hansard*, vol. 190, col. 1525, 12 March 1868.

But the Mill that the working classes knew was not the Fortnightly Reviewer, but the writer of the *Political Economy*. Even the last edition of that work which was revised by Mill, that of 1871, did not contain his current thinking on the wage fund and on land questions, published in the reviews. The Mill the working-class *élites* supported, was the relatively orthodox economist who had no real concord with the main working-class objectives. As with Gladstone and Bright, there was a puzzling incongruity between the undeniable popularity of Mill, and his clear detachment from the interests of his supporters. The explanation may be that, though the organized working class had no difficulty in keeping their independence of outlook where their interests were concerned, to maintain indefinitely a posture of protest against instructed opinion, cost a good deal of anxiety, anxiety which might be marvellously relieved by authoritative re-assurance, and a chance of winning the sympathy of the fair-minded. Mill gave something of both, and left no intellectual obstacles to sympathy with the main aims of the organized working class.

Mill also removed, for those who were willing to listen, any intellectual difficulties that might exist about the merits of State interference in social arrangements. He thought a government might compel universal insurance, though he doubted its expediency.[48] He spoke in favour of State aid to the sea fisheries of Ireland, explaining this was entirely justifiable on general grounds. In the *On Liberty* he demanded a compulsory (though not State) education. But above all he looked to the cities as the next area for the extension of State action:

> One marked feature of the political movement, of which the passing of the Reform Act was a part, is a demand on the part of the people . . . for more administration. It is not only sanitary measures, properly so called, but control over the dwellings provided for the working classes, and a hundred similar arrangements, which are now required at the hands of Governments. . . .[49]

[48] Mill, *Letters*, ed. Elliott (1910), 22 April 1868.
[49] *Hansard*, vol. 191, col. 1860, 5 May 1868. His Metropolitan Government Bill was an attempt to make a start on the problem, by destroying the vestries.

and was confident that poverty, in any sense implying suffering, might be completely extinguished by the wisdom of
society:[50] 'The present wretched education, and wretched
social arrangements, are the only real hindrance to it (sc.
happiness) being attainable by almost all.'[51] (As with Bright,
we find that Mill's expectations of improvement were hardly
founded at all on prospects of scientific innovation or
economic growth: contrary to the received notion of their
blind absorption in material progress.)

Despite the above evidence of good intentions, and many
noble attempts to bring Chadwick back into public life, Mill
in practice concurred in old-fashioned conceptions of 'advanced' politics, to an extent that took him to the opposite
pole from Chadwick.

*   *   *

For, as Leslie Stephen pointed out, the philosopher who took
many-sidedness for his motto, was a good party man in Parliament. Impartiality never led him to think the Tories had the
better case. He had not always seen things so: in 1859 he
deplored the change of ministry and 'the well worn useless
shibboleths of Whig mitigated democracy . . .' But, under the
attractive power of Mr Gladstone and with a bond forged
between the working-class movement and the Liberal left, he
became an admiring reader of the *Daily News*[52] and an (unrequited) admirer of Gladstone. In 1868 he asked the new
electors to send men not only to support Mr Gladstone, but
to help him:[53] this object ought not to be sacrificed to any
other:[54] 'Gladstone and the Disestablishment of the Irish
Church' issued as a slogan from the philosopher as from every
other candidate.

Mill proved the reality of his convictions by giving rather
large sums of money to political objects, about £700 being

[50] *Utilitarianism* (Everyman edition), 14.

[51] Ibid., 12. Though some of their lines of development were the same,
I have failed to trace any explicit influence of Ruskin on Mill, though
this cannot be ruled out.

[52] Mill, *Letters*, ed. Elliott (1910), Mill to Thornton, 29 October 1863.

[53] Mundella Letters, Sheffield University Library: Mundella to
Leader, 24 July 1868.

[54] Mill, *Letters*, ed. Elliott (1910): to his Election Committee, 27
September 1868.

given by him in the four years for which his accounts survive;[55] not a large sum perhaps in relation to his income,
which varied between £2,000 and £3,000 annually, but large
in relation to the resources of those he supported. He supported the National Reform Union and the National Reform
League (with £5 and £10 respectively), the West and Mid-
Kent Registration Association with £11, and some character-
istically Liberal but formally non-party bodies like the
Commons Preservation Society, the Women's Suffrage
Society, and the London Municipal Association, received his
generous support. His main efforts were, however, directed
towards the election of Liberal candidates: between 1868 and
1871 he helped these as follows:

	£
Gladstone	25
Beales	155
Odger	60
Dickson	10
Sandwith	10
Bradlaugh	10
Howell	10
Angerstein and Lubbock	1
Chadwick	100

Though he repudiated formal connection with the Reform
League,[56] he was beyond doubt in earnest over the principle
of working-class representation. What working-class representation was to lead to, his practice did not spell out. His
concern for rationality—in poor law administration and
metropolitan government[57]—and for humanity—in Jamaica
and Ireland—on the part of government were unexception-
able and admirable: but they were not that politics of the
future, for which Mill in his prophetic books had created a
demand quite beyond his power to satisfy.[58]

[55] All information about Mill's finances comes from the Mill Papers,
Box IX.
[56] v. *Autobiography* (World's Classics), 247, for this statement: also in
Hansard, vol. 184, col. 1905, 2 August 1866.
[57] His wish (about the vestries) that 'they would not tolerate hole and
corner government for any purpose whatever' typified his clear sense of
direction on such themes.—*Hansard*, vol. 185, col. 1609, 8 March 1867.
[58] He did not speak on the substance of the Health Act of 1866.
Probably there was no need for him to do so.

Nothing more clearly denoted the irresistibility of Mr Gladstone than the homage done him by the most powerful speculative intellect of his generation. Mill was capable of striking out courageous new trains of thought quite of his own making: moreover, in his *Autobiography* he imagined himself a veteran socialist; yet Mill the politician turned away from the productions of his own mind, from all the themes traced out in his books, to state, and to proselytize, with an enthusiasm he never allowed for himself, the alien, essentially Peelite, creed furnished and embodied by Gladstone in action: Gladstone, 'the man who spoke from his own convictions',[59] the 'statesman in whom the spirit of improvement was incarnate',[60] the 'greatest Parliamentary leader the country had had in the present century, or, perhaps, since the time of the Stuarts',[61] was the central theme of his speeches. In this, Mill led the way, taking a tone that only became general at the time of the anti-Turk agitation. The Apostle of Rationalism left the uncertainty of theoretical creeds, for what was to him a certain personal relation: and what Mill might do, would be generally true for less distinguished minds.

Respecting Mr. Gladstone (Cheers). What was the use to speak of him on a question of sincerity? (Cheers). Every year of his official life had been marked by a succession of measures—no year being without them—some great, some small, but all aiming at the public good—to the good of the people of this country, and especially of the poorer classes. These measures were not even suggested to him: they were the offspring of his own mind, will and purpose —the free gift from him to his countrymen, unprompted, unsuggested. (Loud cheers). And his countrymen would reward him as they had done already (Hear hear and cheers).

Mr. Gladstone seemed to be the first statesman who has come up to the idea of a great modern statesman: . . . If we

[59] Mill Papers, vol. LV, f. 63: Mill to Cairnes, 12 December 1864.

[60] Mill Papers, Box V: report in *Daily News*, 23 July 1866, of a Cobden Club dinner.

[61] Mill Papers, Box V: Westminster Reform meeting reported in *Daily News*, 25 June 1866.

do not stand by him . . . we shall not easily find another to serve us in the same way. (Loud cheers).[62]

Bright's life considered as a whole was strangely marred by inconsequence and interruptions. Only in the ten years before the reform agitation between 1858 and 1868 did he find himself acting to great purpose. Not more than a minor member of the League, he shared in the later futilities of the Manchester School, till he lost his seat and his health in that cause. His first twenty years in politics gained him only the recognition and respect of those he attacked in exchange for what he felt to be the treachery of the middle classes whom he sought to represent, and there are some indications that this waste of half his adult life was a permanent source of pain to him.

Bright was out of politics from autumn 1855 to autumn 1858. Cobden was out of politics from early in 1857 to the autumn of 1859. Bright then returned on his own account with an individual policy in 1858. For ten years he went straight as an arrow on Reform. All that he had urged came to pass, and as the result of a type of agitation he had long foreseen and in some part led. His later life was almost without achievement.

Bright's singular effectiveness at this period of his life was in fact due to his coming to represent two great movements when there was no one else to do so. He stood at the confluence of the working-class movement and of political Dissent. Both movements failed to produce an inspiring leader in their own mould, and had to learn to accept Bright, cast in the mould of the League's social theories, which were only moderately sympathetic either to the working class or to militant Nonconformity. In accepting Bright, the new electors

[62] Mill Papers, Box V: speech by Mill at the Westminster Reform meeting, reported in *Daily Telegraph*, 13 April 1866. Mill attended Gladstone's breakfast parties occasionally in the 1860's, but personal contact played little or no part in the relationship between the two men.

of the great towns were learning to accept a Liberal Party not heartily anxious for the good of the people, learning of Mr Gladstone's great merits, and of the importance of ordinary folk in enforcing righteous conduct upon statesmen. Finally, with Bright's disappearance from political life via the Cabinet, he left Mr Gladstone as legatee both of his supporters and of his method.

Professor Asa Briggs remarks that Bright made Liberalism a creed. He certainly did not provide an intellectual creed, such as the school of Mill invoked to rationalize their political preferences: but he connected the politics of reform with the highest feelings of common folk, touching every question of the day with poetry, moral earnestness and a romantic glow which were comparable with Midlothian, rather than with the mundane speeches Mr Gladstone gave when beginning to speak out of doors in the 1860's.

Reform no doubt would have come without Bright. But without Bright it could have had very different consequences for the Liberal Party. The grand symphonic effect of Palmerston uniting the Parliamentary Liberals in habits of stable co-operation, of Gladstone spanning, by personal stature and legislative ability, the gulf between electors and elected, would have been inadequate without the work done by Bright, as Gladstone's bulldog, in holding together the centrifugal confessional and working-class interests outside Parliament in a broad-bottomed Radicalism. Bright, the great destroyer by nature, made the work of his prime the turning of discord into harmony and it was he, not Gladstone, who first greatly extended and deepened the range of meanings that could be read into support of a party. By such means the question of democracy was successfully kept apart from the struggle of Dives and Lazarus, allowing the more clement treatment of both issues.

*   *   *

What is loosely called character may be treated under various heads: but two large groups of facts stand apart. One great part of his character was inherited, or taken by coloration from his Quaker milieu: and this traditional character fought, with great success on the whole, to dominate both what was

a matter of his individual temperament, and also the circumstances of his health, wealth, and occupation. Any attempt to
diminish Bright would founder, not on political grounds, but
on the remarkable example he presented of admitted weakness transcended by a coherent social faith not of his own
making. Bright's social theory proper will be treated later;
here it need only be pointed out how greatly he was soaked
in the seventeenth century. To Lady Amberley he said he
thought Milton 'the greatest man who had ever lived',[63] and
in the midst of his greatest agitation he wrote to a fellow
Quaker: 'I know where I am, or try to know it, and that
in the midst of a great war, blows must be struck—our fore-
fathers thought so also, 200 years ago.'[64] In 1865 again, he was
reading 'the life of Sir John Eliot till near midnight';[65] like
Miall, he was dyed in the vat of a certain interpretation of
history.

Since his policies were much milder than those of the
Liberation Society, his striking animus against the Church
dignitaries represented all the more a witness to inherited
resentment. To no one else was he as rude as to the bishops
whom, as spiritual peers, he denounced as 'of monstrous, nay
of adulterous birth'; but Church subjects did not have for his
intelligence the interest that they had for his feelings. In the
home, his son related, Bright never touched on religious
topics, adding 'he was, however, a deeply religious man, as his
speeches show'.[66] In conduct, he held very fast to the old ways.
Novels were for long unacceptable, then, these accepted, he
still found Shakespeare not fit to read: the action of Byron
on radical Dissent, as portrayed by Mark Rutherford, and of
which Bright was a good example, only went as far as politics.
His ideas of manners cut him off from any relaxed enjoyment
of society: in 1851 he wrote of this incompatibility: 'An evening foolishly spent through the folly of Osborne, who prefers
jokes and ridicule and nonsense to any useful and agreeable
conversation.'[67] Similarly, the traditional outlook led him to

[63] *Amberley Papers*, II, 21, 19 March 1867.
[64] To S. Fox, 25 October 1866: Street mss.
[65] *Diaries*, ed. R. J. Walling (1935), 283, 11 February 1865.
[66] Ibid., xi.
[67] Ibid., 122, 2 April 1851.

moralize his narrow range of interests and to depreciate what was not strictly concerned with justice: 'I don't believe in the regeneration of a people or the saving of a country by pictures or statues or by any amount of fiddling' he wrote of the great Art Treasure Exhibition at Manchester in 1857. Sanitary reform and law reform likewise hardly appealed to him: he specialized to an extraordinary extent on the kind of moral issue that needed little outlay of thought and argument.

'Ah, here at last is one of those terrible men of 1832,' Peel is supposed to have said after an early speech of Bright's.[68] Bright's lack of capacity showed how little the university men had to fear for their monopoly of government in this age. What the age demanded of a public man, Bright could not supply. One may give three illustrations of this. In the autumn of 1858, Bright found it necessary to draft a Reform Bill: how was it done?

> Mr. McLaren has worked hard on the statistics of the question, and during my stay there, he arranged the schedules of the proposed Bill. We also went through [former Bills] ... and found that many of the clauses would meet our case now by filling up the blanks differently.[69]

That is, Bright delegated the arrangements of a measure with which he was most intimately identified. Similarly, he can be cited to show the incapacity of businessmen for the business side of government. 'I don't understand this question and I know nobody who does, so as to convince me that he is right, so I never speak on it, and never have, in public, said a word upon it,' Bright wrote on the question of Bank Charter suspension in the commercial crisis of 1857.[70] Further evidence exists of his administrative inability: a Bradford merchant, an ardent Cobdenite, whose support was worth having, wrote of Bright as the 'most incapable Presi-

[68] *The National Protest on Manchester's Rejection of John Bright* (Manchester 1857).
[69] B.M. Add. mss. 43,384, f. 149: 29 December 1858.
[70] Bright to Cobden, 24 November 1857: B.M. Add. mss. 43,384, f.

dent of the Board of Trade who ever took office'.[71] Since
Bright only held office in effect for one session, that of 1869,
no judgment could fairly be formed of his powers quite so
adverse as the above, yet the above examples do illustrate well
the failure of Bright outside the realm of feeling.

On the few occasions when he set out to master a question,
he became overwhelmed with the illusion of knowledge. No
man in England, he said, had studied the Devon Commission
more than he, and on Indian cotton as on Irish land, he trans-
muted a little reading into a great authority. On one subject
only was his knowledge and judgment fully equal to the facts
of the case and the position he took up and that was on the
issue of Reform, where he was thoroughly at home in debating
great masses of detail; but in general, Bright strikingly indicated the lack of a middle-class alternative to aristocratic rule,
and the large share that education had in sustaining aristocratic monopoly.

Bright bore the stamp of trade. He was never free, like Peel
or Gladstone, to rest on the achievements of a previous
generation, and he always counted himself, with what justification cannot now be said, a poor man: poor, that is, by the
standards of Lancashire manufacturers, and hence poor in
relation to the great landowners. His arrangements in
London were sometimes straitened by economy: and Birmingham always paid all his election expenses.[72] But business
worries probably cost him more in time and anxiety than
in cash; he refused many lucrative railway directorships on
grounds of overwork.[73] At the end of the session of 1861,
Cobden was afraid Bright would have to retire from public
life, being 'nailed to the desk at the mill' owing to his
brother's ill-health.[74] Between 1861 and 1866 he spoke very
little, and this may have been due to pressure of work in
Rochdale. An intricate lawsuit with Crossley's of Halifax was
not settled until 1864: 'The award is in our favour, and
Crossley's patent is smashed',[75] and Bright had to introduce

---

[71] *Memoir of Sir Jacob Behrens*, 61.
[72] *Hansard*, vol. 192, col. 265, 14 May 1868.
[73] Bright to Fenton, 11 October 1864: Rochdale Public Library.
[74] B.M. Add. mss. 43,655, f. 229, 31 July 1861. Cobden to Hargreaves.
[75] To his daughter Helen, 8 March 1864: Street mss.

modern machinery under the threat of being ruined in pocket by the leader of political Dissent in Yorkshire.[76] But it is not possible to trace clearly the effect of his occupation upon his political activities, save that it added to other factors that tended to make his grip on events precarious, for no evidence of his financial position has come to light.

Cobden suggested to old Mr Bright in 1837 that young John had the makings of a politician. 'Oh no, no, no,' said the old gentleman, shaking his hand. 'He must attend to business, he has got to look after the mills.'[77] To pass from this traditional quietism to middle-class agitation was a long step; to move on as Bright did in the 1860's to become in some measure a working-class leader, was to compress into twenty years a transformation which took generations to accomplish in the sphere of national life.

Bright was at the mercy of his nerves to a degree unknown in any other public man of the age. He was miserably conscious that the political role he could do best in, was the one most dangerous to his health, and his closer friends such as Cobden felt he was pressed into agitation by interested persons, against his better judgment. His illness between 1855 and 1858 struck Cobden as very grave: he had a 'horrid fear of his falling into a state of mental imbecility'.[78] Even in Italy he dreamt of the House of Commons: 'I have been in it apparently all night, and my dream seems as clear before me, as if it were a reality'.[79] In 1863 he was dreaming about America, '. . . seeing telegrams that I could not read . . .'[80] Each year he spent several months fishing and recuperating in Scotland, in absolute idleness.

During his decade of agitation for Reform, he was never more than one step ahead of his bad health. In his first speech at Birmingham, he spoke of his diminished fire and lessened force: in 1865 he was on the verge of a repetition of his earlier breakdown, and had to retire from Parliament for the greater

[76] He had a pocket interest in Cobden's French treaty: 'We are greatly satisfied with the carpet duties . . .' he wrote to Cobden. Add. mss. 43,384, f. 231, 8 November 1860.
[77] C. S. Miall, *Life of Henry Richard* (1889), 130.
[78] Cobden to Henry Richard, 19 October 1856.
[79] To Mrs Bright, 13 April 1857: Street mss.
[80] To Mrs Bright, 19 July 1863: University College mss.

part of the session, not speaking on the Reform question, for instance. In the middle of his great tour of 1866 he was writing to his wife of his great longing for quiet. Finally, his nature caught up with him. He announced to Mr Gladstone: 'I have distinct warnings of an attack something like that from which I suffered 14 years ago, and I dare not disregard them. I am quite unable to work . . .'[81] Bright did not speak in Parliament in 1870, nor again till 1875, when he spoke only twelve times and even then he did not speak in support of Trevelyan's motion for reform of the county franchise. When he returned in 1875, his hair had all turned silver, and his position in politics was entirely different.

Properly appreciated, his ill health supports Bright's claim to have undertaken political work as a trust, a burden laid upon him at no light cost to himself. 'I have not sought the office [of promoting Reform] . . . I did everything I could to decline it . . . how ill qualified I am, in many respects, for the work I have undertaken'.[82]

Many have accused him of intense ambition. It is quite true that he was very tender on the subject of his possible entry into the Cabinet—quite naïvely so, for he showed it to all the world. This, perhaps, is a touch of nature, of the old Adam. But, even if he were greatly ambitious for office—and the evidence only showed that he was disturbed at the prospect, as a Quaker might well be—can any connection between this ambition and the great things he actually did be shown? In fact, it is remarkable how much evidence there is against a Tartuffian view of his character. In 1859 and 1866 he gave loyal support to a ministry, hardly, in his view, Liberal, which could not do without him, and yet without attempting to draw advantage from his position: and he did everything possible to allow Gladstone to reap, from fields which Bright had long tilled and sown.

Bright in the 1860's, naturally indolent except when ex-

---

[81] B. M. Add. mss. 44,112, f. 112, 8 February 1870. According to the Speaker's diary for the same day, Bright was suffering from dizziness, confusion, and paralysis of one leg.—J. E. Denison, *Notes from My Journal when Speaker of the House of Commons* (1900), 251.

[82] Speech at Manchester, 10 December 1858: *Speeches*, ed. Rogers (1869), 303.

cited, depressed, certainly in health, probably also by heavy business cares and family anxieties, isolated by Cobden's death from his strongest support, and without the capacity for detail and bulk needed for Parliamentary success, was quickened, and saved from the inertia of his later life, by the dynamism of his inherited social faith and tradition, on the one hand, and of militant Dissent and the working-class movement on the other. The attitudes of a household in Rochdale, reaching back to Commonwealth times, harmonized remarkably with the great new movements of the day, and what Bright did was not so much to apply old feeling to present circumstances by formulating measures, as to state old feelings with unequalled confidence and clarity. As an advocate of detailed policies, Bright is not to be found. What he did was to state the grounds, the attractions, and the general theories lying behind the various kinds of Radicalism of his day. Hence it is of the first importance to examine what his general theory was.

* * *

Bright's theory of history and of politics did not derive from any abstract attachment to *laissez-faire* or political economy, or from any construction of his business interests. Later on, his tenuous connection with *laissez-faire* principles in the 1860's will be remarked on: but it may be said immediately that he drew little inspiration from ideas which had no moral colouring.[83] When he dealt with the land question, he dealt with it in the spirit of Naboth's vineyard. He claimed support from the 'great laws of political economy', but he never enumerated these laws. The appeal of Free Trade was not scientifically argued, but phrased morally as a manly renunciation of 'relief' gained by Protection. Nor was he in any way the mouthpiece of the moneyed interest—more than any other M.P. from the great towns. When asked to speak at a dinner on behalf of commerce, he replied he was not its representative.[84] Only in the case of creating a popular press did he act

[83] 'What he hated was injustice: what he abhorred was cruelty, whether of war or slavery: what he cared for was the comfort and prosperity of common people'—Holyoake, *Sixty Years of an Agitator's Life*, II, 580.

[84] Letter to Mrs Bright, 1868, no date: University College mss.

with a personal stake in a great industrial question, as will be shown in due course.

Bright's views on taxation, economically considered, were puerile. Considered, however, as symptoms of disturbance in mind unable to reflect more creatively on Dives and Lazarus, they may be said to show good feelings. His views amounted to three propositions. Land, he held, got off too lightly, citing only one example of this, the working of the succession duty, without relating it to the argument that land paid the great part of local taxation. Secondly, like so many reformers from the great towns, he disapproved of income tax ('most odious because most unjust')[85] and at the same time asked for removal of the remaining indirect taxes—a demand ending in the 'Free Breakfast Table'. Thirdly, taxation should not mount beyond the fifty millions a year raised in Peel's time, no matter what might have changed since. Time and again Bright declared that 'this insane and wicked policy' would lead to an 'exiled royal family . . . an overthrown aristocracy, and . . . a period of recurring revolution; . . .'[86] while never giving any account of any mechanism whereby an increase of taxation to the extent of two to three per cent of the national income—no more was involved— could depress the condition of the nation, to any degree much greater than two or three per cent. In short, he had a crotchet, and he used it like a demagogue. 'Profligate expenditure' was his main cry in his first Reform agitation. In this respect, Bright carried the torch of electioneering parsimony on from the old Radicalism, and made an agitator of Mr Gladstone with this enthusiasm, which so greatly failed to come to anything in 1868–74.

But taxation was only a crotchet, and after Cobden's death, it fell into the background. What Bright really sought to do was to destroy the *ancien régime* in England, and all its principles and policies, only one of which was profligate expenditure. He had the most vivid conception of this *ancien régime*: and much biting information on its iniquities. He knew the number of acts passed sanctioning capital punishment under

[85] *Speeches*, ed. Rogers (1869), 484.
[86] Speech on Fortifications, 2 August 1860: Robertson, *Life of Bright* (1912), 281.

each dynasty. In his own words, the social structure appeared to him thus:

> The Aristocracy in this country are almost, and really are altogether on one side—because they have special privileges to sustain, to surrender which would make them no longer an aristocracy. Our government was purely an aristocratic one from 1690 to 1830. Nearly the whole period was one of war, and war wholly needless.[87]

The resulting evils can only be removed by 'an admission of the democratic element'; and he, Bright, will play the part of Samson in the temple, 'lifting up our population into freemen' and bringing down 'the lofty pretensions of the ruling class'.[88]

The main social problem then was seen as Privilege, privilege existing in some close connection with poverty, no doubt, but still it was Privilege and not poverty that was the central question of Bright's politics. The extreme form of Privilege was 'monopoly', whether in the form of an Established Church or of the Corn Laws. The rest of Bright's politics followed coherently from this principle. The train of thought used was this. The basis of the power of Privilege was its social and economic basis in landed property. To end this ascendancy, a great social change would be necessary in the counties. But this the counties could not achieve by themselves. The towns would have to come to their aid. Now the towns did not contain Privilege: flunkeyism, backsliding, ingratitude, yes, but not Privilege, and hence they might not be thought to be in need of reform. But, though Bright did not think the towns needed social and economic changes as the counties did, he thought a measure of political reform in the boroughs essential. If the towns were to come to the aid of the counties in overthrowing Privilege, it would be through an increased weight being given to the artisans in the towns, and to the towns, in Parliament—for the middle class, the ten pounders, had lost their political *élan*. From all this it followed that a good measure of reform in the towns was the only possible way to get things started, and the only thing

[87] To S. Fox, 24 October 1865: Bright Papers, Street, Somerset.
[88] Bright to Cobden, 21 August 1859: B.M. Add. mss. 43,384, f. 154.

worth working for. There was a minor way of achieving reform, by creating a popular Press, and there was the great method of agitation proper.

Such were Bright's arguments. They account for, and do much to justify, the great bulk of his political activity: at least they make it thoroughly coherent and rational, and something of an attempt to realize 'a higher and a better civilization'[89] in the counties. It was not a case of seeing the Tory mote and neglecting the Liberal and urban beam. Inheriting the mental habits of the Commonwealthsman of rural England, nothing was more likely than that Bright should see the new possibility of applying the old feelings to change the social order of the countryside. On the other hand, one could not expect a mind of Bright's order to originate measures equal to the pauperism, paganism, and ignorance of the great towns. His merits were to draw attention to pauperism as a datum of politics, though propounding no remedy: to create, from the frustrations of rural society, a genuine Liberalism which was 'of human bondage', and had a long and useful life: and by applying his general theory outside England, to bring forward a new and sometimes profounder view of overseas problems. An orator pressed into the mould of a teacher, he did his best work when insisting on the scope, seriousness, and possibilities of a problem, not when proposing his often trumpery solutions.

Bright felt a general complacency regarding social conditions in the boroughs: 'Their wages are such that the bulk of them could live moderately well on half their present incomes—and they and their employers might well learn something useful by a little suffering', he wrote of the distress during the Cotton Famine,[90] and the view that philanthropic legislation was the last refuge of a scoundrel kept him apart from currents of practical improvement: 'Don't you observe how our "great" men run into sanitary reforms and social science oratory, fearing to touch politics at all?'[91] Despite his general complacency, he made a candid exception of pauperism. The figure of one million paupers turned up everywhere

[89] The phrase is often used by Cobden.
[90] B.M. Add. mss. 43,384, f. 256, 29 July 1861, to Cobden.
[91] B.M. Add. mss. 43,384, f. 140, 24 October 1858, to Cobden.

in his speeches. It was his touchstone of misgovernment. 'With all our boasted civilization and freedom, I believe we have a greater number of paupers than any other country.'[92] Matthew Arnold, choosing to imply that Bright neglected the darker side of things, did him an injustice:[93] in fact, both occupy the same ground in juxtaposing pauperism and the growing prosperity to enforce the conclusion something was wrong, while avoiding any more specific conclusion. From the time of the Crimean War, Bright's feelings were engaged in sympathy with the working class alone, and his ultimate sanction was in the relation he perceived between pauperism at the bottom and Privilege at the top: a relation only to be changed by political reform.

> Since I have taken part in public affairs, the fact of the vast weight of poverty and ignorance that exists at the bottom of the social scale has been a burden on my mind, and is so now. I have always hoped that the policy which I have advocated, and which has been accepted in principle, will tend gradually but greatly to relieve the pauperism and suffering. . . .[94]

As the only remedies Bright admitted were public economy, peace, and land reform of a Voluntaryist kind, it needed an effort of invective to make Reform highly desirable. The social gains offered being slight and improbable, Bright had to rely on the metaphysical value of the vote in itself, and as a way of expressing antipathy to Privilege unconnected with any plan for social improvement. Bright did not (and it is his most glaring omission) advert systematically to working-class education as the subject most likely to benefit from Reform.[95] When pressed to state how the working classes would benefit from Reform, his chief answer lay in the good it would do to

[92] Robertson, *Bright* (1912), 217: speech at Rochdale, 28 January 1859.
[93] cf. *Culture and Anarchy*, ed. J. Dover Wilson (1935), 186.
[94] Robertson, *Bright* (1912), 288: speech at Edinburgh, 5 November 1868.
[95] Bright, in sharp contrast to the other Liberal candidates at Birmingham, made no mention of the education question in his 1868 election address, and in the cabinets of December 1869 and January 1870 he spoke against introducing an Education Bill in 1870, probably for tactical reasons.

their 'minds and morals and general condition'.[96] At elections, he had seen thousands of non-electors 'with looks of great anxiety, and often with looks of great dejection'. Bright was a great Reformer in spite of the narrowness of his views of what was involved: he relied entirely on the staples of the flesh and blood theory, that one man is as good as another, and on the retrenchment crotchet. Such questions as the efficiency, social composition and ability of the members elected, did not trouble him. He never met Lowe's arguments. He did not discuss working-class representation. All he wanted was to bring into politics a class disposed to redress the injustices of Privilege, as the middle class could not, and the question of justice put aside any thoughts about the quality of Parliament which so preoccupied other Reformers. Another severe criticism is that his ideas of retrenchment were liable to opportunist changes. To the end he held that 'the public exactions and expenditure have much to do with poverty',[97] but the taxes falling on the poor were presumably chiefly the excises on malt, tea, coffee, and sugar. Yet Bright never held the reduction of these more important than the reduction of the middle class and industrial taxes: principally the paper duty and the income tax. From 1863 he was consulted by Mr Gladstone on the question of income tax—in company with the Whips—and would, therefore, if only by his silence, seem to be implicated in Gladstone's habit of turning fiscal policy to electioneering rather than social purposes for the benefit of the middle-class income-tax-paying elector.

Bright, then, was a Reformer, not so much on social grounds as because he inherited antipathies to aristocracy, while after the Crimean War, he came to feel a complete alienation from Parliament and the middle class. He was the earliest analyst of the process by which men of property in the great towns swung back to Toryism:

There is an inveterate flunkeyism which pervades nearly all the newly rich in these districts—and I have little faith

---

[96] Speech at Glasgow, 21 December 1858: *Speeches*, ed. Rogers (1869), 312.

[97] H. J. Leech, *The Public Letters of the Right Hon. John Bright, M. P.* (2nd ed. 1895), 251: letter written in 1878.

in their latent power. When it comes to be latent, we shall probably find it against us.[98]

Even before his defeat, he was not sanguine about his own order. Of one of them he wrote: 'I hope he may turn out well: though after what we have seen of our commercial members, I hope with fear.'[99] Even of an old and close friend of the League days, Moffatt, he noted: '. . . he is a follower of Palmerston, for whose Saturday invitations his very soul hungers.'[100] By such standards, the number of true believers became very small indeed. Bright did go so far as to make two further attempts to act with the organized middle class, in the first place in the fundamentally middle-class agitation of 1858–60: in the second place, by acting with the rising Chambers of Commerce in support of Cobden and Gladstone. The Reform agitation took no hold: the Chambers of Commerce turned out to be as unsound as everyone else, the Manchester Chamber, for instance, refusing to assist Cobden with experts to negotiate the details of the cotton duties. By the beginning of the American War, Bright was left with only the working-class movement to turn to. Bright continued to leave the door open for the middle class, never venturing to attack it outright in public. He admitted 'The rich are personally kind enough, but they do not care for the people in the bulk.'[101] But he was never sanguine that they would really amend, and urged only that they should fall in behind the leadership of the working class, emphasizing the uniting 'of all those persons who compose the vast population of the country below the great privileged and titled classes of society' and wishing there were no such terms as middle and working class.[102] Loss of faith in the distinct mission of the middle class led him, not to a Chartist isolation of the working class, but to the old opposition between People and Privilege. It was logical for Bright to believe, given his *idée fixe* about taxation, that the interests of both classes were the same:

[98] B.M. Add. mss. 43,384, f. 264, 6 September 1861: to Cobden.
[99] Ibid., 21 January 1857: to Cobden.
[100] Bright to Cobden, 14 October 1863: B.M. Add. mss. 43,384, f. 313.
[101] *Speeches*, ed. Rogers (1869), 383: speech at Glasgow, 16 October 1866.
[102] Ibid., 311: speech at Glasgow, 21 December 1858.

> If the middle class prefer an alliance with the aristocratic or ruling party, to the cordial co-operation and help of the great nation now excluded from the franchise . . . they must be content with a profligate expenditure, and a taxation burdensome from its amount, and insulting from its inequality and injustice.

In the towns, then, Bright conspicuously failed to give Reform that social meaning which would have justified the effort and hopes expended upon it. In the counties, he was less entirely at sea. The objects of reform were, for him, Justice, Self-Respect, Retrenchment—and a reform of rural society. But again, while his perception of the problem was remarkable, his proposed remedy was quite inadequate, and bounded by his *idées fixes*. The problem had two parts. One related to the unequal ownership of the land:

> Are you aware . . . half the land in Scotland is in the possession of 10 or 12 men? Are you aware . . . that the monopoly is growing constantly more and more close? And the result of it is this—the gradual extirpation of the middle class as owners of land, and the constant degradation of the tillers of the soil.[103]

Bright's statistics were badly wrong, but the account of the general tendencies of landownership was confirmed by later statistics: and later in the century a certain amount of evidence for land hunger in the villages came to light.[104] The comparison with France was striking: 'The division of the land is the grand source of the property and wealth of France . . . probably no other country has made such strides in increasing wealth and comfort as France has since 1790.'[105] Bright, it will be seen, had little faith in the progress of industry as a remedy for human ills: he was not the blind worshipper of the Industrial Revolution that Arnold made him out to be.

[103] *Speeches*, ed. Rogers (1869), 381: speech at Glasgow, 18 October 1866.

[104] In 1871 half of the land of England was owned by 7,400 persons (Bateman: *Great Landowners*): Bright had claimed that 'less than 150 men' owned half of England.

[105] In a letter written by Bright to George Wilson, 24 September 1853, while Bright was on holiday in Normandy: in the Wilson papers.

The second part related to the abuse of power by squire and parson. Bright here saw clearly the central issues which were to keep Liberalism alive in the counties. There was a genuine issue of human bondage, much wider than the question of the game laws: it involved justices' justice, the rule of property and the resentment at living under the will of a local tyrant. Thomas Hardy, writing with extreme scrupulousness, said the labourer's greatest hardship was not plain poverty or the workhouse in old age, but the anxiety arising from 'not being his own man'.[106] Bright did not touch financial boards and county councils, but he did start to question the local basis of gentry rule when he raised the game laws and the land laws in Parliamentary questions: 'They do not care a rap for the Irish Church here: Game Laws and financial boards interest them much more . . .'[107] The existing constitution was quite inadequate, even for the task of holding the balance between landlord, tenant, and labourer: for Palmerston's Parliament passed Baldwin Leighton's game act, converting the rural constable into a game warden, and the Trespass (Ireland) Bill of 1864, increasing the landlord's power of preserving game in Ireland. On such a question it was reasonable to claim that real change could only come through a large measure of Reform.

But Bright also tied himself to a narrow and crotchety panacea: to allow the operation of economic law to produce a yeomanry:

> I think we are bound, as free men—and we townsmen are especially bound, for we only have the power to take the initiative in this great question . . . (and I have no doubt it will be one of the first consequences of a real Reform Bill), to apply those great principles of political economy, which are the gospel and charter of industry, as fully to property in land as we have already applied them to property engaged in trade.[108]

[106] Thomas Hardy: 'The Dorsetshire Labourer', in *Longman's Magazine*, July 1883, 252–69.

[107] *Amberley Papers*, II, 125: Kate Amberley on the Devon election, 16 October 1868.

[108] *Speeches*, ed. Rogers (1869), 315: speech at Glasgow, 21 December 1858.

Now certainly the laws of entail and primogeniture were unnecessarily restrictive: certainly nothing but a great measure of Reform could create a Parliament willing to alter them: but even if the policy of 'Free Land' were carried to the uttermost, there was not the slightest guarantee that economic law would restore to England a yeomanry; for although the reforms Bright wanted would tend only in the desired direction, they could only have a slight effect at best, and that in the long run. What Bright may claim merit for, is that he was one of the earliest leaders to educate the public mind in the importance of the land system and the land laws and their operation on everyday life, and to inculcate a sense that these laws were affected by the political structure of the country and might, with advantage, be changed.[109] India, Ireland, France, and Prussia all enlarged the field of comparison: historians, economists, philosophers, and anthropologists gave colour and shade to the picture, but Bright, more than anyone, brought the social structure of rural society before the public mind as a proposed subject of political action. Whatever his fallacies, his presentation of the problem alone was a great contribution to the mental enlargement of Victorian England.

Bright engaged in the practical business of altering English life in one respect only, by having a personal stake in the penny press. As in the Reform agitation, the principle was an appeal from the folly of the rich to the sober good sense of the poor, with the added motive of getting round the impasse in education. In this spirit, Cobden had written:

> The difficulties in the way of setting up any system of education in this country seem to be so great, that I am inclined to think the best thing we can do is to pull down all impediments to the diffusion of knowledge . . .[110]

Bright played a leading part in repealing the duties in 1854 and 1860–1, especially in the latter year when his forbearance over Reform was needed to drive the Budget through, in the

---

[109] In 1875 he presented a petition for reform from the Agricultural Labourers' Union, signed by 60,000 labourers: *Hansard*, vol. 225, col. 1061, 7 July 1875.

[110] B.M. Add. mss. 43,655, f. 13, to Hargreaves, 3 April 1852.

face of the strongest lobbying from *The Times* and the paper-makers, of whom he said: 'No man could get in or out of the House without having them upon him . . .'[111]

It was quite impossible not to view the question in a partisan and interested spirit. Urging repeal from a peace point of view, Bright told Aberdeen that removal of the stamp was the only way to improve the character of the press.[112] To Russell he said 'it would gain the Government the general support of the Press for their financial scheme'.[113] Above all, it would overthrow the ascendancy of *The Times*, Bright's great adversary since the Crimean War.[114]

Bright had a personal stake in the penny press through the *Star*. In 1856 Cobden wrote: 'Neither Bright nor I can afford to lose £1,000 . . .'[115] Whether or not Bright remained a shareholder, he retained an interest in its affairs: in 1859 he wrote: 'Personally, as you know, I want the paper duty off most of all . . .'[116] and in 1860: 'The *Star* wants the paper duty off to do well—it costs it now more than £120 a week.'[117]

In fact the *Star* had little influence compared to that gained by the reports of Bright's speeches generally, or to that provided locally by the *Manchester Examiner*, the largest daily paper in the north west. Bright was highly conscious of the new possibilities of the press as a political weapon: 'It is a pity the meeting is on a Friday—for the report is wholly lost for all the London and country weekly papers.'[118] At Bright's meetings, from 1858 onwards, there were generally forty to fifty reporters present and, with the penny daily press, it had become possible to address a national audience without using Parliament. Bright created the opportunity given by the cheap press and demonstrated the right way to use it. Again, Gladstone reaped where Bright had sown.

[111] *Hansard*, vol. 160, col. 1116, 10 August 1860.
[112] *Diaries*, ed. Walling (1935), 165: 22 March 1854.
[113] Ibid., 247: 1 February 1860.
[114] Before the war *The Times* was not unsympathetic to the Manchester School.
[115] Wilson mss. 21 June 1856: Cobden to Wilson.
[116] B.M. Add. mss. 43,384, f. 158, 6 October 1859, to Cobden.
[117] B.M. Add. mss. 43,384, f. 182, 5 February 1860, to Cobden.
[118] Bright to Wilson, Wilson mss. 20 November 1858.

Bright was conscious that the penny press amounted to a new enfranchisement, an extension of the political nation.

There are newspapers published at a price which was once deemed impossible, and these find their way into the agricultural villages. And the labourers will begin to open their eyes, and to see that a change of their position is not so impossible as they once thought.[119]

Though Bright never went into the villages to preach Reform, and never advocated agricultural trades unionism, his influence on a Warwickshire villager might still be significant, as Joseph Arch pointed out: 'As a lad, every time I earned a penny by doing odd jobs or running an errand, I would buy some old papers . . . I would read Gladstone's and Bright's speeches and from them I formed my opinions.'[120] The revolution effected in the 1850's in the cheap press, though hardly an achievement personal to Bright, provides a striking example of a small and interested group engineering, with little fuss or outside awareness of what was involved, a complete change in the real working constitution of the country, entirely altering the balance between Parliament and electorate.

In Ireland, Bright was again at his work of proposing agrarian and political remedies to urban audiences. There was nothing in his speeches to interest the Irish towns as such: nothing on the issue of national as against religious education, nothing on Irish railways, taxation, universities, or on the Galway packet station. He confined himself to those aspects of the Irish question congenial to a Dissenting Radical, Disestablishment and the land question. His views on Disestablishment, defined in 1852 and held until 1869, were peculiar to himself, had no influence on the course of events, and were chiefly interesting as indicating his loose ties with Dissent. The first time Bright spoke to any purpose on Ireland after his return to Parliament was in 1864, when he clearly identified himself with the popular cause in Ireland, but without going beyond advocating equalization of the poor

[119] Speech at Birmingham, 26 January 1864: *Speeches,* ed. Rogers (1869), 457.
[120] Joseph Arch: *The Story of His Life, by Himself* (1898).

laws as a remedy.[121] At the end of that year he was writing to the Lord Mayor of Dublin:

> If the popular party in Ireland would adopt as its policy Free Land and Free Church and would [join the English Liberals], and especially for the promotion of an honest amendment of the representation, I am confident that great and beneficial changes might be made in a few years.[122]

He had no hesitation in giving detailed instruction on Irish land to Irishmen for, as he told the Dublin Trades, no man in England had more fully studied the evidence given before the Devon Commission.[123]

The Liberals gained seven Irish seats in 1865 and eleven more in 1868, amounting to a gain between 1859 and 1868 of thirty-six votes on a division. The quality of the loyalty too was better: Bright said the Irish members in 1869 were more honourable, more patriotic, and more intelligent than ever before,[124] and this was clearly from a party point of view. The 1868 elections returned a body of popular candidates 'possibly more clearly pledged to the English Liberal leadership than at any time since the famine'.[125]

Bright, Gladstone, and Mill played a part in this realignment. But it was Bright who, in 1864, was first in the field, who crossed to Ireland and spoke there three times: who was in touch with popular feelings as represented by the tenants' paper, the *Freeman's Journal*, of Dublin, and who pressed Gladstone on while holding Mill back. Bright condemned Mill's scheme of 1867–8 as 'vast and extraordinary'[126] as Mill, in his *Autobiography*, declared he wanted him to do: while a constant pressure from Bright, leading as usual forces he had little in common with, was necessary to get Gladstone to move at all. A broad hint from Bright in a speech at Birmingham in 1868 was evidently intended to stir Gladstone into action over the Irish Church.

[121] *Hansard*, vol. 173, col. 1880, 11 March 1864.
[122] Leech, *Letters* (1895), 112: 22 December 1864.
[123] *Speeches*, ed. Rogers (1869), 199: 2 November 1866.
[124] *Hansard*, vol. 198, col. 89, 16 July 1869.
[125] D. Thornley, 'Irish conservatives and Home Rule 1869–1873', *Irish Historical Studies*, 1958–9, 202.
[126] *Speeches*, ed. Rogers (1869), 203: speech of 14 March 1868.

On Ireland, Bright proposed measures, disingenuous and inadequate if operated within the Voluntaryist framework within which he conceived them, but which if made coercive, would have represented a working solution. Bright's object was to 'restore a middle class proprietary of the soil . . .'[127] for he held, like Parnell, that the 'poor man, in the ordinary meaning of the term, cannot be the possessor of land . . .'[128] His aim was certainly not to shelter the weak from the struggle of life.

The methods he looked to were security for tenants' improvements: abolition of primogeniture and entail, and other legal restrictions; and the sale of land by willing sellers, from among the absentee landlord class, to willing buyers, aided by the *deus ex machina* of cheap State credit at three and a quarter per cent, all to be repaid. Such proposals resulted, so far as land purchase went, in the Bright clauses of the Irish Church and Land Acts, which were not without value, but indicate clearly the unresolved contradiction in Bright between a desire for results only attainable by coercive social engineering and an intellectual background which forbade interference or compulsion.

This completes the survey of Bright's contribution to the policy of the Liberal Party. Foreign and imperial affairs did not concern him much in the period between 1855 and 1875: between 1858 and 1860, he spoke a great deal on India, but subsequently only infrequently, and without any of the force with which he spoke on Irish affairs. His polemics on American and Canadian questions were essentially occasional speeches, as were his running fights with most of the House of Commons during the war scare of 1859 to 1861. None of these matters had the same importance for the Liberal Party as Bright's avoidance of any clash between Dives and Lazarus in the great towns, and his concentration of setting the people at the throats of Privilege in the counties and in Ireland. These tactics, deeply ingrained in Bright's outlook rather than consciously adopted, explained much of the paradox that Gladstonian Liberalism remained a party of property and position while moving rapidly to the left: while Bright's

[127] Ibid., 189: speech of 30 October 1866 at Dublin.
[128] Ibid., 203: speech on 14 March 1868 on Maguire's motion.

attempt to wear the mantle of Burke in regard to America, Ireland, and India, though mainly a matter of intention, added cubits to the moral stature and propriety of the Liberal Party in retrospect and did a great deal to create the illusion of the Liberal Party as a charitable organization for the weak and helpless everywhere.

*   *   *

Bright joined forces with the working-class movement, perhaps as an exile from middle-class politics, but not as a penitent for former bourgeois failings. In the year when he covered the gap between the two worlds, he wrote of finding his 'bitterest assailants by crowds in the very class on the public Exchanges of the United Kingdom, for whose benefit we have given twenty years of our lives'[129] and he could entertain no hope about the Chambers of Commerce. Yet he could not change his stripes for this contumely. He never said a good word for trades unions or for Factory Acts. In 1861 his firm prosecuted four of its workpeople for picketing.[130] In 1860 he wrote to another employer that while he had never denied the right to combine, he believed that there was not one case in a hundred where it was wise to do so: and he looked to Reform to end trades unionism, by breaking down the wall between classes and teaching labour to strike, not at its friend Capital, but at its enemy, Privilege.

' They will contend for themselves, by themselves, if condemned to remain a separate and suspected order in our social system . . .'[131] Bright, certainly, was no flatterer.[132] Nor could he very well be, as even at his most revolutionary, most of his speeches were delivered to audiences mostly well-to-do, or else at least collected under the auspices of the well-to-do. In the great demonstrations of his autumn tour in 1866,

[129] B.M. Add. mss. 43,384, f. 272, 24 October 1861, to Cobden.

[130] *Manchester Examiner*, 23 November 1861 and 10 January 1862. Ernest Jones defended the men.

[131] Leech, *Letters* (1895), 246: 3 November 1860.

[132] Bright's link with the working class was through trade unionism alone. The equally numerous Co-operative Movement he left alone, though he gave Parliamentary assistance and neighbourly counsel to the Rochdale Pioneers (see Holyoake, *Sixty Years*, II, 595) and praised them in a Reform debate (23 April 1866).

after the scores of thousands had attended the great open air meeting in the daytime, there was a meeting most important, most influential, omnipotent indeed within that town in which it was held. In the town of Leeds, I was told, nearly 1,000 persons paid 5/- each to attend the Town Hall meeting, and I think that is some sign of the class of persons who attended.[133]

Bright was far more under the necessity of applying soft soap to those who were 'omnipotent indeed', than of having to eat fire before the mob. Only three times did he speak under distinctly working-class auspices: to the Leeds Working Men's Parliamentary Associations (11 December 1860) and twice to the London Trades in the St James's Hall (26 March 1863 and 4 December 1866). He did not speak at the open air meetings in the daytime nor, to my knowledge, did he speak in the open air at all. It was therefore not surprising that he should have neglected aspects of Reform which would have strikingly increased working-class influence. In 1859 Cobden made the suggestion of single-member constituencies, on the express ground that this would allow working-class quarters to elect members of their own colours.[134] This proposal, which had such radical results after 1884, Bright quite ignored, though it was probably the quickest way to advance working-class representation. Secondly, Bright never encouraged the entry of working men into Parliament, at least in his campaign speeches: in 1858 he thought some men without property might enter the House on a salary from their constituents. 'He should be very glad to see such a case.'[135] But clearly he expected no change of consequence in the pattern of rule by men of property, beyond a new pressure being put on the men of property to be earnest radicals.

It is sometimes made to appear as if Bright's demands for reform succeeded beyond his wildest dreams. In the case of

[133] *Speeches,* ed. Rogers (1869), 386: Manchester, 20 November 1866.

[134] Quoted by Sir J. Pakington, *Hansard,* vol. 157, col. 1043, 22 March 1860: and not repudiated.

[135] *Hansard,* vol. 149, col. 1033, 13 April 1858. In later life he was not in favour of payment of members, nor of 'what is called a Labour Party'—Leech, *Letters* (1895), 234: letter of 23 September 1887.

the 'residuum' of unintelligent artisans who were enfranchised, this was partly, but only partly, true. But in general, what is most striking is the surrender by Bright of point after point, up to the very moment when popular agitation caught fire in autumn 1866. When attempting to enforce his own programme on parallel lines to the agitation of the League, he failed, and completely acknowledged his failure. This self-knowledge was important in making him a good and loyal party man, giving up most of what he had demanded as essential. On the defeat of the Liberal Bill in 1866, Bright, far from being master of the situation, was completely at a loss, and far from sanguine of any further progress. The next few months showed how complete was the contrast between what Bright could do by himself, and what he did when borne on a wave of feeling he had not even expected.

The changing nature of Bright's demands must be outlined. First there was the shifting relationship between the franchise and redistribution. Bright saw and taught that redistribution mattered far more than the franchise: that under the arrangements of 1832, the middle class were 'almost altogether defrauded'[136] and that a grant of the franchise to the working class, with no corresponding measure of redistribution, might well be equally fraudulent. Between 1858 and 1861 he expended a great part of his energies on expounding that redistribution was the 'very pith and marrow'[137] of Reform, a point not easily obvious to popular audiences, who were exhorted never to 'take your eye for one moment' from this great subject of dispute.[138] The transfer of members was to be from the small boroughs to the large. Any Reform Bill, he said, worth a moment's thought, ought to more than double the representation of the metropolis and of the great cities.[139] And the draft Bill that Bright prepared at this time was remarkable among Reform Bills for the extent of its redistribution measure.[140] Also, at this period he gave the ballot

[136] *Speeches*, ed. Rogers (1869): speech of 21 December 1858 at Glasgow.

[137] *Hansard*, vol. 157, col. 896, 19 March 1860.

[138] *Speeches*, ed. Rogers (1869), 287: Birmingham, 27 October 1858.

[139] Robertson, *Life of Bright* (1912), 207: 2 February 1858.

[140] This Bill, 'ready to be introduced any night' (Robertson, op. cit., 227, 7 December 1859) was never brought forward.

much greater prominence than he ever gave it later: in short
he wanted everything at once, and he was far too sanguine.
By 1860 he was advising Russell to separate franchise from
redistribution, and to give franchise priority. As early as 1857
he had in fact recognized this was necessary: 'A good Bill
cannot be carried giving suffrage and redistributing seats
except by a revolutionary movement as in 1832, and this is
not very likely, nor is it very desirable . . .'[141] He went on to
declare his preference for concentrating on the franchise, and
leaving to Parliament elected on the wider suffrage to secure,
at a later date, a good measure of redistribution. This was the
course he adhered to from 1864, and stated openly as his
policy in the debates of 1866. In 1868 his election address did
in fact attempt to set the second stage of the process in motion.
'The small Boroughs are still to be got rid of, and the large
populations will still demand their fair share of political
power.'[142] But to drop redistribution so completely as Bright
did in his second agitation, to abandon the general grievance
of fraudulent representation in favour of the class issue of
the borough franchise, was to become very much less radical.
If Bright had focused the popular feeling on redistribution
in 1866, as he tried to do in 1858–60, the second Reform
movement would have had a far more revolutionary poten-
tiality. There must be at least a suspicion that a part of
Bright's mind, which had grasped so clearly the essence of
the situation, was at work to neutralize the passions he engen-
dered, by removing the intellectual substance from the question.

On the question of the suffrage, there were no such am-
biguities in Bright's course. He was a consistent advocate of
'parish' suffrage, or measures approximating to it such as
household suffrage or £5 or £6 rental suffrage, and upheld
this level consistently as the true principle, while remaining
very willing to compromise on other figures with those elements in the Liberal Party whom he trusted. His principles
did not change, but in his application he became more and
more a party man, because the ministry, 'founded and acted

[141] Bright to Cobden, 16 April 1857, B.M. Add. mss. 43,384, f. 94.
[142] J. A. Langford, *Modern Birmingham and Its Institutions* (1877),
II, 369.

upon the principles of trust and confidence in the people',[143] became increasingly sympathetic. In 1859 he told Russell he would not go across the street for a £6 rating suffrage: Russell said he should adhere to the £6 rental,[144] and Bright gave mild support, though pointing out that only 100,000 working men would gain the vote by the Bill of 1860. In 1866 he claimed that he never was in favour of a £6 franchise, and would never have proposed it: but, *faute de mieux*, he found himself supporting a £7 borough franchise, a proposal for which he had never said 'one syllable'.[145] In the interval between the defeat of the Liberal Bill and the introduction of the Tory Bill, he insisted that the next Liberal bill would have to be household suffrage, and he believed the Liberal leaders were converted to this.[146] From this it is clear that while holding to his principle, he had given up any real hope of obtaining it at least till the autumn of 1866: the following passage, in support of the £7 borough franchise, was a remarkable instance of his recognition of failure in the face of the Palmerstonian world: 'I think that a Franchise Bill which does not adjust this question for at least as long as the Bill of 1832 settled the question of Reform, is a Franchise Bill which it is not desirable to consent to'.[147] If this means anything, it meant that he accepted the 'useless' £7 franchise as final till 1899. (He made a feint in the direction of reducing the county franchise from £14 to £10, but the county franchise was throughout of quite secondary importance.)

Bright's position in regard to upward revisions of the franchise he wanted was then quite honest, if extremely fatalistic. In regard to manhood suffrage he was on thinner ice. He said, he had to say, that he was not against it: he could not condemn it. He was not afraid of 'the principles of the Reform

[143] *Speeches*, ed. Rogers (1869), 375: at Birmingham, 27 August 1866, on the outgoing Liberal ministry.

[144] *Diaries*, ed. Walling (1935), 237: 3 June 1859.

[145] *Speeches*, ed. Rogers (1869), 346: 13 March 1866, House of Commons.

[146] Ibid., 390: speech at Manchester, 20 November 1866.

[147] Ibid., speech on the second reading of the Reform Bill, 23 April 1866.

League'.[148] He had 'not the smallest objection to the widest possible suffrage that the ingenuity of man can devise'.[149] Yet in his own mind all this was quite consistent with the statement: 'I have never uttered a word in favour of universal suffrage either in this House or elsewhere.'[150] What did all this mean? Certainly, taking his speeches as a whole, nobody could be in any doubt that he wanted the ancient household or municipal suffrage: there was no serious deception. But there was no doubt that he tried to have the best of both worlds, the respectable one and that of popular radicalism, and on the whole it was the democrats whom he deceived, by keeping back his idea of the 'residuum'. One phrase slipped out that admitted his reserve about democracy: he said 'the £5 franchise would probably admit nearly all of them that can be admitted'.[151] It will be remembered that in his treatment of the Irish land question, Bright held the same almost penal view of the residuum.

It is now time to turn to the actual course of Bright's various agitations, and his movement from 'Morley's lot' to 'Howell's lot'. Bright, from the beginning of his return to public life, concentrated upon Reform. He would never again advise an agitation for any other purpose. Above all, he was not to become, what Nature seemed to intend, a great political Dissenter—not with the scales of the constitution tipped against him as they were. 'It is but rolling a stone up to see it roll down again, and our experience since 1846 should be sufficient for us—it certainly is for me.'[152] The wave of Reform that first swept him up came from the Liberationist and Radical gains at the 1857 elections, which led to a middle-class agitation backed by Miall, Morley, and Roebuck, for household suffrage, with George Wilson conducting a League-type agitation locally around Manchester. Bright's fiery speeches terrified other reformers, the Dissenters could

---

[148] Ibid., 377: speech at Birmingham, 27 August 1866.
[149] Ibid., 284: speech at Birmingham, 27 October 1858.
[150] *Hansard*, vol. 158, col. 2020, 4 June 1860.
[151] *Speeches*, ed. Rogers (1869), 298: speech at Manchester, 10 December 1858.
[152] Bright to Cobden, 6 October 1859, B.M. Add. mss. 43,384, f. 158.

not hold on to their gains made in 1857, and it became clear
that the franchise could not be to the already enfranchised
what bread had been to the starving in the days of the
League. The whole conception was wrong, and Bright was
quick to spot this, and by 1860, he was seeking to put the
Reform movement on a working-class, and probably a trades
union, basis. But having arrived at this point, Bright failed to
make the unions meet him there. In these early years, Bright
was moving in two opposite directions: at a Parliamentary
level, through his various negotiations with Russell and
Baines, he brought himself to accept measures very seriously
compromising his proposals, dropping his own Bill and in
fact, eating his own words in order to bring about 'that Union
of moderate Reformers which seems above all things to be
necessary in prospect of next session . . . on Mr. Bright's proposal they cannot unite. If Lord John fails, the Tories come
in, and their next Reform bill will be carried.'[153] On the
other hand, out of doors, Bright left behind the old radicalism
of mayors, banquets, soirées, and conferences in coffee-houses,
which had proved once again a thing of words. The city
fathers wrote criticizing Bright's Bill,[154] the lesser fry were
very doubtful. After a thorough canvass of the Leeds electors
in 1865, Frederick Baines wrote to his brother: 'It is a fact
that very few indeed of the liberal voters favour an extension
of the suffrage: the great body promise for our candidates in
spite of their convictions on this point.'[155] Bright in 1861 had
not so much started an irresistible movement, as achieved a
shattering failure by attempting to move on the lines of the
League. The ministry, in breach of most explicit pledges
given in 1859, which Gladstone wished to honour, was able
to drop Reform with equanimity, to Bright's great anger.
Bright had started by telling Cobden: 'You and I could do
much in a couple of years, and crown the former labour by
one still greater almost.'[156] Cobden told him he was wrong,

[153] Edward Baines to George Wilson, 7 November 1859: Wilson mss.

[154] e.g. in Baines' letter of 1859 cited above and in a letter from
William Brown, the Liberal millionaire who was M.P. for South Lancashire, an old Leaguer, disowning the Bill, in Wilson mss., 7 February
1859.

[155] To Edward Baines, 7 April 1865: Baines mss., 'F. Baines' bundle.

[156] Bright to Cobden, 21 August 1859, B.M. Add. mss. 43,384, f. 154.

obstructed the Reform issue by placing the French treaty in greater prominence, and left matters alone: though Cobden was a strong reformer. And Cobden's sense of the situation was right. Bright therefore changed from promoting an extreme policy of his own backed by the old hierarchies of the great towns, to massing behind a moderate policy not his own, the newly born working-class institutions. That defines, almost, the change from Radicalism to Liberalism in the great towns.

In 1860 he wrote to his wife that argument never wrested anything from the monopolists of power, political and ecclesiastical, and 'something more is wanted to bring about change in this country'.[157] At the end of the year, the 'something more' emerged, in the shape of the Leeds Working Men's Parliamentary Association, at whose meeting he spoke for the first time under truly working-class auspices;[158] 'specially called for them and by them', Bright writes. This resulted from a correspondence many months old: Bright referred to it as a capital meeting, but for Bright it remained an episode, and he did not encourage repetitions. Thereafter he refused all the invitations he received, 'for I cannot undertake the weight of an agitation which does not seem able to sustain itself'.[159] From the time of the Leeds meeting at the end of 1860, he did not speak seriously on Reform again till the beginning of 1865.[160] There was no one like Bright for retiring to his tent to sulk: Cobden had to try to persuade him to be more active. At the time of Baines's motion in 1864, Cobden wrote: 'I have been trying to persuade Bright to speak. He ought not to be silent when the question is brought forward. Indeed, I think his silence for the last three years on the subject has been a mistake.'[161] Bright had many reasons for this long retirement: probably business cares,[162] possibly health, above all the American war and the certainty of Palmerston's early departure. He wrote to his wife that till

---

[157] Letter to Mrs Bright, 28 April 1860: University College mss.
[158] In Leeds Town Hall, 11 December 1860. Baines also took part.
[159] Bright to Wilson, 7 January 1861: Wilson Papers.
[160] Speech at Birmingham on Reform, 18 January 1865.
[161] Cobden to T. B. Potter, 10 May 1864: Cobden Papers, Chichester.
[162] He plunged into a Welsh gold mine at this period.

America was disposed of, he could not care deeply about English or European affairs.[163] About the same time he thought Reform would 'rise again and march to success' when the North won in America and Palmerston went.[164] He was, in short, indolently optimistic. In 1865, with Cobden's death, he still did not feel he 'could do anything in the political field'[165] and he only spoke twice that year out of Parliament. Altogether his public appearances between 1860 and 1865 could have hardly affected the state of the Reform question when the Liberals took it up again in earnest in 1866.

Bright, from the time of the Leeds meeting in 1860, was an advocate of the working-class solution, and willing to work with that class. But, as he stated in retrospect, the unions took no part in Reform 'until they were challenged to it by the acts of a great party in the Parliament of the kingdom',[166] that is until the autumn of 1866. That they were so tardy was not Bright's fault. In 1861 he published a letter to the Glasgow Trades Council, congratulating them on their political activity, and hoping the trades unions would everywhere unite for reform. 'I know how opinion has grown, and that only accident and combination are wanting to make it [unionism] an omnipotent force on this question.'[167] W. E. Forster deplored Bright's suggestions:[168] Ashworth wrote to Cobden that Bright's most ardent admirers were shaken by his 'coquetting with Trades Societies'.[169] Cobden replied that it was a mistake: 'He could not have meant to invite Potter & Co., the trade unionists, to agitate for the suffrage. He must have alluded to other clubs of working men.'[170] That Bright could shock his closest associates so much, while failing to

---

[163] To Mrs Bright, 22 June 1863: University College mss.

[164] Wilson mss., 28 December 1863: Bright to Wilson.

[165] Wilson mss., Bright to Wilson: 14 May 1865.

[166] Speech to London Trades, 4 December 1866: *Speeches*, ed. Rogers (1869), 394.

[167] *Manchester Examiner*, 19 November 1861: Bright's workpeople were sentenced the same month for picketing.

[168] Ibid., 20 November 1861.

[169] B.M. Add. mss. 43,654, f. 128, Ashworth to Cobden, 12 December 1861. Ashworth was a Bolton cotton master of the best type.

[170] B.M. Add. mss. 43,654, f. 132, 13 December 1861: Cobden to Ashworth.

gain working-class support, showed the originality and difficulty of his situation. He had to admit that his initiative at
the end of 1861, like that at Leeds in 1860, was no use: 'The
working men have no leaders of their own class, and they have
little faith in any others. I wait therefore for some accident to
bring about a change . . .'[171] Cobden agreed with him in a
typically sound diagnosis:

> Until the non-electoral class can have a bona fide organisa-
> tion in every large town, composed of their own class, and
> self sustained, it is a pure waste of life and strength for
> a man of Bright's genius to advance their cause in that
> packed assembly the House of Commons . . .[172]

Even the meeting in support of the Northern States, organized by the London Trades in the St James's Hall,[173] had no
immediate effect on Reform, but it brought Odger, secretary
of the Trades Suffrage Society, into correspondence with
Bright,[174] and by 1865 Howell was also concerting measures
with Bright. The London working men in particular were
impressed:

> The men in the Bee Hive were talking about a public
> meeting to express their sympathy (*sc.* for Cobden in his
> controversy with Delane) but they are disposed to reserve
> the occasion till Mr. Bright and Mr. Cobden are ready to
> open a campaign on the suffrage. I believe the leading
> Radicals among the London working men are ready to
> adopt their lead in a way they never were before. This is
> chiefly due to common sympathy with the North in
> America.[175]

These new co-operators were from the sector of the political
working class which had most keenly cherished the old
Chartist distrust of Bright. The way the conflict ran on under-
ground in the 1850's and 1860's, and the memories that had

[171] To Cobden: 6 August 1862, B.M. Add. mss. 43,384, f. 296.
[172] To Hargreaves: Add. mss. 43,655, f. 317, 5 April 1863.
[173] On 26 March 1863. Bright was chairman.
[174] Marx, *Selected Works*, ed. Adoratsky (1933), II, 603. Marx to
Engels, 4 November 1864.
[175] Frederic Harrison to Cobden, 26 February 1864. Cobden mss.,
Chichester.

to be overcome, come out well in such a Chartist reminiscence as this:

> I think there is one very important incident that ought to be recorded. It is this. During the agitation for the Six Pound Franchise, a meeting was called in Birmingham in support of the measure. John Bright, and the Financial Reform Leaders were the speakers in support of it. The Chartists of Birmingham invited your father to come to move an amendment in favour of manhood suffrage. A lot of roughs were hired for the occasion, and when your father got up to move the amendment, a rush was made for the Platform, your father was scared, his coat and waistcoat torn from his back, and was thrown down the steps from the platform amid the yells of the Middle Class supporters, without a single protest from John Bright and the speakers on the platform, thus showing the true from the sham Reformers. I think it would be in 1853 or 5.[176]

However, the trade union *élite* in London were as incapable as Bright of securing mass interest. What really rallied the feeling of the town populations behind Bright and the trade union leaders was the excitement caused by the trampling down of the Hyde Park railings by the mob. This incident, the Sarajevo of Reform, took place on 23 July 1866, and led to the rapid and unforeseen creation of a popular front.

A month later, Bright was on tour, denouncing the police action as Lord Derby's 'declaration of war on the working classes',[177] and the Reform League began expanding incredibly quickly.[178] Yet, in the two months preceding the

[176] From a letter of 5 January 1892, written by a Mr Thomas Garbutt of Attercliffe to the son of Ernest Jones, which is in the Instituut voor Soziale Geschiedenis, Amsterdam.

[177] At Birmingham, 27 August 1866: *Speeches*, Rogers (1869), 375.

[178] At Northampton, the local branch was founded on 16 July 1866, and grew as follows:

16 July 1866	31 members
31 August 1866	124 "
31 September 1866	151 "
31 October 1866	555 "
23 February 1867	639 "

From the *First Report of the Northampton Branch*, in Northampton Public Library.

incident, Bright had had little confidence in the Reform League, the working class, or himself, and a remarkable scepticism about political action. For him, the crisis simply fell from heaven: when the Liberals resigned in June 1866 he had had no plan:

> The working men want more organisation and more life, but whether through their trades unions or not, I cannot tell. The Tories care little for the middle class call for Reform—It is only numbers and the fear of force that can influence them. . . . We seem to have no definite plan of action, and I am not able to suggest one—and I feel too old to go 'on the stump' again for any public question. . . .[179]

Unfortunately, his diaries from June 1865 to February 1867 are missing: but a letter shortly before the Hyde Park riot showed how much Bright was a handmaid of Fate:

> I do not know what can be done that is important. I cannot see my way to any formidable organisation, or movement . . . To call Conferences merely to have a few speeches and nothing more, is to make conferences useless . . . What are we to do and say, that others may do? Meetings? well we have had meetings and the result is not considerable. Petitions?—yes I think a great movement for petitions in the winter might be very proper and useful—but what else? Elections? But we have no great friend as we had 20 years ago,[180] to go into anything costly . . . I am puzzled, just now.—I do not wish to come to a meeting which cannot lead to anything substantial . . . You will think this letter unsatisfactory, and so it is, but I write exactly what I feel.[181]

On the eve of his greatest triumph, the great agitator had to confess himself politically bankrupt and at his wits' end and his problems were solved for him by changes in very deep and obscure parts of society. Bright was the constitutional monarch of this movement: he warned, exhorted, and advised, looked with equal favour on Reform League and Reform Union, appeared on the platforms of both with a

[179] Bright to Wilson, 27 June 1866: Wilson mss.
[180] The great Sir Thomas Potter?
[181] Bright to Wilson, 10 July 1866: Wilson mss.

message of unity and organization—there should be a Reform
society in every factory, a conclusion that had escaped him in
the preceding decade. He pressed the Irish to form societies in
their towns, and did a good deal of liaison work between
sections of reformers as no one else could have done: but
though he reigned, he did not rule.

*   *   *

Bright had most of the Dissenting attitudes, but a habit of
independent reasoning and the secular discipline of the Manchester School cut him off from the orthodox Dissent of his
generation. Quakers, moreover, with no ministry, were traditionally less involved in ecclesiastical squabbles; besides
which, Bright would not easily forget the large section of
Dissenting notables who had supported the Crimean War.
But on the whole, it was character and intellect which separ-
ated him from the Dissenting programme. His opinions—
backed by a great deal of reasoning—'had always been very
adverse to maintaining an armed squadron for the suppression of the slave trade'.[182] The supporters of the permissive
Bill, 'fanatical promoters of well intending but impracticable
measures'[183] did, in his opinion, much harm, and he could
not vote for Lawson's bill.[184] Education, he argued, was the
sheet anchor of temperance reform: but Bright did little
enough for education. On the Sunday question, he sat on the
fence, but freely admitted that the opposing needs of the
working class and the feelings of the middle class, and not
Scripture, were what was involved.[185] Unlike many of his
friends, he was not an officer of the Manchester Peace and
Arbitration Society:[186] and there is some evidence that the
London Peace Society found him hard to get hold of for their
campaigns. Cobden and Bright refused to attend a peace conference in London 'and therefore the project was relinquished'.[187] Again, unlike many Dissenters, he thought his

[182] *Hansard*, vol. 151, col. 41, 18 June 1858.
[183] To Mrs Bright, 10 May 1873: University College mss.
[184] *Speeches*, ed. Rogers (1869), 511 ff.: speech of 8 June 1864.
[185] *Hansard*, vol. 188, col. 105. (1867: speech on Sunday lectures.)
[186] Thomasson, Ashworth and Wilson were. See list in Annual Report,
Wilson mss. 1866, No. 95.
[187] *Peace Society Minute Book*, 10 March 1862.

generation would never be called upon to decide the question of Disestablishment,[188] and he did not want Disestablishment to come about through 'violence, hatred and angry discussion' leading to a bare and naked Church. That is, he had qualms about disendowment. He abandoned the voluntaryism in education that went with Liberationism at least as early as 1854. The *Morning Star*, the paper most closely representing Bright's policy, had great difficulty in finding its bearings on such issues as the Sabbath, State education, and peace, as letters in the Wilson papers show, and their paper in the 1850's represented the honest doubters rather than the militants of Dissent. The above points, however, do indicate the distance between Bright and darkest Dissent.

On one leading issue he maintained views wholly opposed to those of the Liberation Society, which criticized him severely in public (in 1869 he emphatically repudiated any connection with the society). In 1852 he advocated a limited endowment of the Catholic and Presbyterian Churches in Ireland, as an atonement for past errors, the funds to come from the Protestant Church, which was itself to have a small compensation upon Disestablishment,[189] all three Churches to be entirely independent subsequent to the transaction. In more detail, he wished every Roman priest in each of the 1,000 parishes to receive a house and fifteen to thirty acres of land, costing £1,000 per parish. Shortly before the form of disendowment was fixed, he made the same suggestions to the House of Commons, mentioning the great objection the Liberation Society had to it.[190] In 1869 he made it plain that he preferred his own plan to Gladstone's, or to the plan the Dissenters forced on Gladstone: Bright coldly recognized that the Dissenters relied on the *ultima ratio* of brute votes and prejudice. There had been, he said, no more powerful minister than Gladstone, but 'all my right hon. friend's influence and power would break and shiver like broken

[188] *Speeches*, ed. Rogers (1869), 545: speech of 27 April 1860 in the House of Commons.

[189] Letter to Dr John Gray, 25 October 1852: *Speeches*, ed. Rogers (1869), 550 ff.

[190] *Speeches*, ed. Rogers (1869), 211: speech of 14 March 1868 in the House of Commons. Matthew Arnold managed to avoid giving Bright any credit for this scheme.

glass if we were to propose with these funds' to endow Rome.[191] To have proposed to endow Rome, even if not very much, in the face of such prejudice, and as an admission of English guilt, showed in Bright a strain of high and literal Liberalism, as it must lower the estimate of the Liberal Party that had so little interest in the best side of him. Also of great credit to his integrity was his abstention from jockeying himself into place and position by putting himself at the head of militant and organized Dissent, as he could so easily have done as a matter of calculation. The contrast with Chamberlain is striking.

On the other hand, on a fair number of matters he acted as one would expect any back-bench Dissenter from the provinces to act. On such matters as Church Rates and the Deceased Wife's Sister Bill he took a humble part in the general labour. He was on the committee for the prosecution of Governor Eyre, that question which, with the American War, united the Liberal intelligentsia with the Nonconformist conscience to produce the *Fortnightly* school of politics. He felt as a Dissenter: 'I don't like the Church so long as it steals silver spoons . . .'[192] but he could not, like Miall, conjure series upon series of abstract arguments out of these feelings. He voted silently with Miall on Disestablishment in 1871, but the evidence showed more of a personal than an ideological sympathy. In 1850 Miall stayed with Bright in Rochdale, where he was elected in 1852, Jacob Bright being an especially hearty supporter of Miall there, and later John Bright wrote of Miall as a 'capital member, most intelligent and faithful, and no man in the House is more to be relied on than he is'.[193] In 1862 he spoke very warmly at the presentation to Miall of £5,000.[194] In 1868 he spoke in the House of Mr Miall as 'not only a good man, but he is a great man', while indicating disagreement with him.[195]

But he was not a follower of Miall—he was not a follower of anyone. In the Irish Church question, he was a bridge

191 *Hansard*, vol. 197, col. 1931, 15 July 1869.
192 To his daughter Helen, 20 January 1868: Street mss.
193 To Mrs Bright, 15 March 1857: Bright papers, Street, Somerset.
194 *Life of Miall*, 245.
195 *Speeches*, ed. Rogers (1869), 209.

between the Cabinet and Dissent: on the education question, had he been well, he would also, from his independence of both sections, have stood in the position of conciliator and mediator, so far as his position in the controversy can be discerned.[196] Bright's devotion of his splendid oratorical talents and national prestige, solely and single-heartedly to Reform, account considerably for the comparative failure and present oblivion of the great movement of political Dissent.

*　　*　　*

Bright's renown exceeded his achievements and survived his failures and indolence. A great part of it was contributed by his opponents. The well-to-do educated Anglicans who almost monopolized the higher positions in society were well aware that year by year the old landmarks which secured their privileges were being shifted. Yet there was no agreed solution to the problem of where the centre of disturbance in the history of the age lay, and what the dynamism of the process was. It required far more insight to see the demographic and technical roots of change than to see the social and political ones. And with all the answers to the question, what was undermining Palmerstonian England?—that is, with Democracy, Dissent, Capitalism, Commercial Principles, Americanization, the Rule of the Great Towns, Bright, and only Bright, could be identified. Only Bright, of active men in politics, saw the system of Privilege as a whole, which should and could be overthrown, and no one could doubt that this was no form of words. Hence Bright could always depend upon his opponents for his prestige. Every Tory attack would increase his standing outside Parliament, while not diminishing what he could never have, a following inside Parliament. Bright profited extremely from the misunderstandings of those he infuriated; the constant senseless attacks upon him by the stupid, served to draw the attention of the discerning to his many sterling qualities. To those whose good opinion was worth having he was fundamentally safe and compatible. To give one example: the Speaker wrote offering him a rod on

[196] See C. A. Vince, *John Bright* (1898), 154–61. Vince was a Birmingham man well acquainted with the local situation around 1870.

the Helmsdale river.[197] Yet in 1866 he was the 'great terror of the squires—they seem to be seized in a sort of bucolic mania in dealing with me'[198] and he felt the Tories could 'easily excite themselves to serve me as Gordon has been served in Jamaica'.[199] A gentleman connected with a great estate told him: 'You have no idea of the terror which your speeches create amongst landed gentlemen.'[200] Clarendon once felt 'an almost unconquerable desire to give him a good thrashing, which he felt he could do, and would have liked intensely . . .'[201] Mr Kendall, the member for East Cornwall, called him 'the most disloyal, the most mischievous and the most dishonest member'[202] of the century. Thus Bright could neglect Parliament almost entirely in 1862, 1863, 1864, and 1865: he could fail to achieve the connection with the working classes that he aspired to, and yet emerge again in 1866 with little exertion as a national symbol. He personified all the tendencies making for the transience of the established order.

*   *   *

The geography of Bright's relationships may now be sketched. Those with 'popular social forces'—with Birmingham, Lancashire, the Society of Friends and with his family circle all over the country—were, so far as they can be traced, uneventful and without development compared with his impact on individual ornaments of the aristocratic régime. Bright was a solitary figure by his own desire. His letters to his wife showed him, before the Crimean War, mixing in the London Quaker aristocracy, and otherwise being outside social life almost entirely. It would be hard to distinguish anyone who was his friend rather than his colleague, Cobden, of course, apart. Cobden educated Bright, and after his death, Bright never really found intellectual sustenance elsewhere. Cobden made Bright his mouthpiece, and gave him

budgets of facts upon the war, newspaper stamp and other

[197] Bright to his daughter Helen, 2 August 1861: Street mss.
[198] To Mrs Bright, 18 February 1866: University College mss.
[199] To his daughter Helen, 19 February 1866: Street mss.
[200] *Speeches*, ed. Rogers (1869), 455: at Birmingham, 26 January 1864.
[201] *A Vanished Victorian*, by G. Villiers (1938), 297.
[202] *Rochdale Observer*, 5 January 1867.

debates which he has always hurled about him with his usual force. He had a genial aptitude for bringing out in his speeches . . . ideas or facts with which he was prompted.[203]

Bright's reliance on Cobden's researches and his own consciousness of always speaking from an unanswerable brief, led him to remain a completely unorganized element in politics, the last great lone wolf. Nowhere in his life or Cobden's, for instance, can one find any interest taken in the electoral minutiae that Chamberlain noted down in his little black notebooks. What evidence there is, goes to show the shallowness of his roots in provincial politics. Only once did Bright organize a round-robin of provincial Liberalism, as Chamberlain was to do: 'I have written, and caused to be written, letters to many principal towns urging them to give a warm and immediate support to the Budget when it appears . . .'[204] and this attempt was not very successful. What Bright had, was a family connection with the local hierarchies which was extremely useful to him, his brother-in-law Leatham in the West Riding, his brother-in-law Duncan McLaren at Edinburgh, and his own family in Rochdale and Manchester. What he did not have was a finger in local politics.[205] Not a comment escaped him upon the singular process by which Lancashire became Tory. The Manchester election 'that passionate and ungenerous treatment when I was stricken down and was enduring exile'[206] rankled very deeply:

after what occurred in 1857 . . . I should feel it a deep humiliation to assume a friendship for men whom I hold in utter contempt. I can act in Birmingham and in Rochdale, and in other towns to which I may be invited, but I can never obtrude myself on any Manchester meeting of a public or general character.[207]

It was noted that, for whatever reason, he did not take a

[203] Cobden to Parkes, 11 November 1856, B.M. Add. mss. 43,664, f. 58.
[204] Bright to Cobden, 5 February 1860, B.M. Add. mss. 43,384, f. 181.
[205] He made no electioneering speeches on behalf of other candidates.
[206] *Speeches*, ed. Rogers (1869), 278: at Birmingham, 27 October 1858.
[207] B.M. Add. mss. 43,384, f. 271, 24 October 1861.

prominent part in the relief of the Cotton Famine. Ashworth wrote of his absence from meetings called to aid the distress: Cobden asked 'why does he refuse all participation in this life and death movement for the support of the people . . . ?'[208] Bright did, later, lead a Lancashire deputation to the Poor Law Board,[209] and speak on the subject in Parliament: but his friends' questions do suggest how far he was from being a Lancashire leader. A letter written on his brother's election for Manchester in 1867 underlined the estrangement: 'It restores Manchester to the Liberal party, and punishes the fools who disturbed its true position ten years ago.'[210] At no single point was Bright involved in the negotiations which began in 1857, to draw Gladstone to fight South Lancashire: he was ostentatiously excluded· from the arrangements. In Birmingham he always remained a stranger, never re-finding there what he had lost in Lancashire in 1857. He went there under the auspices of the local party managers, who always paid all his expenses,[211] and formed no close personal connections there. His fellow member Scholefield he found 'rather Palmerstonian'.[212] Chamberlain when a very young man opposed him, and even in 1878 was writing to him 'as a stranger'.[213] Like his hero, Sumner, Bright took it to be no part of the business of a statesman to arrange majorities.

Bright's hold on the political organization of the provinces was as weak as his hold on its opinions was strong. It emphasizes the regional variations of experience that he had nothing whatever to do with the Liberal revival in Wales in the 1860's. In the same period, he never spoke at Newcastle—where Cowen had Chartist doubts about him—or at Liverpool, Bristol, Norwich, Sheffield, or the East Midland towns. To some extent, the new press had made it possible to obtain national coverage without canvassing every town in turn: but it also meant that great areas of Liberal England never had the slightest contact with Bright.

208 B.M. Add. mss. 43,654, f. 241, Cobden to Ashworth, 12 December 1861.
209 Robertson, *Bright* (1912), 242.
210 To his daughter Helen, 26 November 1867. Street mss.
211 *Hansard*, vol. 192, col. 265, 14 May 1868.
212 Bright to Cobden, 6 January 1862: B.M. Add. mss. 43,384, f. 286.
213 Chamberlain to Bright, 14 May 1878: B.M. Add. mss. 43,387, f. 180.

The significant relationships of Bright were those with highly developed individuals with views very different from his own, with the intelligentsia of politics, Russell, the Peelites, Gladstone, and Mill, whom he did something to bring together for common aims based on very divergent principles.

Little can be said about Bright's relation to Mill.[214] Despite Bright's attack on Mill's cherished East India Company as a nest of jobbers, Mill, particularly in the session of 1866, entered politics almost as a follower of Bright: a lady wrote of Mill looking up at Bright 'with that warm look of admiring love',[215] but Bright found that philosophers were all he had feared. Mill's minority clause outraged common sense and, worse, endangered Bright's seat at Birmingham, and when the election came, Bright felt he could not subscribe for one 'who voted for the minority clause, against the Ballot, and spoke in favour of hanging. I do not believe in the philosophy so much boasted of . . .'[216] But the spectacle of Bright and Mill[217] co-operating on such issues as the American War, the Jamaica agitation, Irish coercion, and Irish land, lent force to the vague impression late Victorian Liberals had of their intellectual ancestry and ultimate irrefutability.

The Peelites had an attraction for the Manchester School on similar, but larger, grounds than that which led them for a time to act with Mill. The Peelites acted on rational and coherent principles, did not set their sails to catch gusts of popular passion, and what they attempted, they brought to a sound and practical conclusion. Cobden looked back to Peel's ministry as a time when more progress was made in the development of great principles than in twenty years of Liberal rule.[218] Peel represented 'the idea of the age, and it has no other representative among statesmen'. The long struggle to maintain and extend Free Trade developed a fellow feeling

[214] In 1859 Mill saw Bright as the 'mere demagogue and courtier of the majority'.—Mill to Chadwick, 20 December 1859, in *Letters*, ed. Elliott.

[215] Mrs McLaren to Helen Clark, 9 January 1868: Street mss.

[216] To his daughter Helen, 3 August 1868: Street mss.

[217] Bright voted for Mill's motion on female suffrage, as he afterwards said, from personal respect. It was the only mistake he ever admitted making.

[218] B.M. Add. mss. 43,664, f. 211. Cobden to Baines, 11 April 1857.

between the two sections. As early as 1851, the Duke of Newcastle was habitually friendly to Bright, who urged the Peelites to 'throw themselves more on the people' and outbid the Whigs on Reform.[219] As the issue of Free Trade receded, two further ones emerged as a bond between the sections: the Crimean War and Palmerston's foreign policy in general. Much later Bright was to claim that his views of foreign policy were precisely identical with those of Peel.[220] Likewise on religious questions, Bright joined with the Peelites in opposing such illiberal measures as the Ecclesiastical Titles Bill. The result of all this was that on resignation in 1855, Aberdeen was ready to act along with the Manchester School, and Bright urged Gladstone to take a new start 'in a Liberal and useful public career', well away from Oxford.[221] The cordiality continued. Bright stayed with Lord Aberdeen more than once, and Aberdeen's son became friendly with Bright and Cobden. Cobden is stated to have intervened to save Graham's seat at Carlisle in 1857.[222] Graham 'rejoiced much' in Bright's return to Parliament, and later 'was in raptures' at the defeat of Palmerston, 'seizing my hand . . . as if we had met with a deliverance'.[223] Partly on the ground of a common doctrinal approach to politics, partly on account of common experience and practical co-operation, the Peelites by the end of the 1850's had long lived on terms of mutual respect and regard with Cobden and Bright, without the least trace of patrician disdain, and Aberdeen had clearly laid down the principles of fusion which were to lead to a popular Liberal Party. One Peelite alone, Mr Gladstone, would have no part in this accord, and Cobden and Bright, and especially Bright, viewed him with corresponding suspicion. When Gladstone came to Manchester in 1853, he had no contact with the Manchester School, who were then engaged in 'war to the knife' with him over the advertisement duties.[224] Gladstone, unlike the other Peelites, could not unbend: in 1855 he

[219] *Diaries*, ed. Walling, 126: 24 May 1851.

[220] *Speeches*, ed. Rogers (1869), 467: at Birmingham, 29 October 1858.

[221] *Diaries*, 22 February 1855.

[222] See Bean, *Parliamentary Representation of the Northern Counties*, under Carlisle.

[223] B.M. Add. mss. 43,384, f. 119: Bright to Cobden, 1858.

[224] Bright to Wilson, July 1853: Wilson mss.

scolded Arthur Gordon for sitting next to Bright, though
Lord Aberdeen approved warmly of his son's friendship with
Bright.[225] Bright could admit Gladstone's superiority to all
other men in the House,[226] but he could not, right up to 1869,
trust him. He thought it worth while to dissuade Gladstone
from joining Derby in 1858, but later in that year he did
'not see any good to be done' with him: 'he dare not accept
the lead of a popular party—Oxford and tradition bind him
fast'.[227] Bright, like Aberdeen, found no difficulty in seeing
the role in which Gladstone was to make his place in history:
but he found great difficulty in believing Gladstone would
rise to the opportunity. Even with the French treaty well
under way, Bright nursed his distrust: 'I shall never trust any
man again, who went into and supported the Russian war.
And Gladstone, whom I was told yesterday, you regard as a
saint, is no more to be relied on than the rest.'[228] The French
treaty by no means forged a bond between the two men,
though it started a correspondence composed of complaints
and exhortations on one side and excuses and evasions on the
other. Between 1860 and 1864 Bright was in two minds about
Gladstone's good faith: thereafter he simply doubted his
ability as a statesman. He began to feel the attractions Gladstone later became noted for: 'There is a fine conscientiousness in Gladstone, and a *reverence* which touches everything
sacred with beauty.'[229] But despite this, and despite the
French treaty, Bright felt in 1861 that he would not be able to
support Mr Gladstone if he contested South Lancashire, 'as a
member of the Palmerston government, with no policy of his
own,'[230] and in 1862 Gladstone's 'vile speech' at Newcastle,
showing he was 'as unstable as water' cast a chill over
things.[231] In 1863 he was surprised to find himself rising in
the House to defend Gladstone; he found his action curious.

[225] Gordon to Gladstone, 7 June 1855: B.M. Add. mss. 44,319.
[226] *Diaries*, 201: 3 August 1855.
[227] B.M. Add. mss. 43,384, f. 132: 2 September 1858, Bright to Cobden.
[228] Bright to Cobden, 16 November 1859: Add. mss. 43,384, f. 167.
[229] To Mrs Bright, 19 April 1860: University College mss.
[230] B.M. Add. mss. 43,384, f. 251: 28 March 1861, Bright to Cobden.
[231] *Diaries*, 262: the phrase was used in a letter to Sumner.

In 1864 Bright entered into close consultation with Gladstone, a consultation which—though there is no record of it—did much to settle the course of policy for the rest of the decade. They discussed finance (18 February 1864), Reform and taxation (9 March 1864), the budget (13 March 1864) and the Irish Church (13 April 1864). For tactical reasons, Bright appears to have parted company with Gladstone in 1865 and 1866: both were conscious that either might be used by opponents to blacken any measure of Reform. But the entente of 1864 remained, and Bright's conduct over Reform, crowned by his panegyric of Gladstone at Birmingham (22 April 1867), left nothing to be desired. Bright's attitude remained didactic. In 1866 he referred to Gladstone as the only man who spoke as if he comprehended the Irish question, and urged him on to further endeavours.[232] But Bright was still anything but a follower. He could not conceive that the pupil would ever reach the level of the master:

> Mr Gladstone hesitates, and hardly knows how far to go. The material of his forces is not good, and I suspect he has not studied the land question . . . The Liberal party is not in a good position for undertaking any measure of statesmanship. We want a strong man with a strong brain and convictions for work of this kind, and I do not see him among our public men.[233]

What Bright meant chiefly, no doubt, was that the Liberal Shadow Cabinet was still two months away from adopting his Irish schemes, and might yet back out: but to be unable to see 'a strong brain and convictions' in the Gladstone of 1868, showed that though they might mass their followers in a common body and a common enthusiasm, the two men had little common ground on which they could influence each other. There was no real question of Bright following Gladstone (what was there to follow, but an intricately reluctant assent to what had been plain sense to every Radical cobbler in 1830?) but rather, Bright mitigated his disapproval of Gladstone in proportion as he found Gladstone (who still

---

[232] *Speeches*, ed. Rogers (1869), 179: 17 February 1866, House of Commons.

[233] Leech, *Letters* (1895), 113: 27 January 1868.

in 1867 spoke of him privately as an impracticable demagogue),[234] willing to learn from him. That willingness was
never very great.

Bright kept his dealings with the old Whigs to a minimum.
He thought them useless and heartless, with a personal reservation in favour of Argyll, who supported the Northern States
and lionized Bright, and a personal and political reservation
in favour of Russell. Definitely not consulted in the drawing-
up of the 1866 Reform Bill, he had little even of business
contact with the Liberal leadership before 1869. But before
he became politically respectable, he achieved social recognition and he achieved it chiefly through the young Whigs, the
Cavendishes, Amberleys, and Trevelyans. Trevelyan paid
homage to Bright in the House, Mrs Gladstone had him to
dinner with Wilberforce and Dean Stanley,[235] the Amberleys
gave a dinner for him and Lady Frederic Cavendish.[236] Lady
John Russell had a pleasant little dinner with Bright between
herself and Lord John. She wrote, 'he is warm-hearted and
very much in earnest . . . He said reading poetry was next to
the greatest pleasure he had in life—the greatest was little
children.'[237] Lady Frederic Cavendish was struck by his ease,
and his unaffected simple manner. In short, the great Radical,
without changing any of his political views, became a fascinat-
ing and charming diner-out, at the moment when he appeared
to have aristocratic society by the throat.

Bright made the young Whigs more radical: but the unsus-
pected charm they discovered in him was hardly responsible
for the curious figure of poacher turned gamekeeper that he
presented in later years. His relations with Russell had a
much stronger political content. It was always on the cards
that rash, impetuous Lord John might be lured into being the
first leader of a popular Liberal Party. Palmerston, Russell,
and Bright were quite aware of the opportunities which were

[234] Brand to Clarendon, 31 January 1867: Maxwell, *Clarendon*, II, 330.
[235] *The Diary of Lady Frederic Cavendish*, ed. J. Bailey (1927), II, 33:
29 May 1867.
[236] Ibid., II, 9: 14 June 1866.
[237] Lady Russell to R. Russell, 1 March 1866: *Lady John Russell*,
by D. MacCarthy and A. Russell (1926). George Eliot found Bright a
charming dinner companion: *The George Eliot Letters*, ed. Haigh, VI,
373.

first really made use of by Gladstone. On reform, Russell had no intellectual difficulty: '. . . while agreeing in Bright's ends, I cannot approve of his means'.[238] And Bright in his early speeches was obviously setting his cap at Lord John: 'Lord John Russell . . . has probably, from his own reading and study, and from his own just and honest sympathies, a more friendly feeling towards Parliamentary Reform than any other man of his order . . .'[239] and in 1859 he bargained away his agitation very readily for promises that the Whigs could not perform.

Such sympathy arose more readily while Russell was an alternative to Palmerston. Russell was writing to Cobden in 1855: Bright commented that the Whigs were opening their eyes to the need for a better staff and a new programme.[240] In this spirit, Cobden exerted pressure on Samuel Morley to secure Russell's return for the City in 1857, as he had exerted pressure on behalf of Graham. But in 1861 Russell jocularly disavowed Reform and avowed a foreign policy distinctly Palmerstonian. Bright cut him dead after a fierce attack in the Commons at his breach of pledges. Bright refused all invitations from Russell in 1864 and 1865, and did not speak to him once between 1860 and 1866,[241] when he received Russell's frank apologies—shortly before his support was needed for the Liberal Reform Bill. (About this time he wrote 'I have never had so many invitations.')[242] Considering the slight to his feelings involved in the reconstructions of the Cabinet[243] without his inclusion, he showed great tolerance, as usual, of neglect, by speaking of Russell in the highest terms of party praise:

> Lord Russell had no fear of freedom. He could be much more easily persuaded to give up . . . for ever the name of Russell, than he would give up his hereditary love of free-

[238] Russell to Argyll, 24 November 1858: Argyll, *Autobiography*, II, 131.

[239] *Speeches*, ed. Rogers (1869), 283: at Birmingham, 27 October 1858.

[240] B. M. Add. mss. 43,384, f. 33: Bright to Cobden, 29 November 1855.

[241] To Mrs Bright, 5 February 1866: University College mss.

[242] To Helen Clark, 3 March 1866: Street mss.

[243] 'Nobody's asked me to dance, and I wouldn't, even if they did.'— *Punch*.

dom. [His ministry] was founded and acted upon the principle of trust and confidence in the people.[244]

Russell was similarly broadly tolerant of Bright 'if he renounces his allegiance to President Johnson'.[245] The old grudges between Whigs and Radicals came to an end long before any active, day-to-day co-operation ensued. Bright and Russell both remained lonely figures. What continually strikes one is that Bright, by being extremely accommodating and far from intransigent, was always on the edge of some striking and original new political combination—with Russell, with the Peelites, with the trade union *élite*, with Gladstone—that there was no further personal barrier to overcome—and yet neither side was able to push the large degree of mutual understanding reached, to any political conclusion. The general fatalism induced by the ascendancy of Palmerston was stamped upon all these manœuvres.

*　　*　　*

There remain a few points, connected with patronage, education, *laissez-faire* and the relation of Bright's Liberalism to the authoritarian pattern of his home life.

The great opponent of outdoor relief for the aristocracy did not allow his principles to stand in the way of doing good to those he represented. Several times he dabbled in the appointment of Lancashire magistrates: he was involved in an attempt to get a job for Miall's son-in-law, Skeats, at the Board of Trade: he forbade the imposition of a gun tax in the interest of his Birmingham constituents. His most audacious importunity was a very strong attempt to make Gladstone appoint a Bishop of Manchester 'of known Liberal views' in order to offset the political opposition of the clergy to his friends in Manchester,[246] and again, during his campaign against the Crimean War, he solicited the ministry for a place in the Navy for a client.

In education, he hardly stood ahead of his age, his children

---

[244] *Speeches*, ed. Rogers (1869), 375: at Birmingham, 27 August 1866.
[245] Asa Briggs, *Victorian People; some reassessments of people, institutions, ideas and events, 1851–1867* (1954), 238.
[246] Bright to Gladstone, 1 January 1870: B.M. Add. ms. 44,112, f. 119.

receiving the old Nonconformist education of a sound business training and no frills. He never gave prominence to the cause of popular education or showed any sign that he regarded it as one of the great tasks of the age. But if he stood with the more hysterical Voluntaryists in the 1840's, he had come to his senses, under Cobden's influence, by 1854. In that year, he spoke for an hour at the Manchester Mechanics' Institute, showing that the arguments of the voluntaries were untenable, though giving them high credit for their labours,[247] thus playing at least a respectable part in the process which led to the final acceptance of State education. And, judging from a protest by Sturge, it seems the *Morning Star* advocated a national system.[248]

Bright was at his silliest when questions of *laissez-faire* were involved, when, for instance, he moralized on a Free Breakfast Table, but did not encourage the Board of Trade to prevent the food on it being adulterated. But he was not so silly as is often implied. As in the case of education, *laissez-faire* was easy enough to abandon when one so wished, and the gap between social necessities and social legislation after 1850, and still more after 1860, did not arise particularly from any presumption among educated and disinterested persons against state interference. (An enormous evil was done by the rule that made it necessary for a bill to pass in a single session.) There was never any sign of recantation of the abstract principle. In 1884 Bright still held legal limitation of hours worked by adults was 'unwise, and in many cases oppressive'.[249]

But on the whole Bright decided for or against a Bill on practical grounds. In the case of the Permissive Bill of 1864, he opposed interference as grossly unfair to the trade, but urged municipal control of all establishments on quite stringent terms, as preferable and necessary. 'I am in favour of adding to the dignity and authority of our municipal government . . .' and he wished elementary education had been put in their hands.[250] What he disliked in the state, he applauded

[247] *Diaries*, 156, January 1854.
[248] Wilson mss., 1856, Sturge to Wilson.
[249] Leech, *Letters* (1895), 253: 1 January 1884.
[250] Ibid., 204: 27 November 1873.

in the corporation. And the remedies he suggested for India and Ireland, though retaining some *laissez-faire* scruples, really involved large scale economic planning from the centre quite alien to the old economic creed.

On only three measures in the 1860's did Bright speak from a perverse point of view. In 1860 he spoke against a government Bill for the formation of highway boards, on rather slight grounds. In 1863 he joined with Cobden in modifying the Alkali Bill in favour of the St Helens manufacturers. In both cases the clauses chiefly at issue were those which gave more power to the county magistrates, and in neither case was resistance based on principle. In 1869, as President of the Board of Trade, Bright was placed in connection with measures raising the question of *laissez-faire*. What emerged was that he was daunted above all by the legislative difficulties involved, and that he made no effort to alter the established tradition of the Department in favour of his own views. 'Adulteration is only a form of competition . . .' is a remark imputed to him,[251] but I have not found it in these debates, nor the attitude it represents. The Liberal ministry did in fact pass Food Adulteration Acts which annoyed 'every milkman in Leeds'. But, though Bright's reluctance to disturb trade with ill-framed legislation was not a proselytizing creed, neither can it be said that he showed real inclination to overcome the difficulties involved.

The Achilles' heel of his Liberalism lay in his creed of the family. His household suffrage amounted to a confederacy of absolute despots: and in his opposition to Home Rule, he was applying the principles of family life to Irish insubordination.[252] He would not have his wife discuss suffrage questions with his daughters,[253] and he observed 'evil results' to women who entered into political discussion[254] (as his sister and daughter had done). Let his sister speak last.[255]

[251] G. Saintsbury, *Manchester, a Short History* (1887), 170. Saintsbury, a hostile writer, gave no reference for this quotation.

[252] He wrote to his daughter: 'It is strange that some of my children should think themselves better informed on the Irish question than I am . . .' Street mss., 17 March 1887.

[253] To Mrs Bright, 10 May 1873: University College mss.

[254] Leech, op. cit., 235: 21 October 1882.

[255] Priscilla McLaren to Helen Clark, 8 April 1893: Street mss.

. . . he could praise women, but not Woman—he could worship what he called charming women, but he could *never* bear women to assert themselves—he could bear this less after his second marriage which taught him what a resolute woman could be and what she could not be—one who would assert her power over a £5 note to even a postage stamp, not to name the comfort of a smoke in his own home. Whilst he could be beautifully influenced by the women he loved and admired, as I said he could only like this influence to be exerted through a feminine deference to the power of man. I remember how displeased he was once in the Highlands, with Esther and me, when his back was turned I got over an awkward style unaided—she *waited* for his help—he exalted this in her, while he expressed disgust at what I had done. He did not think his sisters had a right to think for themselves with regard to any offer of marriage—one to Esther which fell into his hand he would not have let her see but for me . . . One evening [when Bright had gone to visit his friends], he was very angry with me because I had seen McLaren in his absence and he reproved me severely because he said I appeared to think marriage was necessary to my happiness.

He once told me that daughters had no right to have the money their father had left them if it would be of use to their brothers in business . . . Like his father, Albert[256] clings to the 'respectable' in religious matters—the only son who does—and John was the only one in his family who did—he has the same adhesiveness in family matters, the same *reverence*—the others have little or none. There was the same kindness and benevolence to the poor and to our poor relations.

The significance of Bright's career, concentrated in his ten years' siege of the British Constitution, lay not in tangible achievements but in clearing the ground for a popular national party outside Parliament under Gladstone. He was able to do this work supremely well because, governed and restrained by a fine tradition, he spoke aloud, what for centuries had been felt in silence, although his character and

[256] John Albert Bright, Unionist member for Birmingham.

attainments did not fit him for political work in general. Ignoring, though without disloyalty, the obvious career available to him as a leader of Dissent, he tried to enlist working-class support. His conscious efforts to do so largely failed, and his great campaign of 1866 was the improvisation of a disheartened man. Much of his stature resulted from the needs of his supporters and opponents to clothe their hopes and fears in flesh and blood, rather than from activity on his part. Yet Bright was exactly what he always appeared to be. There was no one freer from economic Liberalism. Nearly all his effort was devoted to treating politics by the standards of the meeting house: his decisive limitation was lack of knowledge, not of intentions. His courage and disinterestedness were beyond dispute. From all this, several hundred commonplace gentlemen, who had hardly any point of agreement with him, benefited for a generation: more important, at a time when vigorous working-class societies were, in practice, denied Parliamentary representation by their own class, Bright provided an acceptable assurance of the good faith of the Parliamentary Liberal Party.

GLADSTONE

> These later-born Theresas were helped by no coherent social faith and order which could perform the function of knowledge to the ardently willing soul. . . . A certain spiritual grandeur ill-matched with the meanness of opportunity.
>
> *Middlemarch*

If Gladstone was a Liberal, it was not because of the point of departure of his thought, for behind his view of public life lay a theory of the mutual duties of classes in their private relations, drawn from his experience as a landed proprietor. If he was a Liberal, it was because he was a landowner, and it is to his views on landownership in general and his Flintshire estates in particular that one must look to grasp his social theory.

Though Gladstone had industrial knowledge, industrial

connections, and a mercantile background, by middle life he had come to invest the rural social order with a special moral significance. It was not only that 'agriculture is by far the most satisfactory of all pursuits . . .'[257] but that the hierarchy based on agriculture was the best of all possible hierarchies. Of all kinds of property, landed property most 'involved kindly and intimate relations between the higher and the lower classes'.[258] He regarded it 'as a very high duty to labour for the conservation of estates, and the permanence of the families in possession of them, as a principal source of our social strength . . .'[259] and when the Hawarden estate ran into heavy debts, he made great sacrifices of income sooner than part with an acre of land.

He accepted the manners of the landed class, not merely without demur, but with enthusiasm, believing in old traditions and mourning their passage. He liked shooting and saw little harm in the game laws.[260] He disliked equally the innovations of a teetotal dinner and of smoking.[261] On the subject of 'that incomparable and most wholesome article which we term bitter beer',[262] his eloquence was unrestrained, and must have shocked many good Temperance Liberals. It is even possible that Gladstone may have regarded the Hawarden tenantry, *more antiquo*, as 'his' voters: Brand, the Liberal Whip, seemed to think they were.[263]

These were individually small things, but on them was impressed the stamp of generality. Hierarchy and antiquity meant more to Gladstone, as he complained, than to the Conservatives,[264] and he sought to strengthen and assist the aristocratic and archaic element in that party. 'I am a firm believer in the aristocratic principle—the rule of the best. I am an out and out inequalitarian.'[265] He liked to have young men of

[257] Speech at Mold: *Manchester Examiner*, 26 September 1862.

[258] F. E. Hyde, *Mr. Gladstone at the Board of Trade* (1934), 11.

[259] Morley, *Gladstone* (1901), I, 347.

[260] Viscount Gladstone, *After Thirty Years* (1928), 64.   [261] Ibid., 44.

[262] Sydney Buxton, *Gladstone as Chancellor of the Exchequer* (1901), 54. See also L. A. Tollemache, *Talks with Mr. Gladstone* (1898), 62.

[263] Brand to Gladstone, 2 May 1861: B.M. Add. mss. 44,193, f. 41.

[264] L. A. Tollemache, op. cit., 78.

[265] L. March–Phillipps and B. Christian, *Some Hawarden Letters* (1917), 37.

good birth around him, and his appointments were systematically favourable to whatever was aristocratic in the Liberal Party.

Of such stuff are diehards made: but Gladstone was not a diehard. There was an unbroken chain linking his conception of landed property with his position as the leader of the Liberal Party. The creed of the country gentleman, made militant and energetic, brought into contact with a thousand aspects of life, led inevitably to the idea of the State as embodying the moral effort of the upper class; to a fierce hostility to the 'Upper Ten Thousand', to Business, and to Socialism, as equally enemies of the general interest: and to a view of democracy, which regarded it as the supplementary and occasional engine of the principles of true aristocracy. High Toryism in private life, led by strict logic to conclusions directly opposite about public affairs.

Gladstone's view of the duties of landed property was hardly a secular one. One could no more become a proprietor than the incumbent of a parish without recognizing the serious moral and social responsibilities attached.[266] Applied to public life, such views demanded an almost episcopal character in the upper class. Privilege was to be functional, or it was nothing. Its justification was 'the strong conviction of the people that its existence is beneficial to the community at large'.[267] It was in order to make privilege useful and moral that Gladstone defended rotten boroughs in 1859, and drew up tinkering schemes to enable the titled young to serve a political apprenticeship in the Commons.[268]

Something like this episcopal principle was in fact necessary. For England, though equally divided between town and country, had to be ruled through the *élite* of the rural half of the nation. The landed proprietors were the only class trained for government, and urban society was not ready to enter upon national responsibilities. But the landed proprietors had no clear *locus standi* in relation to the large towns. Their position in relation to them was not one of power or of economic

---

[266] Morley, *Gladstone* (1901), I, 345.

[267] Speech at Edinburgh: *Manchester Examiner*, 13 January 1862.

[268] See a curious draft of 16 March 1869 by Gladstone in the Russell papers: P.R.O. 30/22/16.

position or class representation, but of natural detachment, at odds with an involvement necessary to carry out national purposes. Such a situation could only be handled in terms of service, episcopacy, disinterestedness, and Christian steward-ship, for more worldly connection there was none.

Gladstone simply dealt with the towns as though they were not towns at all. He desired to see in them the best features of the hierarchic rural social order: the mutual attachment of classes, the aristocracy recognized and ruling by consent and merit, the achievement of public good by the performance of private duty, were the notes he struck in his provincial speeches when attempting to characterize social well-being.

For the towns as they were, he had no specific theory. He had no theory of history, little historical perspective, and he had no sense of the scale of the transformation the world was undergoing and was still to undergo. 'The future is to me a blank. I cannot guess what is coming.'[269] He thought of the England of 1990 as one in which the great landed estates would still be intact.[270] There was an extraordinary gap between his education and his historical experience. Both remarkable, they never met for mutual enrichment. For in-stance, his work on Aristotle's *Politics*, which he translated in 1860, did not suggest that among Aristotle's unrivalled qualities was any relevance to the nineteenth century.[271] End-less experience educated Gladstone in the logic of Parliamen-tary action, taught him to hear the talk in the corridors, clubs, and houses, to move inside the minds of other politicians with similar problems; but the larger drama of nations, classes, and technologies escaped him.

Hardly seeing that the end of the traditional rural order was only a matter of time, Gladstone regarded the preserva-tion of hierarchy and wealth, even when not well used, as a matter of like importance with its right use. As among the English rulers of India, disinterestedness was not only a matter of the most earnestly felt principle, but a prime con-dition of security. Gladstone's comments on his Legacy Duty revealed the note of precaution that was one element in his calculations:

[269] Tollemache, *Talks with Mr. Gladstone* (1898), 166.
[270] Ibid., 70.   [271] B.M. Add. mss. 44,750, ff. 35-147.

In my humble but sincere opinion, differentiation of the Income Tax is the true mother of confiscation to the land: and this new Legacy Duty, so far from introducing it, will be the present and I hope the permanent means of averting that fearful risk.[272]

Justice in details was to be the mainstay of a system of hierarchy and ascendancy; disinterestedness was in part a defensive class policy. The problem for a public man feeling his way towards some generalization of the principles of the rural order, which might serve to govern a half urban country, was to embody disinterestedness in flesh and blood, and to find an appropriate tone and temper and line of policy.

Gladstone's commendation of Childers—a man of no particular ties or colour—suggested what he was looking for in men. Childers, he wrote, 'pleases me exceedingly, not only by his capacity for work but by the general manliness and unselfishness of his character as it comes out in affairs'.[273] To govern with the support of some class was necessary: to govern only with the support of particular classes was intolerable. Barbarians, Philistines, Populace—to none of these classes, as classes, could the essential principles of English life be entrusted. The formula eventually settled on, was to combine the rude but sturdy morality of Nonconformity and the working class, with the otherwise forceless 'principled' minority of the Upper Ten Thousand. In Peel's day, the conception of the Queen's Government had given ministers a freedom of manœuvre, which they could use to act on behalf of the general interest. That ebbed, and Gladstone was left trying to square the circle. Gladstone's creation of a national ascendancy for himself was much more than a matter of crusades and electioneering; it was a much needed attempt to introduce a balancing element into the constitution during a critical period of transition, to create an area where rationality and the general interest could be enforced and class will rebuked, and to provide a reserve of power sufficient to do a difficult right or prevent a popular wrong.

[272] Guedalla, ed., *Gladstone and Palmerston*, 94.
[273] Gladstone to Russell, 3 January 1866: Russell Papers, P.R.O. 30/22/16.

To hold in check the appetites and passions of three classes might seem no light choice of pastime. But his intensity of conviction left him no choice in the matter. *Fiat justitia, ruat coelum*; his opposition to the lower selves of each class was as absolute and peremptory at eighty as at forty. The young Peelite of 1843 warned

> of our deadness to the denunciations of Scripture concerning the perils of wealth, and the difficulties it interposes in the way of salvation: of our insensibility to the Christian equality, or (should it not rather be said?) the Christian superiority of the poor . . .[274]

In his last years, he spoke of being not so much afraid either of democracy or of science as of the love of money.[275] In the 1870's Gladstone made the opposition of 'class' and 'mass' part of the public vocabulary: even in 1871 he spoke in such terms. 'In London it is that the interests of class are particularly concentrated.'[276] His criticism of the 'classes' was a religious one:

> . . . the burden of his [Gladstone's] song is always the deterioration of the Governing Classes in comparison with the poor. He said very solemnly that our Lord's teaching goes very deep in this direction, as to the poor being better and wiser than the rich . . . He had just said the clergy must rely more on the poor and less on the rich and high social ranks.[277]

If his criticism of the aristocratic rich was in religious terms, his strictures on business were of Benthamite and administrative origin, and his strictures on working-class claims were based on the orthodox political economy and on the morality of self-help.

A Chancellor of the Exchequer must regard the business world with a jaundiced eye. What was unusual about Gladstone was the degree of his malevolence towards the appetites

---

[274] Gladstone, *Gleanings of Past Years*, V, 119.
[275] Tollemache, *Talks with Mr. Gladstone* (1898), 166.
[276] Speech at Whitby: *Whitby Gazette*, 2 September 1871.
[277] Acland to his wife, 1878: *Memoir and Letters of Sir Thomas Dyke Acland*, ed. A. H. D. Acland (1902), 323.

of business, and its combination with extreme popularity on the Exchanges and Chambers of Commerce. Cornewall Lewis might have shrugged at anomalies, but not so Gladstone. The shipping interests, Gladstone wrote, were meditating violent assaults upon the public purse, 'infected with the disease of the time'.[278] He abhorred 'the great mischief of State intervention' in undersea telegraphy, and the 'vicious habit they have contracted of looking for Government money in order to overcome the difficulties of novel enterprises . . .'[279] He thought dockyard lobbying and the Dockyard Superannuation Act of 1859 the greatest Parliamentary scandals of his time.[280] His savings banks and government insurance enterprise attempted to put the Exchequer in a stronger position in relation to the City. To maintain such implacable opposition to the lobby, demanded that Gladstone should find unusually strong support in other quarters. Not from wantonness, but from necessity, he turned away from Parliament to bring fresh elements into politics:

> . . . the unreformed Parliament used to job for individuals, while the reformed Parliament jobs for classes. I do not adopt the rudeness of the phrase, but the substance of the observation is in my opinion just. I think that the influence of the public interest properly so called . . . is too weak . . . I speak much from my own experience as Chancellor of the Exchequer . . . I believe the composition of the House might be greatly improved; and that the increased representation of the working classes would supply us more largely with the description of members we want, who would look not to the interests of classes, but to the public interest.[281]

The function of the working class in politics was to curb the appetites of other classes. But Gladstone also sought working-class support to prevent their tendencies to error leading

[278] Gladstone to Russell, 1 September 1859: Russell Papers, 30/22/19.
[279] Guedalla, ed., *Gladstone and Palmerston*, 201.
[280] Gladstone to Russell, 3 April 1866: Russell Papers, P.R.O. 30/22/16.
[281] *Selected Speeches*, ed. A. T. Bassett (1916), 372: quoting Gladstone's speech on the Second Reading of the Reform Bill, 1866.

to 'jobbing for classes'. He sought to apply the same discipline to the working class as to any other, as a matter of equal justice, without regard to difference of circumstances. Gladstone's ideal of a State dissociated from class, organized by an aristocratic *élite* and maintained by popular love of and interest in justice, had not one streak of Socialism in it. It could have been otherwise, for the ideal as such had no logical connection with a particular brand of political economy.

Yet, as his private secretary said,[282] Gladstone was the strongest of anti-socialists. He even deplored essays in what he called 'construction' which had little doctrinal implication one way or the other, like Mundella's extensions of education. The Budget of 1874, which gave special relief to poorer income-tax payers, appeared to him as dangerously socialistic.[283] In matters of political economy, divergence from the path he had learnt in youth was no more possible than in matters of religion. Only the intellectual or moral aberration could account for such schemes as land nationalization: 'Do you mean to pay for it [land], or do you not? If you mean to pay for it, it is folly: if you don't mean to pay for it, it is robbery.'[284] It was unfortunate that Gladstone's ideal of the mutual relations of the classes and the State should have been tied to points of doctrine so likely to be taken amiss by others; especially so as his intransigence on the subject of State action was much greater in later life, when the working-class movement was at the turning of the ways, than in his early or middle period.

Posterity, looking through the eyes of Morley and the Labour Movement, has taken the Hawarden windows, which look away from the coalpits, as the epitome of Gladstone's diehard social policy. In fact, the record was curiously uncertain and various. If the G.O.M. became something of a diehard in his last years, it at one time seemed as if the Chancellor of the Exchequer, 'who could not repress a carnal satisfaction' in the myriad processes of industry, might become for England what Chamberlain was for Birmingham, the reconciler of material order and industrial progress.

---

[282] Lord Kilbracken, *Reminiscences* (1931), 83.   [283] Ibid., 84.
[284] E. H. Fowler, *Life of Lord Wolverhampton* (1912), 507. He heaped anathemas on Harcourt's death duties.

Although encased in education from tip to toe, he knew the world of business as it was, and he knew the world of poverty as it was. As Chancellor of the Exchequer, and in a private capacity, there were few branches of trade, manufacture, and husbandry with which he was not concerned. Coal and corn were the twin pillars[285] of the Hawarden estate. In London, his social interests were extensive and peculiar, and highly to his disadvantage as a public man: how extensive they were may never be understood, for only by chance does one stumble on Gladstone visiting Millbank Prison,[286] reading the Bible to a sick crossing sweeper,[287] and giving a dinner party for sixteen skilled artisans.[288] And Mrs Gladstone, the miraculous survivor of the East End cholera wards, could have had nothing to learn from *The Bitter Cry of Outcast London*. Where Gladstone adhered to *laissez-faire* and Voluntaryism, it was with full knowledge of the consequences, and after giving the most convincing testimony of desire to promote improvement by other means. But that he did adhere to a very scanty social policy, was not entirely due to abstract rigour, but to a fortuitous precedence of claim on the part of purely political questions:

> What relates to health and the well-being of life, to the good order and comfort of the community, to the reasonable supplies of those necessities of air, water, and the like, wherein the action of public authority is almost necessarily involved . . . if little had been achieved upon those important and non-political questions, it was not for slight cause, but because we had been compelled by overwhelming motives of public duty to give the first place to the great national overruling subjects. . . .[289]

Though he never took full measure of the political aspects of industrial progress, Gladstone was the great prophet of the beneficence of industry. No other Liberal struck these

---

[285] Morley, *Gladstone* (1901), I, 348.
[286] Viscount Gladstone, *After Thirty Years* (1928), 66.
[287] *Autobiography of Newman Hall* (1901), 265.
[288] Ibid., 263.
[289] *Selected Speeches*, ed. A. T. Bassett (1916), 415: speech at Blackheath.

apparently insensitive notes of 'gorgeous reckless optimism'.[290]
The diction of Bossuet enforced the speculations of Pangloss.
He looked forward to the utilization of the enormous wealth
lying in London sewage: he fully expected cheap gas to lift
the pall of smoke over the great cities. He was sanguine
enough to believe

> that the day was not far distant when the estuary of the
> Dee, which now meant a vast surface lying entirely useless,
> would be recovered from the surface of the sea and brought
> into cultivation, while the mineral enterprise of this great
> country was at work underneath. . . .[291]

As the largest proprietor in Flintshire, he took a leading part
in its industrial enterprises, carrying the Wrexham Railway
Bill through Parliament, and cherishing a lively hope that his
little county was still 'a very young coal mining district . . .'[292]
The diehard who lamented the abolition of noblemen's gowns
at Oxford, wished to create a Ruhr on the Dee.

Elsewhere there was the same inability to repress a carnal
satisfaction in the growing wealth of the country. At Sunderland, it was a positive pleasure 'to observe that your ships are
almost knocking one against the other';[293] he lauded the
declining mortality rates of Blackburn; and at Bootle, he rose
to exaltation:

> This Bootle, gentlemen, which we now see covered with
> the houses of thinking citizens, I remember it a wilderness
> of sandhills with its grouse and wild roses. What has
> changed it? In no small part, the beneficial legislation
> which has struck the fetters from the arms of human indus-
> try.[294]

To side with the villas of the thinking citizens, against the
wild roses—evidence of coarseness of fibre to many critics—

[290] The phrase was Lord Salisbury's.
[291] Speech at Mold: *Manchester Examiner*, 3 January 1865.
[292] Ibid.
[293] Speech at Sunderland: ibid., 10 October 1862.
[294] W. E. Williams, *The Rise of Gladstone to the Leadership of the
Liberal Party, 1859–68* (1934), 169.

was to place oneself with the cause of humanity, villadom
representing a great escape from subjection, increased opportunities for domestic life, and greater economic security, but
it was both more and less than Liberal party politics. Like
Turgot, Gladstone felt the state was gigantically involved in
the material well-being of its citizens, chiefly through a wise
abstention and the emancipation of productive forces. No
collectivist could have taken a more social definition of the
aims of politics: if 1860, he wrote, were to pass 'without anything done for trade and the masses, it would be a great
calamity . . .'[295] The taxation of charities was a measure of
justice to 'the labouring poor, to elevate whose character and
to improve whose condition is one of the main objects of
legislative action'.[296]

There is some mystery as to what Gladstone might have
done, had he found himself in office with sympathetic colleagues between 1853 and 1865. There were hints of some
great scheme. 'I greatly felt being turned out of office, I saw
great things to do. I longed to do them. I am losing the best
years of my life out of my natural service . . .'[297] Tariffs,
finance, the reform of the Civil Service, the abolition of the
Duchy of Lancaster and the Lord Lieutenancy of Ireland—
could there have been something more? Dissension in office
and fruitless opposition out of it before 1865, pressure of
political business after 1865, took away from Gladstone the
chance to do the work of a Turgot. But he alone of public
men, while his mind was at work on the subject, had risen to
a conception of industrial progress as a great aim of State and
social policy, to be achieved only through the wise action of
government, and he moved to an almost callous optimism
through a massive and compassionate understanding of the
far-reaching elevating effects of industry.

His practice, as it was, was full of parentheses, full stops, and
contradictions. In 1843 he established a central employment

[295] Gladstone to Cobden, 3 December 1859: B.M. Add. mss. 44,135,
f. 75.
[296] Selected Speeches, ed. A. T. Bassett (1916), 343: speech on taxation
of charities, 4 May 1863.
[297] Wilberforce's Diary, 13 October 1857: A. R. Ashwell and R. G.
Wilberforce, Life of the Rt. Rev. Samuel Wilberforce, D.D., with selec-
tions from his diaries and correspondence (1881), II, 349.

office for the London dockers, hitherto debt slaves to the publicans: on one occasion he attended a coal whipper's meeting in Shadwell from 6.15 p.m. to midnight.[298] He thought the merits of an Exchequer grant to hospitals were an open question,[299] and that national ownership of the railways might be 'a very great and fruitful measure . . .'[300] But when Florence Nightingale wished to advise him on Army reform, he cautioned her that his duty was to 'watch and control on the part of the Treasury, rather than to promote officially departmental reforms',[301] and he looked with horror on the State management of railways: 'I contend that under no circumstances, and for no time, however limited, ought the working of any railway in the country to pass under the direct superintendence of Government.'[302] When the question of State management of Irish railways arose in 1870–1, Gladstone was decisively against it, though Hartington, the responsible minister and no radical, thought the idea sensible. On national education, Gladstone's lack of attitude was entirely at odds with his reputation and his general conception of his work. Like most of his colleagues, he admired the Revised Code of 1862, that epitome of administrative orthodoxy, which certainly did not naturally lead on to national education. So far as he viewed the question at all, it was from the point of view of the Church and the Exchequer, to neither of which could national education appear attractive. The Treasury grant to education indeed fell from about £800,000 to about £600,000 between 1861 and 1865.[303] But even so his mind did not enter into the subject as it warmed, say, to his projects for the abolition of the Duchy of Lancaster. At this level, and without bad faith, the public was grossly and seriously deceived about what Gladstone, left to himself, really was. Their error did not emerge, for the public were quite right in their belief as to what Gladstone would do for them once he was in their hands. But the initial lassi-

[298] Viscount Gladstone, *After Thirty Years* (1928), 90–3.

[299] *Selected Speeches*, ed. A. T. Bassett (1916), 337: speech on charities, 4 May 1863.

[300] *Gladstone and Palmerston*, ed. P. Guedalla, 291.

[301] Sir E. Cook, *Life of Miss Nightingale* (1925 edition), 227.

[302] *Hansard*, vol. 178, col. 919, 7 April 1865.

[303] Brian Simon, *Studies in the History of Education* (1960), 346.

tude was striking: '. . . in affairs generally I follow others, Bruce for example on education, and wait for a breeze.'[304] Even loyal colleagues had to admit it: '. . . Mr. Bruce said that there was only one subject on which Uncle William [Gladstone] did not seem well up and interested, viz. National Education: A large one.'[305] Age and knowledge only increased his distaste for this part of his labours. A reliable record states that Gladstone 'regarded the Board School as a most unsatisfactory solution of the problem of popular education',[306] while a much less reliable witness, the royal journal, noted that Gladstone 'entirely agreed that it [education] ruined the health of the upper classes uselessly, and rendered the working classes unfitted for good servants and labourers'.[307]

Yet in politics it is consequences that matter, not attitudes, and in particular not retrospective attitudes. And close study[308] of the working of the Bill of 1870 through the Cabinet shows that the educational consequences of Gladstone's drive towards reaching conclusions, towards making the machinery of government work, were decisive. His contribution was much larger than Morley suggests. Gladstone made the key appointments of denominationalists which made a moderate solution possible. He started the wheels of legislation moving by asking Ripon to prepare a Bill on 2 October 1869, a week before Forster's diary mentioned the subject. He worked closely with Forster and Ripon in preparing the Cabinet papers in accordance with which the Bill was drawn up, and in the December and January Cabinets he backed Forster's desire for a Bill in the coming session. This was certainly bold and generous on his part, considering the demands on Parliamentary time and party management which were bound to be made by the Irish Land Bill, then his main preoccupation. Probably he made some calculation that

[304] Gladstone to Russell, 2 November 1867: Gooch, *Later Letters of Earl Russell*, II, 363.

[305] J. Bailey, ed., *The Diary of Lady Frederic Cavendish* (1927), II, 67: entry of 20 March 1869.

[306] C. R. L. Fletcher, *Mr. Gladstone at Oxford, 1890* (1908), 42.

[307] F. Hardie, *The Political Influence of Queen Victoria 1861–1901* (1938), 139.

[308] David Roland, *The Struggle for the Elementary Education Act and its Implementation, 1870–1873, passim*: Oxford M. Litt. thesis.

an early solution would give the best terms the denominational schools could get, but in general the Education Act passed in 1870, in very difficult parliamentary circumstances, because of Gladstone's especial commitment to the strenuous prosecution of government business, not because he was keenly interested in teaching children to read.

*   *   *

On the Reform issue in the 1860's there was the same divergence as on the education question, between the public view of Gladstone, his own view of his part in the matter, and what he actually did. The *obiter dicta* of the later Gladstone were stiffly unprogressive. He described himself as an 'out-and-out inequalitarian'. He thought a wide franchise was not an advantage to the cause of reform, and that the real reforms of 1830–80 would all have been carried by the unreformed House of Commons.[309] He also held that Catholic Emancipation would never have passed through a reformed Parliament. But *obiter dicta* of a retrospective sort establish little, whatever their insight.

In the 1860's Gladstone impinged on Reform at three levels. First, there were his well-publicized bouts of democratic inflammation, surrounded by rather more significant periods of *détente* which excited little attention. Second, there was his actual handling of the question in the party counsels and in Parliament, where a different pattern of intention and motives was apparent. Third, and probably most important, was the public misconstruction of what he was about. In the event his nature had to imitate his hagiography, but at the time the discrepancy was rather large.

In 1862–4 he importuned public opinion on behalf of Reform (unaccompanied by any attempt in party counsels to make it palpable) on two sorts of ground—the personal commitment to a good statistical case and to the effective completion of Parliamentary business, and the party consideration that a Conservative minority government might come in and either steal the Reform card from the Whigs, or else handle the Bill in a scandalous way. After August 1865, with a Commons majority increased to eighty and no pledge to

[309] C. R. L. Fletcher, op. cit., *passim*.

Reform like that of 1859, Gladstone clearly did not fight in Cabinet for an early Reform Bill. The gossip in December was that 'Gladstone talks Conservatism and sneers at Lord Russell . . .' Between August 1865 and the time when his Bill ran into difficulties in the Commons in the following spring, Gladstone remained successfully on the fence, as did most of the Cabinet. His exasperated commitment to Reform in the second quarter of 1866 was that of an untried party leader fighting for his hold over the House and the party. The question for him as for many rebels, was his personal acceptability as leader, as much as Reform itself. After the climax of June 1866, Gladstone carefully mended the fences he had broken in a democratic stampede which had lasted barely two months. Not only did he not repeat his appeal to the public at Liverpool of April 1866, but he spent a long autumn holiday in Rome, where there were several other Liberal ministers, while England was turning itself upside down. The democratic excess of the Baines speech of 1864 and of the spring speeches of 1866 were both isolated incidents tailored, in the first case, to the imminent probability of the Conservatives coming in over the Danish question; in the second case, to the need to drum up outside support to beat down opposition to his position as leader in the Commons. From June 1866 till the time in 1867 when it became apparent that the democratic side was after all the right one to have been on, Gladstone assiduously planted in the minds of his interlocutors a sense of his malice towards Bright, Disraeli, and democracy. His perception of Bright's virtues corresponded exactly to the latter's importance for his and Liberal Party strategy. Before the 1865 election, when the context was economy, Bright was an intimate counsellor. After mid-1867, when the context was the coming election on the new franchise, Bright was accepted without delay into the ruling circle of the party. But between August 1865 and mid-1867 there is a nice distinction between the Gladstone who used Bright as a trusted lieutenant in the House, and the Gladstone who planted barbs in him in private conversation. Gladstone began his withdrawal with a published letter in August 1866:

I do not agree with the demand either for manhood or for

household suffrage: while I own with regret that the conduct of the opponents of the Government measure of this
year has done much to encourage that demand, which, but
for such opposition, would scarcely have been heard of.[310]

For almost a year, Gladstone at least had the ground prepared for consolidating his position as a moderate standing
out against agitation and opportunism. He told Lowe in
February 1867 of his alarm at the idea of household suffrage
and thought it an evil day when such a thing was proposed by
the Government. He told Elcho in March that the lowest
orders were unfitted to exercise even a share of political
power. Gladstone distinguished between Bright out of doors
and indoors—'he had no sympathy whatever with him out of
doors, but thought on this question he had been fair and
moderate indoors'—as he had accepted the Bill of last year.
Selborne stated that Gladstone would have been ready to
oppose Disraeli's Bill as a whole, if he could have overcome
the reluctance of his followers.[311] Gladstone's richly am-
biguous position in 1867 could pay off in three ways. First, if
for any reason the Conservative Bill had to be shelved, as
appeared likely till the end, Gladstone could come before a
Palmerstonian electorate and House of Commons to claim
Palmerston's legacy of the moderate centre. Secondly, his attitude to Disraeli's Bill in 1867, which to the right and centre
could be made to mean that he was a guardian of order,
should an anti-Reform closing of ranks follow the failure of
the Bill, could equally be explained to the Radicals on exactly
the opposite grounds. The crux here was a Morton's fork
about the payment of rates. If Disraeli enfranchised only
those who paid rates directly, then he enfranchised only an
arbitrary few. But if he abolished the compound payment of
rates, then he landed great numbers of the urban poor, who
had not paid rates before and who were in no position to find
the relatively large sums involved, in great misery. An enormous number of cases of distraint of the goods of poor people
did, in fact, follow the Bill. Hence Liberal moderates were

---

[310] Gladstone to W. Horsfall, 8 August 1866, in W. E. Gladstone,
Reform Speeches in 1866 (1866), 309.
[311] Cited by Morley, *Gladstone* (1901), II, 232.

able to challenge Disraeli's proposals for enfranchisement without necessarily challenging their Radical wing. The final contingency, of a permanent change to a more democratic political climate, had been so fully insured against by Gladstone in his reform speeches of 1864 and spring 1866, that he was free to pursue unrelated or opposed courses of action with impunity. Gladstone, having secured from the start that if the democracy came to a share of power, they would know what they were meant to know about him, then showed that his main preoccupation was not to change the unreformed system of politics, but to establish his position in it.

* * *

Gladstone did not give to the pursuit of public esteem, that systematic and lifelong attention which he devoted to his official, Parliamentary, and scholarly cares and to acts of private service. He conceived political life chiefly in terms of Parliamentary party. He never went more than half way to meet the Liberal rank and file. It was a public mischief, he said, to look beyond the walls of Parliament for the influences that were to determine legislation.[312] But Gladstone's position out of doors, little cultivated as it was in comparison with the daily burden of his other interests, was his greatest source of strength, not least because of the change it wrought in him.

Gladstone ruled Parliament through the electorate. He was a minister given by the people to the party. 'Your hold over the country is a very different thing from your hold over the present House of Commons.'[313] 'Gladstone exercises such a sway over the constituencies, that the members are afraid to call their souls their own.'[314] Before his fiftieth year, there were few signs of popular ascendancy in his career; after 1859, Gladstone became associated, in the space of a few years, with the conflicting aims of half the great interests of the country.

[312] Gladstone to Russell, 8 June 1867: Russell Papers, P.R.O. 30/22/16.
[313] Argyll to Gladstone, 3 February 1868: Argyll, *Memoirs* (1906), II, 241.
[314] Argyll to Goschen, n.d. 1881: P. Colson, ed., *Lord Goschen and His Friends*, 83.

He stood at once for the serious aristocracy, the High Church-men, the industrialists, the cheap press and radical agitation, the provincial towns, Dissent, and the working class. So quickly did he evolve, that differing impressions of him, mutually exclusive in the long run, but all favourable, were co-existent in the minds of great classes, and Gladstone obtained that support of the general interest he looked for, from a party which was a confederation of all classes, each acting in their own interests. By the velocity of his evolution towards many-sidedness, he temporarily squared the political circle.

Gladstone's public character up to 1859 was still simple. He was the *vir pietate gravis* of the Oxford High and Broad Churchmen, and the budgetary virtuoso of the politically skilled and earnest section of the aristocracy. Hard reasoning, scholarly aristocrats like Argyll, Carlisle, and Granville, were the people who most fully appreciated the merits of Gladstone's finance: [315] for his successes, useful to them politically, were successes for the qualities they most valued in themselves. He was appalled by frivolity, and frivolity was appalled by him. A great Whig lady compared him with Peel for parvenuism:

> . . . something in the tone of his voice and his way of coming into the room that is not aristocratic. In short, he is not frivolous enough for me: if he were soaked in boiling water . . . I do not suppose a single drop of fun would ooze out.[316]

And easy-going men like Clarendon would poke fun at 'our Jesuit' and his 'benevolent nocturnal rambles'.[317] Thus, before 1859, Gladstone was cut off from wide popularity among the Parliamentary class by stiffness and political isolation, and his only source of support was the approbation of an exclusive few, and the votes of the resident electors of the

---

[315] See Argyll, *Memoirs*, I, 418–35, and II, 155. Carlisle wrote: 'How I envy those who heard G.'

[316] Miss Emily Eden to Clarendon, n.d. 1860: Maxwell, *Life of Clarendon*, II, 224.

[317] Clarendon to the Duchess of Manchester, 6 February 1860: *My Dear Duchess*, ed. A. L. Kennedy (1956), 90.

University.[318] Owing to ancient and strict tradition that a University candidate must maintain silence in word and in print during election campaigns, Gladstone was not even able to issue an election address in the years 1847–65. It was an apparently incurable case of political introversion.

Five years later Gladstone wrote, 'I am become for the first time a popular character. As far as I feel justified in appropriating and enjoying any of this popularity, it is on account of what I did, or prevented from being done, in 1859–1861 . . .'[319] That is, Gladstone first became popular with the industrialists and with the provincial press, and through the excitement of his contacts with them on what were basically pocket questions, he moved on to the wider popularity of a Dissenting and a working-class hero.

When Gladstone visited Manchester Exchange, he was received with 'loud and repeated cheering'.[320] His popularity in Middlesbrough, the Potteries, and the West Riding was equally founded on the hearty good will of the employers. As the member for Bradford said on behalf of his constituents, Bradford was in a more flourishing state than ever previously, and the French Treaty caused a great part of that prosperity. Similarly, a Bradford ironmaster wrote, after hearing the Budget of 1860: 'Gladstone was grand last night . . .'[321] Gladstone was not asked, but pestered, to stand for industrial constituencies: South Lancashire wanted him in 1861 and subsequently, Leeds asked for him in 1864.[322]

Gladstone was good for trade, but he was good for the provincial press in a quite special degree. For that press, closely tied to Radicalism, owed, not a little more or less of trade, but its very existence to Gladstone's paper duties. When Gladstone visited Newcastle in 1862, the arrangements were formally in the hands of the old Liberal oligarchy, but the

---

[318] For the Oxford University election of 1865, see Noble, *Reformers' Manual* (1883), 30, and J. Campbell, in *Oxford Magazine*, 9 November 1961. The resident dons were for Gladstone by two to one, and his defeat was due, not to a change of opinion in the University, but to new legislation enabling country clergy to vote by post.

[319] Gladstone to A. H. Gordon, n.d. 1864: B.M. Add. mss. 44,320, f. 44.

[320] *Manchester Examiner*, 23 April 1862.

[321] F. W. Wickham to Wilson, 11 February 1860: Wilson Papers.

[322] Letter by W. Rathbone, 5 June 1864: Rathbone Papers.

excitement was stirred up by the Radical party under Cowen, the owner of the penny daily, the *Newcastle Chronicle*, and by Holyoake, who wrote a series of eulogies of Gladstone in that paper. The word passed from the newspaper to the workmen, Holyoake said later, and they

> came out to greet the only English minister who ever gave the people right because it was just they should have it . . . Without him a Free Press in England was impossible . . . If not the first Chancellor of the Exchequer with a conscience, he was the first who was known to have one, and when he went down the Tyne, all the country heard how 20 miles of banks were lined with people who came to greet him.[323]

For a statesman to form connections with the provincial employers and the new cheap press, meant sooner or later entering into relations with militant Dissent and with the Reform movement. But there was an intermediate stage, in which Gladstone formed liaisons with provincial towns as corporate entities. In Stoke and in Newcastle, he was more than the patron of editors and industrialists, he was simply a friend of the town. Almost anyone would have filled the role, for these proud, isolated towns trembling on the verge of civic and ceremonial life, were bound to respond in excess to any kindly interest taken in them by a celebrity.[324] Ovations were ends in themselves, and the life of a place like Stoke offered few pretexts for junketings. But Gladstone, utterly strange and marvellous, filled the role supremely well. He had pondered well the doctrine of classes and State which he now fitted to the ritual of the provincial great occasion: it was the only doctrine which could meet the needs of the occasion, and nourish and sustain an intense sensation of good will. These occasions, not overtly political, contained in their very arrangements a kind of liturgical equivalent of Gladstonian political theory.

Gladstone was all his life reluctant to admit his creation

---

[323] G. J. Holyoake, *The Liberal Situation* (1865), 29.

[324] Since Newcastle also invited Cobden, Russell, and Palmerston to receive its civic good will, precise shades of Liberal politics cannot have been very important there.

of popular democracy. He tried to go on believing that Parliament was all the world:

> Throughout my public life, until the Eastern question arose, I never, except in explanation to constituents, pursued Parliamentary action, except within the walls of Parliament. It [his Eastern question agitation] was a thing that had rarely been done before, and which I hope will rarely have occasion to be done again.[325]

Gladstone did indeed take pains to cover himself against imputations of demagogy:

> I am not going to the North on an economical crusade. . . . This dinner affair [at Newcastle] has risen in a great degree out of the French Treaty. It came to me through, and was recommended by, Headlam and Hutt; and Brand concurred in their view.[326]

Gladstone, his son argued, no doubt rightly, did less 'stumping' in his election campaigns of 1868 and 1880 than the average candidate in a county division was expected to do. In 1865 and 1874 he carried on no real campaign at all. Even judged by the strict old standards, he did not formally misbehave or innovate.[327] But of course, for a man like Gladstone to make 'explanations to his constituents', even in the old way, was bound to be an innovation in an age of great meetings, cheap daily newspapers, and impending political changes. His speeches were, on the one hand, a great step in themselves towards popular democracy, while on the other hand they were far too few to lend support to accusations of ambition. So obviously was the platform the way to power, so few were the competitors, and so great was Gladstone's mastery of its use, that had he really been ambitious, he would never have kept to so limited a programme. In 1861 and 1863, he made no outdoor speeches. In 1864, he spoke less often

---

[325] Leech, *Life of Gladstone* (1893), 145.
[326] *Gladstone and Palmerston*, ed. P. Guedalla, 236.
[327] '. . . I have never been as a stranger into a County, and do not like the precedent.'—Gladstone to Granville, 26 March 1880: *Pol. Corr. of Gladstone and Granville, 1876–86*, ed. A. Ramm (1962), I, 116. See ibid., II, 455, for the references to Gladstone's stumping in 1886.

than Palmerston. He did not speak in the West Riding before 1871, in Birmingham before 1876, or in Wales before 1870. His topics were innocuous, his views studiously moderate. He trod the road to popular power with innocent and casual dilettantism, not incompetently certainly, but quite without his usual passion for fullness of achievement.

Gladstone had to overcome no obstacle in dealing with the employers, the press, and the Reformers, such as his High Churchmanship was when faced with Dissent. Political Reform, from 1858 onwards, he took as a matter of course, but his change of opinion on church rates and the Irish Church was delayed till 1862 or later. When he stood for Lancashire, a leading Rochdale Liberal wrote: 'Under any circumstances it will be difficult to carry him, because his opinions on Church Rates will prevent many Dissenters supporting him . . .'[328] Difficulties persisted. Gladstone, agreeing with Bright and Russell that distribution and concurrent endowment was a better Irish policy than the one eventually adopted, nevertheless had to give way to Dissenting *force majeure*.[329] Education controversies reopened the gap, which was eventually closed by the least attractive of Gladstone's coups, the publication of his pamphlets attacking Rome. Those parts of Dissent who had been aloof hitherto on religious grounds, now found they had a Daniel amongst them:

> I shall esteem it a high privilege to meet the Great Gladstone, of whom I have read and heard so much—the Gladstone who has fixed a thorn in the side of Pio Nono, which is affecting the hearts of millions and will continue to fester, till Babylon be thrown down and be no more found at all. . . .[330]

Heartened in mutual esteem by this English version of anti-Semitism, Gladstone and Dissent were never again parted. They discovered common social pleasures:

[328] W. Fenton to Wilson, 17 June 1865: Wilson Papers.

[329] See, for evidence of Gladstone's personal preference, Gooch, *Later Letters of Earl Russell*, II, 366, and W. E. Williams, *The Rise of Gladstone, 1859–1868*, 163.

[330] Dr Robert Moffat, missionary, to Newman Hall, 6 February 1874: Hall, *Autobiography* (1901), 210.

For two hours we discussed Papal decrees and Disestablishment . . . [Gladstone] then asked that as on a former
occasion, we might have a hymn together. He heartily
joined in singing four verses of 'Sun of my Soul'. Then we
had supper and general conversation,[331]

wrote a Free Church minister of one evening party given for
Dissenting industrialists, M.P.s, and clergy.

The Nonconformists came late to the fold, and on predictable grounds. It was the working-class support given to Gladstone from the early 1860's that alone gave him the character
of a folk myth. Its irrationality was perhaps shown by his
cult being strongest among the country workers who must
have known least of him, the books of Joseph Arch and Flora
Thompson and the biography of Joseph Ashby of Tysoe
giving a good idea of what he meant to the peasantry. He
embodied the hope of ultimate justice in an immediately
oppressive world. The town workers, more politically conscious and less reliant on bush telegraph, created a figure
whom they called Gladstone and whom they invested with
their own political ideas, with all the intense unreality of a
cult. 'At a great meeting at Preston, the mere mention of
Mr. Gladstone's name is received with great applause—not so,
I think, Bright—they catch at Gladstone like light at gun-
powder.'[332] The same ardent faith in Gladstone inspired the
Hyde Park rioters and demonstrators of 1866. Beneath a
banner bearing his portrait, ran the motto: 'Gladstone and
Liberty: An Honest Man's the Noblest Work of God.'[333]
'Gladstone and Reform. Gladstone for ever: and such cries
were roared ad libitum.'[334] When Gladstone spoke words
mildly sympathetic to Reform in May 1864, such as he and
most other Liberal politicians of the day had often uttered
before, there was a most disproportionate furore. 'Chartism
itself did not assert more', said the *Star*. 'He has unfurled the

---

[331] Ibid., 210.

[332] E. Howard to G. Glyn, 22 September 1868: B.M. Add. mss. 44,347,
f. 181.

[333] *Henry Broadhurst, M.P. The Story of his Life from a Stonemason's
Bench to the Treasury Bench* (1901), 37.

[334] Lord R. S. Gower, *Records and Reminiscences* (1903), 119.

old, long-lost flag of the Liberal party', said the *Daily News*.[335] 'This is the key principle of the theory of universal suffrage, upon which, for the future, Mr. Gladstone is to act', said the *Rochdale Observer*.[336] A state of expectation clearly existed, which magnified trivialities into historic events, and it existed independently of any effort on the part of Gladstone. Nothing he had said or done, however admirable, could fully account for this address of the York working men to Gladstone after his Reform speech of 1864:

> You have spoken words that have sunk deep into the hearts of every working man in every corner of the land. We thank you from our inmost souls. We look upon you as a powerful and consistent advocate of our cause, and may God long preserve your life. That you may continue to be the sound and impartial statesman—the friend of the poor, seeking simple justice to all—is the fervent wish and desire of the working men of this ancient city.[337]

There was a rather chilling want of reciprocity in Gladstone's comment on his reply to this address: 'My desire was simply to frame that answer so as to discourage a repetition of like addresses elsewhere . . .'[338] Gladstone practised no deception, but many were grossly deceived, when they assumed that Gladstone's conscientiousness implied agreement with their own notions.

*   *   *

In stripping the State and, to a lesser extent, the Liberal Party, of the marks of class, and attempting to form them into organs of the general interest, Gladstone revealed a certain bareness of ideas, not only in himself but in his age, as to what that general interest was. All the promise of his elevated notions of party and his imaginative understanding of what industrial progress meant in terms of human happiness, required to be consummated in appropriate lines of

---

[335] Quoted in Masheder, *The Rt. Hon. W. E. Gladstone* (2nd edition, 1865), 177.

[336] *Rochdale Observer*, 14 May 1864.

[337] *Manchester Examiner*, 9 June 1864.

[338] *Gladstone and Palmerston*, ed. P. Guedalla, 289.

policy. These were lacking. The State was taught justice in details, not in mass. Taxation continued to redistribute wealth in favour of the rich. In foreign policy, England was committed to metaphysical wars, not in the name of the Balance of Power, but of the Public Law of Europe. In education, the approach of the Liberal High Command was extremely oblique. Even with a sparing use of the discipline of public opinion, Gladstone was able to elevate and render rational the conduct of public life to a remarkable degree, but the great political opportunity thus created fell on stony ground. Gladstone's creation of a high-minded democracy did not lead to changes in public policy comparable to the revolution he caused in rhetoric and public expectations.

4 Policy

Policy

No part of Victorian history is more documented or less investigated than that dealing with the formation of policy within the Cabinet and within the departments. What was physically one of the smallest departments of government in the 1860's, the Privy Council Office, has by itself inspired one commanding book,[1] and the work of the Emigration Department of the Board of Trade has served as text for another,[2] yet for the time being these monographs stand almost alone. It is therefore inevitable on these grounds alone that the following sketches of the relation between State policy and the Liberal Party should lack authority. Another difficulty is more than historiographical. It is that the functions of the Liberal Party did not include the discussion and formulation of policy, outside a few issues like Church rates, the Volunteers, or the Museums, in which the rights of a few militants to share in policy-making within a chosen area were admitted. There was, of course, no machinery of party conference or party meetings, though this was compensated for by the amount of time of the House which was at the disposal of private members. This lack of machinery applied also to the Cabinet, which made little use of committees and confined those it had to *ad hoc* terms of reference. But there was more to the lack of discussion than lack of machinery. On a great number of topics, members were not interested, or, despite individual interest, there was no general party opinion. It was difficult to make a House on Indian or colonial matters, Indian budgets, for instance, being generally introduced to a deserted House at the end of July, and approved virtually without discussion.[3] Again, since it was good manners not to interfere with colleagues, there was a tradition of each department acting

[1] R. J. Lambert, *Sir John Simon 1816–1904, and English Social Administration* (1963).

[2] O. Macdonagh, *A Pattern of Government Growth 1800–60: the Passenger Acts and Their Enforcement* (1961).

[3] *Annual Register for 1864*, 134–6.

independently, and carrying out its own legislative programme. The very idea of a party programme, with its corollary of the quinquennial mandate, had no place in a Parliament-centred world. There were no programmes in the 1865 election, because there was no sense in parties or cabinets meeting to decide what they should do collectively, so long as Parliament had the power to treat each of their proposals as a separate case. Policy making as the activity of a party, in the sense of deciding what proposals to present to the public, rather than what actions to take if in office, began in 1867 when it became clear that Reform had triumphed. The Liberals reacted by gathering the leaders together, not to work out Parliamentary tactics as formerly, but to choose what policy to put to the electorate.

Before 1868, then, much or most policy originated outside the party political system, and must be considered in terms of the clannish tradition of ministers grown grey in office, of the special aims of civil servants,[4] and of fluctuations in public opinion as guided by the Press. This book has had as its theme the attachment of the Liberal rank and file to Parliamentary leaders and the Parliamentary party. To such a study in party history, State policy as it actually was, is rather peripheral, for it neither promoted the extension of Parliamentary Liberalism downwards in society—rather the reverse—nor was it greatly affected by party politics. The reforms that never came were important in Liberal Party history: those that did come were less important, and the ordinary, non-reforming continuity of policy was not important at all from the party point of view.

Only the great questions can be discussed here, and even on these, what is put forward here does not claim to be more than a general interpretation of Liberal 'psychology', and is not intended as a comprehensive record of fact. It is argued that though Liberal policy had many merits, they were not those claimed for it. Thus, though it was flexible enough to excite and satisfy democratic feelings, many Liberal sections strongly objected to 'democracy' and even the professedly democratic sections of the party nearly all, like Mill, made

---

[4] See G. Kitson Clark, 'Statesmen in Disguise: Reflections on the History of the Neutrality of the Civil Service', *Historical Journal*, II, 1 (1959), 19–39.

extensive reservations. In foreign policy, there were two changes. Instead of commercially-minded quasi-pacifism permeating the Parliamentary party from below—a process which happened on a small scale—the Whigs made great headway in establishing traditional aristocratic principles of foreign policy as the conventional wisdom of the nation as a whole. On the other hand, the balance within the Cabinet tilted towards extreme prudence in the application of the traditional ideas, giving a false impression of a change of principle. In domestic policy, the traditional Liberal trump card of virtuosity in administration is hardly borne out by the slow progress made in the fields of military reform, electoral corruption, and Civil Service patronage. On the other hand, their attitude to the condition of the people was more variously determined, less governed by *idées fixes*, than usually appears. What is in question, indeed, is less the quantity of Liberal achievement, than its internal distribution and the motives that lay behind it.

THE CONDITION OF THE PEOPLE

The force of Socialist and Conservative criticism of the Liberal Party has fallen on their attitude to the 'condition of England question'. Liberal conduct of foreign affairs, of administrative reform, and in constitutional reform, is hard to censure by their own standards except in details. But in this field of social policy, the charge made against the Liberals is clear and general: the wealth of the age did little to reduce the numbers of those in misery. The offence of the Liberals was not only to do nothing, but to claim that they were doing something. The language of Bright, Gladstone, Mill, and Samuel Morley suggested that their political justification lay in their contribution to the welfare of the poor. They spoke, in Bright's phrase, of the heart of the nation being in the cottage. Yet a look at any representative political publications such as the *Annual Register, Hansard*, or the *Parliamentary Papers*, will show that political attention was fixed chiefly on foreign affairs, finance, defence, Reform, and Church affairs.

Simply regarded as a fraction of time spent and attention given, social questions hardly entered into general politics. The contrast between the rhetorical awareness of the Liberals on the subject and their legislative performance could only excite dismay. They did not approach social questions with a sense of mission, yet their words taken at face value implied a promise to do so.

Having reached this point of the argument, it is now necessary to indicate the three main lines of exoneration. These convert a rather incredible picture of motiveless malignity into one neither damnatory nor brilliant, but more true to life. Firstly, though a sense of mission might be wanting, pedestrian common sense could be relied on to go a long way. Thus, Sir Benjamin Hall, who became President of the Board of Health in 1854 as a bitter opponent of Chadwick and centralization, was converted to the views of his inspectors, and astonished everybody by his zeal in the sanitary cause. In the life of Florence Nightingale, many cases may be found where ministers, otherwise not specially distinguished, proved themselves to be good listeners to her flow of information. Again, Dr Rogers, a reforming physician in the notorious Strand Workhouse, had nothing but praise for the Liberal ministers of the 1860's to whom he appealed.

The second line of exoneration concerns the inappropriateness of the standards of criticism used. If those who lived in an age are to be allowed any understanding of their own needs, what was wanted was not a Welfare State, or a feudal romance out of Scott and Disraeli, but legislation and administration which fell well within the self-defined scope of Liberalism. The social questions which were already in hand, had an urgency which make redistributionary measures, nowhere seriously advocated at the time, appear comparatively frivolous. The question then left, is whether the Liberal Party, measured by those high standards whose creation was a reform in itself, was an effective instrument of Liberal social reform.

The question is partly a comparative one, for an estimate of Liberal policy must depend on whether the Conservatives offered a better practical alternative. There is only room here to suggest that they did not. That Disraeli's novels show some pleasing ideas, that a group of Lancashire Conservatives actually lived up to these ideas,[5] and that Cross and Sclater-Booth carried some excellent Acts in 1874–6, is not denied. This was the best side of Tory social policy, and it is well known. What is less well known are the qualifications that have to be made, even about this best side, and how far their best side was from their average performance over a run of years. On this there is only space to refer in passing to the devious conduct of Disraeli over the Plimsoll Line;[6] the explanation given by Viscount Gladstone[7] of the derivative relation of Tory health legislation in 1874–5 to the substantive Health Acts of 1871–2; and the opposition of Disraeli to Lowe's establishment of the medical department of the Privy Council under Simon. If the Liberals were not a philanthropic organization, neither were the Tories.

What the age demanded was clear enough. The priorities were working-class literacy, some reinstatement of social control over the drink trade, the application of the simple rules of health as taught by Nightingale, Chadwick, and Simon, the application of the rules of humanity, as taught by Shaftesbury, to working conditions and housing, the decent administration of the existing Poor Law, and some relief from what was most cramping in rural life. These objects, labours of Hercules though they were in point of volume of administration, yet formed perfectly practical targets, in the sense that they were politically possible. They naturally excited sympathy, they did not offend the interests of the classes who had to enact them, and they did not grossly conflict with political economy and the other nostrums of the day. Above all, they were not expensive, and most of the costs could be, and were, put on the rates.

All these good causes concerned chiefly the welfare of the working class. Before the working class was enfranchised, these causes had little political prestige. (In the *Annual Register* for 1864, for instance, the Factory Act of that year is not mentioned in the account of the debates.) After 1867, their

---

[5] H. J. Hanham, *Elections and Party Management* (1959), 314–20.

[6] See Speaker Brand's Diaries, 11 August 1875: House of Commons Library.

[7] Viscount Gladstone, *After Thirty Years* (1929), 425–7.

political prestige and legislative prominence grew rapidly. The achievements of the Gladstonian Liberals in social policy were those of men responding to suddenly changed circumstances. Had the political situation remained unchanged, there is good reason to think that the Liberal front bench would have remained undisturbed by the social aspects of Liberalism. If ever there were peaceful sessions in which to drive through large pieces of domestic legislation, it was in the period 1861–5, and the men who failed to take that opportunity, were the same people as those who achieved so much in 1868–74.

A third line of exoneration is now indeed needed. It is that when the Liberals spoke with deep feeling on the condition of the people, their words did not bear the obvious construction: they were not talking of the kinds of social problems mentioned above, but of something quite different. Hence their deep feeling, which referred to what they felt were the moral and political forces which had built up the economy, appears in harmony with their actions, when their rhetoric is once set in the appropriate intellectual context.

The creed of both the aristocratic administrators and the radical capitalists was that nothing acted so powerfully on the condition of the people as peace, retrenchment, and free trade. By applying themselves to these issues, men like Gladstone and Bright felt themselves true philanthropists and great social reformers, without even having to consider social questions proper. The mechanisms by which free trade and economy acted on the dark places of society were not spelt out, but the simple passage of time confirmed their deep conviction that theirs was the part of social beneficence, even of social salvation. For they had truly seen a wonderful thing. Men who were growing up about 1830, who had lived to see how money could fructify in the pockets of the people, and who were nourished by memories of bad trade in the 1820's and 1840's, could look upon peace, free trade, and public economy, as though they were the whole alphabet of the social question. Consequently, even when Liberals of this generation did precious work, their approach was oblique. Such a monument as the Education Act of 1870 came more from Gladstone's majority than from his heart.

However narrow the old conception of social politics was, there was no want of zeal in the manner in which it was applied. Gladstone's budgets and legislation between 1859 and 1865 were the high water mark of one conception of social duty. For Gladstone took a very rough road unbidden. He incurred the displeasure of the banking and insurance interests, who were well represented in both parties. He had to force the Post Office Savings Banks Bill through a mutinous House of Lords. His budgets involved vulnerable deficits and conflicts with his colleagues and with the Lords which no safe politician would have faced. Finally, of course, the labour undertaken was punishing and avoidable. Gladstone's absorption in finance, though a case of the good being the enemy of the best, justified his deep belief in the beneficence of Liberalism.

For want of monographs, Cabinet attitudes on the main branches of social policy can only be stated approximately. The discussions of 1862 on Lowe's Revised Code, for instance, were not those of men who expected shortly to establish a national education system. Temperance was regarded in the light of doctrinaire libertarianism rather than in terms of social fact, Gladstone still being a 'free trade in beer' man[8] in 1872, and the Wine Licences and reduced Wine Duties of the early 1860's worked in the opposite direction. The reform of rural society, in however slight a degree, chilled the numerous landed Liberals: Parliament was still readier to pass Game Laws than to repeal them.

The least satisfactory performance was in the field of humanitarian legislation arising out of the conditions of a trade. It was not always true that when a thing was found to be intolerable it was not tolerated. Also, legislation once passed had often no effect. The main cases of grossly delayed legislation concerned chimney sweeps, coffin ships, agricultural gangs, mines inspection, and evictions for railway termini in central London. The factory acts proper, slightly extended and efficiently administered, were a standing example of what could be done.

In the administration of the Poor Law and in the related field of public health, ministers acted alertly, but were held

[8] Morley, *Gladstone* (1903), II, 390.

back by the nature of the local bodies they had to deal with. Much waited on the creation of a full system of local government which could administer what was already agreed on. In the medical department of the Privy Council, Simon continued and extended a great tradition, and the responsible ministers were well regarded by their officials and by reformers. But they presided over a system which included the Wapping Workhouse of *The Uncommercial Traveller* and the Strand Workhouse with which Dr Rogers was connected. There was a contrast between the steady progress of the Metropolitan Board of Works in creating modern London, and the slight impression that even the best-intentioned ministers could make on the system they were supposed to control.

In general, then, the intellectual context in which ministers thought, and the political situation in Parliament before the Reform Bill, were socially unfruitful; but within the departments, there was steady and laborious progress. Even when there was an apparent reverse, as when the opponents of Chadwick gained the upper hand, the pressure of the officials and of circumstances prevented retrogression. Though some of their best legislation, for instance on liquor licensing and education, was rather a forced improvisation than an expression of inward thought, it was hard enough for ministers to do even as much as they did. Many of the faults were not the faults of a party but of the general thought of the country, yet even so there were many cases where power and will were joined to produce no legislative result. But it must be remembered that it was largely the political education of the public by the Liberals of the 1860's, which produced those high expectations by which they have since been judged.

PEACE AND WAR

This is not the place to deal with the technical questions of execution, which make up most of the history of foreign policy. Differences about facts and tactics were legion; but the number of possible general ideas about foreign policy was necessarily limited. It is these general ideas about peace and war, empire and trade, balance of power and the Concept of Europe, that are discussed here. In a study in party history such as this, two questions are important. The first concerns permeation from below: how did the absorption of new social groups into the Liberal Party and the extension of the electorate affect the broad aims of foreign policy? The second concerns political instruction given from above: did the 'rules of thumb' used by ministers change, so that they moved towards a policy of non-intervention independently of outside pressure? What is suggested below is that in the 1860's two contradictory patterns were superimposed. On the one hand, power within the Cabinet passed into the hands of a cautious set of junior ministers, who curbed the three Liberal leaders in times of crisis. This change, the product of reflection on the Crimean War and of growing doubts about the national defences, was often taken to be something more than a single change from hot to cold in the temper of Cabinet personnel. On the other hand, the middle class, far from permeating the party with the 'peace views' once endemic in it, was itself permeated by the old aristocratic orthodoxy, the 'rules for national safety handed down from Pitt and Chatham'. To support the Parliamentary Liberals meant eventually coming to support the nation-state and its interests; and this meant coming to see things as the great tradition saw them. A timely change within the Cabinet, which had nothing to do with the public and little to do with Gladstone, preserved the essentials of the tradition—Belgian independence, the integrity of Turkey, the security of the route to the East, the general balance in Europe, the avoidance of territorial empire, and commercial supremacy in Africa and China—while shutting the door firmly against more adventures and against the extravagant Palmerstonian interpretation of the tradition. Here began the work of bowdlerizing foreign policy in order to make it an extension of the domestic morality of the public, which was continued in the Alabama arbitration and in the Midlothian campaign. In the 1860's this process had not started even on the Liberal side, because the House of Commons was still the primary field of political action, and its members were generally not men to be shocked by power politics. Between the humanitarian virtues of the home and the economical virtues of business, and the usages of international relations, there was really no relation, and it had not yet occurred to politicians in the 1860's to try to make one. Henry Richard's motion for international arbitration in 1870 was greeted by Gladstone in much the same way as Palmerston had treated Cobden's motion on the subject in 1848. Perhaps, as Gladstone said, the ideal of his life in foreign policy had always been 'the working of the European Concert for purposes of justice, peace and liberty, with efficiency and success',[9] but the transformation of this inward thought into a mystique, humanitarian, and almost pacifist in overtones, that could be put before the serious public did not occur in his popular campaigns in the 1860's.

Liberal opinions on foreign policy ranged from aggressive chauvinism to pacifism: the Tories under Disraeli were the party of sobriety and the golden mean. It was certainly not foreign policy that brought together the Liberal Party. When Samuel Morley organized an economy motion in 1861 signed by fifty-one Liberal M.P.s, Palmerston, attributing it to 'that dangerous lunatic Cobden', added that the true meaning of the motion was 'that we should cease to be an influential Power in the World, that Spain should have Morocco, France Egypt, Syria, and the Rhine, Russia Constantinople and European Turkey, and that our commerce should be shut out from the Mediterranean. That we should hold our existence as a nation at the good will of France and Russia . . .'[10]

In short, there was much disagreement, and the attitudes of the 'economical' Radicals led the old school in the Cabinet —Palmerston, Russell, Clarendon, and often Gladstone—to regard the public as a millstone. For instance:

It would be difficult to convey to you in a letter how strong the peace feeling is in this country, and how very unpopular the Persian War is with all classes . . . the British

[9] Gladstone to his wife, 10 October 1880: *Gladstone to his Wife*, ed. Bassett (1936), 232.
[10] Palmerston to Brand, 15 January 1861: Brand Papers, Letter No. 7.

public are not aware how necessary it is to keep a tight
hand upon a people so false and wayward as the Per-
sians . . .[11]

In short, the participation of the public in the making of
foreign policy, or even their support, was hardly canvassed
because they were presumed to be hostile, wrong, or ignorant.

Within the Cabinet was where the decisions were made.
The parties were not of left and right, or Peelites and
Whigs, but between the three senior ministers, Gladstone,
Palmerston, and Russell, and most of the others. (For instance, Gladstone got on famously with Granville, a Whig,
but was opposed tooth and claw by Cardwell, a Peelite, on
all questions of economy.) Palmerston put this clearly:

> You say that with a less timid Cabinet, we might probably
> have kept Austria quiet in the Danish affair. Perhaps we
> might . . . As to Cabinets, if we had colleagues like those
> who sat in Pitt's Cabinet such as Westmoreland and others,
> or such even as those who were with Peel, like Goulburn
> and Hardinge, you and I might have had our way on most
> things: but when as is now the case, able men fill every
> Department, such men will have opinions and hold to
> them, but unfortunately they are often too busy with their
> own Departments to follow up foreign questions so as to be
> fully masters of them, and their conclusions are generally
> on the timid side of what might be best.[12]

The junior Cabinet ministers did in fact overrule the three
leaders in European and American crises, but their behaviour
in Chinese and Japanese questions showed that they were
acting less as moral reformers than as prudential ones. The
memory of the 1857 election deterred opposition to continued
war in China and naval bombardments in Japan. There was
a growing doubt as to how far England could 'play her part'
in the European system, but there was little objection to
power politics in the East.

[11] Clarendon to Mr C. Murray, 13 March 1857: Clarendon Deposit,
C. 138.
[12] Palmerston to Russell, 11 September 1864: Palmerston mss., ' Private Letter Book 1862'.

The changes in the structure of the Liberal Party in the 1860's brought Parliamentary leaders into contact with groups which, though not always pacifist, traditionally had regarded peace both with a Utopian reverence, and as a peculiar interest of their class. Their refusal to accept the self-interest of the nation state as of overriding importance was best expressed by Cobden and Bright. It was always a tradition of minorities and *élites*, of Nonconformity, of those who had fallen foul of the main national traditions in some other way as well. Torn between 'virtuous passion' and pacifism, orthodox respectability and Bible Christianity, the Radical tradition in foreign policy was absorbed by less absolute solutions. The ascendancy of caution within the Cabinet allowed many who had opposed Palmerstonian orthodoxy, to accept a prudent version of the same principles, while those still unreconciled, found in the popular cry of economy an easy way of avoiding real disagreement.

DEMOCRACY

No appreciable section of the Parliamentary Liberal Party believed in numerical democracy in the modern sense without serious qualifications. Nevertheless a large part of the party was genuinely anxious to enfranchise the upper part of the working class. The controversy, too, was conducted on the wrong ground, for the redistribution of seats affected class strength in Parliament far more than the level of the franchise, and this point was extremely difficult to 'get across' to a mass audience. The whole emotional interest of the Reform agitation centred in the level of the English borough franchise, but the chief consequence of the reduction of this, was simply to give the M.P.s for the great cities and industrial towns more voters to manage. It did not affect the kind of man elected, except in the special cases of the Tory gains in London and Lancashire.

What one might expect would be that, according to the normal variations in opinion, some Liberals would be cheerful and unflinching democrats, just as others were averse to any concession. But those opposed to substantial change were far more numerous than those who actually rebelled against the Liberal Bill of 1866, the 'Adullamites'. The position of the Whigs is probably summed up by the biographer of de Grey:

> He did not conceal his alarm, though party loyalty and a shrewd feeling that the Moderates should keep in touch with the Extremists if the unbound Demos was to be safely guided, imposed upon him a tactful reticence. He only spoke once upon the Reform Bill . . .[13]

The official corps of Whigs placed considerations of leverage far above their own misgivings. They were explicit about their braking role:

> I believe myself to be a Constitutional Liberal opposed to the violent doctrines which Bright and his organs when agitating for Reform propound. . . . Depend upon it, the more moderate Liberals separate themselves from their party, the stronger will eventually be the Radicals.[14]

But it was not only the Whigs, but the party as a whole, including the chief proponents of Reform, who wished to stop far short of democracy. The attitude of the Liberal middle classes in the towns cannot be established from the size of the middle-class audiences at Bright's meetings. Many of the rich industrialists who had supported the Anti-Corn Law League felt that things were going too far by 1860. A full canvass in Leeds in 1865 showed the Liberal electors voted despite, not because of, the party's support of Reform. Granville, visiting thirty principal Liberals in Manchester in 1867, found them 'frightened out of their wits at the borough franchise'[15] and saying the power of the middle class had gone. Behind the rhetoric of brotherhood, the chief reformers knew that there were many technicalities that could be used as safeguards, which greatly diminished the value of their promises. The

[13] L. Wolf, *Life of the First Marquess of Ripon* (1921), I, 222.
[14] Spencer to Elcho, 21 January 1867, refusing an invitation to lead the Adullamites in the Lords.
[15] Granville to Gladstone, 7 September 1867, B.M. Add. mss. 44,165, f. 142.

movement of voters from one address to another,[16] local differences in the methods of payment of rates, and the revision of
boundaries could all be used to produce a 'safe' result. The
result which the Liberal Reformers were aiming at with their
£6 franchise was stated by Edward Baines:

> At present, therefore, only one in five of the male adult
> population in the boroughs has a vote; and the measure
> which I would submit would increase the voters to about
> 1 in 3 of the male adults. Two thirds of the population . . .
> would still remain without the franchise . . .
>
> The proportion which the working class voters would
> bear to the middle and upper classes in the boroughs, if the
> measure I ask you to grant is adopted, would I believe be
> between 1 in 4 and 1 in 3. The upper and middle class
> would still constitute two thirds of the voters in the
> boroughs . . .[17]

This carefully calculated minimum concession represented
fairly well the basis on which the 'convinced Reformers', as
contemporaries saw them, were working. Brand, the Liberal
Whip, Bright, Baines, Mill, and Gladstone all had in mind
some measure of this limited nature. Gladstone and Bright
were to some extent playing a double game when they combined the most highly coloured language with the careful
study of statistics proving the mildness of their aims. In short,
the leading Liberal Reformers were politicians, not democrats. They had indeed a genuine regard for the serious upper
working class, the enfranchised part of which had always been
so electorally important to the Liberals, and they had a good
case for thinking that except for this labour aristocracy,
labour generally was too socially and economically dependent and too corrupt and ignorant to vote. Elections, after all,
meant beer, brawls, and bribery. The Liberal Reformers,
who represented perhaps a minority of Liberal M.P.s, but a
majority of the active Liberals in the boroughs, acted in good

[16] ' Probably one fifth of our voters move from one Ward to another
during the year.'—Chamberlain to Dilke, 14 December 1884, Chamberlain mss., unsorted.

[17] *Speech of Edward Baines on the Borough Franchise Bill, 11 May
1864* (pamphlet), 11.

faith towards the working class, but they were not strong enough to carry the party except with a strong lead from within the Cabinet. They were unable to make the 1865 election turn on Reform:

> This might be necessary if the dissolution had turned on a question of Reform, or if any strong opinion for Reform had been expressed Universally at the elections: but the elections had nothing whatever to do with Reform. At all events it is not for us to begin an agitation . . .[18]

The great debate on democracy in England took place essentially over a minor point, almost an unreal one from the point of view of power—whether Radical M.P.s in the great towns should have more Radical voters to manage. The contest was between two sections of the Liberal Party, much alike in their general attachment to the *status quo* and in the distance at which both sides stood from numerical democracy. More striking even than the guarded proposals made by the Liberal Reformers, was the emptiness of their arguments. The vote was discussed chiefly as a kind of personal reward or certificate of good character, never as an instrument for changing the social condition of the people. The chief democratic argument, that those who wear the shoe know best where it pinches and must be given power to act in their own interest, was as conspicuously absent as were democratic proposals.

[18] Palmerston to Brand, 3 August 1865: Palmerston mss., unsorted.

5 Conclusion

Conclusion

The problem uniting this work has been the creation and extension of popular Liberalism outside Parliament, yet in firm attachment to the Parliamentary Liberal Party and leadership. Though the Parliamentary Liberals remained socially and denominationally unrepresentative of their supporters, and though the Liberalism of the Executive was guided more by a desire to move forward in a well-established tradition of administrative progress, rather than by love for the novelties of popular Liberalism, there was however a sudden change in the structure of extra-Parliamentary politics. In the 1860's, the new cheap Press, militant Dissent in its various forms, and organized labour, joined to form the pillars of a popular party. At the same time Gladstone ratified their emergence, by placing himself in a relation to popular feeling quite new in a minister. His mastery over great audiences enabled him to capture and tame a formidable Radical front for the benefit of the basically aristocratic Parliamentary party. This was done at the price of creating an expectation that the Liberal Party was a philanthropic body, an idea which was hard to live up to. Gladstone's possible rivals for leadership, Russell, Palmerston, Cobden, Mill, and Bright, were either *hors de combat,* willing evangelists for Gladstone, or not willing to go before the public as he was. Oratory apart, Gladstone did not so much create the circumstances of the 1860's, as make good administrative use of the opportunities given by popular support, to reassert the authority of the State over Parliament.

The unification of the Parliamentary Liberals by Palmerston, the building up of a Radical front behind Bright, and the convergence of popular and Parliamentary Liberalism under the spell of Gladstone, were all achievements in the realm of sentiment. The national party, as it began in the 1860's, was not an organization, but a habit of co-operation and a community of sentiment. The few distinct groups within the party were small and not necessarily troublesome.

The majority of Liberal M.P.s were men of good position whose common Liberalism amounted to little more than a common good nature. The party was a coalition of convenience, not the instrument of a creed, and the popular enthusiasm that sustained it, arose reasonably enough from the novelty of participation in politics, rather than attachment to programme or doctrine. So long as most social conflict arose and was absorbed within a local situation, and so long as Gladstone held the Liberal left fascinated, the impetus of popular Liberalism was satisfied by sound government in the aristocratic tradition, improved by the new rhetoric of beneficence.

Appendices

Appendix One

THE CATHOLIC VOTE

Between the two Reform Bills, Catholicism in England was growing as fast as any industry:[1]

	1830	1863
Number of priests in England	434	1,242
Number of convents in England	16	162
Male religious houses	8	55

Two tendencies, and one intrigue, concerning the political situation of Catholics, have to be stated here. The first point was the replacement of the first generation of emancipated Catholic peers, who were chiefly Whig, by a second generation who were often more than Tory. The ostensible point of separation here was Liberal policy towards the temporal power of the Pope, assisted by the reassertion of natural conservatism in domestic matters.[2] Later, when the Eastern question became prominent in the 1870's, it was fancied that Catholic interests were threatened by a Russian advance on Eastern Europe, and this too played a part among those Catholics who knew about such things. The Liberal policy of generosity to Ireland, whether the Irish accepted it as such or not, was not calculated to win the hearts of English Catholic grandees, who already had their own reasons for wishing the Irish Channel wider. The Duke of Norfolk led the way in each generation; the 19th Duke (1856–60) declined an offer of the Garter, by Palmerston, whose policy he disapproved. The 20th Duke, who came of age in 1868, even in that year lent no support to the Liberals. In the 1870's, the Roman Catholic nobility and gentry, and their forum, the

---

[1] W. Ward, *The Life and Times of Cardinal Wiseman*, II, 459.

[2] Though Manning was trying to convert Gladstone to a more liberal Irish policy, he expressed qualms over Reform repeatedly in 1864–6. The speech by Gladstone on Baines' motion in 1864 alarmed him. 'I do not wish to see you even remotely allied to Bright in home policy, or Garibaldi in foreign.'—Manning to Gladstone, 24 February 1865, B.M. Add. mss. 44,248, f. 267.

Catholic Union of Great Britain, had become strongly Tory.[3] The Catholic aristocracy drew apart from the Liberal Party as the Catholic masses were beginning to enter into relations with it.

The great Catholic intrigue of 1859–65 arose from the fact that Palmerston, Disraeli, and Pius IX were each struggling for their political lives. They knew exactly what was going on: the political public heard very little. The English Catholics and Irish Catholic M.P.s were the pawns in the game. The climax came in the Danish crisis of 1864, with a motion of want of confidence moved by Disraeli on 4–7 July 1864. Palmerston had no intention of being defeated, but saw greater advantages in being defeated by Popery, than in conciliating it. 'I have heard, what perhaps you know already, that Monsignores Talbot and Howard arrived from Rome yesterday, with orders to the Catholics to vote to a man against us.'[4] About seventy-three Irish members in fact voted against the ministry, and Disraeli's hopes of a Catholic-Tory alliance appeared justified. But the No Popery principle, as exemplified in Lord Derby, knocked down this house of cards. When Derby insisted on meeting Garibaldi, his Chief Whip in the Lords warned him: '. . . you will mortally affront the Catholics who both in England and Ireland have not only dropped their hostility to the Conservatives, but have in many instances been disposed to support you.'[5] The Whip resigned in protest at such clumsiness. A year later, Derby committed the greater error of talking of the necessity for muzzling Catholics, and near broke the heart of the greatest party manager of all:

> All this is quite consistent with what he [Disraeli] said to me after the General Election of 1865, when he was again greatly disappointed. During the whole of Lord Palmerston's administration, he said he had been labouring assiduously to conciliate the R.C. party, who were naturally much displeased with the foreign policy of the Govern-

[3] Wolf, *Life of Ripon*, I, 313.
[4] Palmerston to Delane, June 1864: Dasent, *Delane*, II, 115.
[5] Bath to Derby, 12 April 1864: quoted F. M. L. Thompson, *English Landed Society in the Nineteenth Century* (1963), 273.

ment. He had met, he said, with considerable success, and he mentioned to me several Lancashire families on whose vote and influence he believed he could depend. A careless, thoughtless speech of Lord Derby's gave deep offence to the R.C.'s, and shattered all his hopes. Here he did speak with considerable warmth, as he sat up in his armchair and showed 'how fields were won' and, alas! how they were lost.[6]

Disraeli's policy of exploiting the divisions between the Catholics and the Liberals was sensible in one respect. At very least, the Conservatives gained fifteen seats in Ireland between 1852 and 1859, and in the years of Italian crisis after 1859 the numbers of non-Conservative Irish members who could be counted on to support the ministry had been greatly reduced. In another respect, however, a policy of conciliation and seduction was unrealistic, because it assumed that the Conservatives in general were as willing as Disraeli to subordinate what really mattered to them, to rather cerebral speculations about party advantage. In fact there were a sufficient number of Conservatives who were unwilling to give ground on anything to do with Catholicism, to make Disraeli's acute and large-minded policies unworkable. In particular, of course, the Irish Conservative M.P.s created an impossible problem. When such cases as the Belfast Riots of 1864 demanded some public pronouncement, it was a matter of antagonizing one group or the other, and sharp things were said about Disraeli's attempt to sit on the fence, when a group of Irish Conservative members met in Dublin.[7] The exceptional weakness of Disraeli's position in the party in 1864–6 must have owed much to his insensitively adopting unacceptable methods in his devoted search for a majority. It was the ancestral fear of Catholicism, not fear of democracy, or desire for his party to be in office, which was still in 1865 the driving force and overriding object of the plain and simple Conservative gentleman, and the politicians and adventurers in the party could not get round this obstacle.

[6] T. E. Kebbel, *Lord Beaconsfield and Other Tory Memories* (1907), 28–9.

[7] The Irish Conservative leaders, Naas, Whiteside, Ball, Napier, and Cairns, were more important in Conservative counsels than their Irish Liberal counterparts were in the Liberal Party.

The isolated Catholics in the Parliamentary world could be worked on as individuals according to the ordinary rules of politics. The Catholic masses in the constituencies, however, created a social division in the nation as massive and unyielding as that between rich and poor.

As early as the 1850's the Catholics in the north of England were trying to exert a united electoral influence. Though they generally succeeded in polling their men *en bloc*, they made little progress since the addition of their votes to one side was more than outweighed by the resulting subtraction of Protestants.

In England as a whole, the Catholic vote was, with little qualification, Irish. But Lancashire, the main reception area for Irish immigration, happened also to have a large pocket of native Catholicism. In 1787 a Papal emissary sent the following computation of Catholic communicants to Rome:[8]

Cheshire	340
Lancashire	23,000
Yorkshire	4,812
Northumberland	3,130
Durham	1,676
Cumberland	300
Westmorland	400
Man	27
	33,685

In Lancashire, therefore, Catholic influence was important in the county constituencies and in higher social classes than elsewhere. For instance, in the South Lancashire election of 1859, the Tory victory was attributed to the priests.[9] In that division in 1868, Gladstone was supported by two large Catholic proprietors, Thomas Weld-Blundell and Lord Beaumont, who were no longer Liberals in 1880,[10] when it was remarked that the Catholics as a class turned against the party.[11] Outside rural Lancashire, Catholic influence was

[8] C. A. Bolton, *Salford Diocese and Its Catholic Past* (1950), 248.

[9] *The Times*, 9 May 1859, quoted in *The Liberal Party and the Catholics*, Anon. (1874), 8.

[10] *Political Correspondence of Gladstone and Granville 1874–1886*, ed., A. Ramm, I, 118–19.   [11] Ibid., I, 116.

practically confined to the urban working class of Irish stock, and was therefore latent till after the Second Reform Bill. In Leeds, for instance, there was a Home Rule vote of 2,000 to 2,500 in 1874, 'under the direct influence of their priests'.[12] In Bradford upwards of 3,000 voters out of 21,000 were Irish in 1868, most of them labouring men earning under £1 a week, and in Liverpool in the 1868 elections, the Catholic voters were assembled in their own schoolrooms, and taken to the poll together.[13]

Before 1867, Catholic influence among the ten-pound householders was weak, even in the North. At Stockport, the Catholics had thirty votes in 1852, which were delivered according to arrangements made between the priest, the leading Catholic layman, and the secretary of the Reform Association.[14] In Carlisle, Catholic support, though organized, was equally marginal: '. . . the Catholics turned against me because I had subscribed to the Garibaldi fund. However, my Committee tell me I can now hold the seat in spite of them. . . .'[15] The Manchester Catholics had not yet grasped the king-making power which they came to have in the 1880's: when the South Lancashire Catholic Electoral Registration Association was formed in 1864, its prospectus lamented:

> . . . [the Catholics were] . . . so little united by any organisa-
> tion . . . no candidate for any office . . . ever thinks of
> consulting their wishes, or deems it requisite to give any
> degree of attention to their interests . . . in Man-
> chester, unconscious of our strength, we have hitherto
> been incapable of using any influence; our support is un-
> solicited . . .[16]

The most striking Catholic vote to come to light before working-class enfranchisement was at Preston, with its free-

[12] Edward Baines to his brother-in-law, 13 March 1874: Whitby mss. unsorted.

[13] *Parl. Papers, 1868–9*, VIII, 121, 133.

[14] Coppock to Smith, 19 March 1852: J. B. Smith Papers, Manchester Central Library.

[15] Edmund Potter to G. Melly, 29 November 1861: Melly Papers, III, 849, Liverpool Central Library.

[16] *Manchester Examiner*, 31 December 1864.

men electors. There, it was said, they were—before the Italian crisis of 1859—the great strength of the Liberals, numbering 500 in a constituency of 2,800. They were 'well disciplined and obedient to orders'.[17]

Catholic politics were based on confession, class, and nationality. At a particular election, any one of these might be dominant. Only in 1868 did confessional, class, and Irish national interests coincide with support of the Liberal Party.[18] In 1859 and 1865 Garibaldi and the Italian question brought Catholic support to the Tories, in England and in Ireland, for the first time, but as working men the Catholics were still attracted to the Liberals. 'The Catholics were divided between Italy and class.'[19] The Catholic vote, naturally aligned with the Liberals, generally failed to find its way to them in the period 1859–85, because the Catholics demanded too much in return for too little.

The streets, not the polling booths, were the real battleground. Every step taken to organize the Catholic Church among the immigrants of the famine years met with violent Protestant resistance. Though the Irish normally lived in their own quarter, religious riots were fairly frequent during the period 1850–70 when the Catholic parishes were being established in the Lancashire towns. Important riots involving attempts to sack Catholic chapels and the extensive destruction of Irish property took place in Stockport, Ashton, Stalybridge, Rochdale, Bacup, and Haslingden, where the young Michael Davitt drove the mob back with a revolver,[20] and outside the county, there were outbreaks in Birkenhead, London, Belfast, and Birmingham. Belfast, where the Catholic population had grown rapidly to reach thirty-four per cent

[17] *Preston Elections 1807–1865*: volume of cuttings in Manchester Central Library.

[18] But 'the *Tablet* writes against us, and I can't get the Duke of Norfolk to help us'.—Glyn to Gladstone, 3 October 1868: Add mss. 44,347, f. 188.

[19] H. A. Taylor, 'Politics in Famine-Stricken Preston . . . 1861–1865': in *Transactions of the Hist. Soc. of Lancs and Ches.* (1955), 132.

[20] F. Sheehy-Skeffington, *Life of Davitt* (1908), 12. Further up the coast in Wigtownshire, the Orangemen were very active against the Liberals. —G. W. T. Omond, *The Lord Advocates of Scotland 1834–1880* (1914), 266.

in 1861, had riots[21] in 1857, 1864, 1872, 1886, 1893, and 1898. The Irish were as militant as their opponents. In Hyde Park, 'a large number of Irish labourers got up a discussion on the respective merits of Garibaldi and the Pope, upon which a fight took place between two of the opposing parties.'[22] The Irish challenge was directed entirely against the English industrial working classes, who reacted more violently to this than to any other issue of the period. Such feelings were strong enough to influence their votes after 1867. Although the Tory Party was a very imperfect means of expressing anti-Popery at a national level, the local Tory parties in Lancashire were far better able to catch the Orange vote than the Liberals, and were thus able to reverse a traditional Liberal supremacy and turn working-class enfranchisement to their advantage.

[21] D. B. Barritt and C. P. Carter, *The Northern Ireland Problem* (1962), 71.
[22] *Manchester Examiner,* 8 October 1862. For the Birkenhead demonstrations *against* Garibaldi, v. ibid. 10 October 1862.

Appendix Two

THE PRICE OF WHEAT AND POPULAR POLITICAL ACTIVITY

The long-drawn-out political crisis of 1866–8 coincided more or less with a period of great economic tension and distress. The economic crisis chiefly affected the political one by stirring the working class and radical middle class into more vigorous action than they showed for a long time before or since. Unemployment affected many after the financial crisis of June 1866, but the rise in prices affected everybody. The chief price involved was the price of wheat. Wheat prices did not rise to famine levels, but then they started very low, rose very rapidly, and stayed high for a long time. People, of course, bought either flour or bread (there was a sharp rise in the price of the 4 lb. loaf in London[1] between 1864 and 1867) but the prices of both simply reflected the changes in the *Gazette* price of wheat.

The following table shows the movement of prices from December 1864, when wheat was at its lowest price between 1851 and 1879, to a maximum in May, 1868, when it reached the highest price between 1855 and the end of the century.

AVERAGE GAZETTE PRICES OF BRITISH WHEAT PER IMP. QTR.

	s.	d.	Events
December 1864	38	1	
April 1865	39	6	
December 1865	46	7	
January 1866	45	10	
April 1866	44	10	
May 1866	46	2	Failure of Liberal Reform Bill
June 1866	48	3	Financial crash
July 1866	54	1	Hyde Park riots
August 1866	50	6	

[1] J. H. Clapham, *An Economic History of Modern Britain; Free Trade and Steel 1850–1886* (1932), 460.

AVERAGE GAZETTE PRICES OF BRITISH WHEAT PER IMP. QTR.

	s.	d.	Events
September 1866	48	11	
October 1866	52	4	Mass Meetings begin
November 1866	56	6	
December 1866	60	3	
January 1867	61	4	A very hard winter
February 1867	60	10	
March 1867	59	9	
April 1867	61	6	
May 1867	64	8	
June 1867	65	4	Further London riots
July 1867	65	0	
August 1867	67	8	
September 1867	62	8	
October 1867	66	6	
November 1867	69	5	
December 1867	67	4	
January 1868	70	3	A very hard winter
February 1868	73	0	
March 1868	73	0	
April 1868	73	3	
May 1868	73	9	
June 1868	67	11	
July 1868	65	5	
August 1868	57	7	
December 1868	49	11	

The movement of prices throws much light on the popular lack of enthusiasm for Reform in 1861–6, and the ardour and activity of 1866–7; and the continued high level of prices in 1867–8 similarly corresponded to a spell of political militancy extending well after the passage of the Reform Bill.[2] Gladstonian Liberalism began in a series of lean years when it became almost twice as difficult for the breadwinner to earn the main article of his diet, bread—if he had a job at all.

[2] The prices quoted were taken from the Statistical Abstract, *Parl. Papers, 1870*, LXVIII.

Manuscript Sources Consulted

I. NATIONAL

The Brand Papers, in the care of the Clerk of the House of Commons.

The Bright Papers *a*) in the British Museum.
b) in University College Library, London.
c) in private hands.

The Chamberlain Papers, in Birmingham University Library.

The Clarendon Deposit, in the Bodleian Library.

The Cobden Papers *a*) in the British Museum.
b) in the County Record Office, Chichester.

The Duchy of Lancaster Papers, Savoy House.

The Gladstone Papers, British Museum.

The Howell Collection, in the Bishopsgate Institute.

The Mill-Taylor Collection, in the British Library of Political and Economic Science.

The Palmerston Papers.

The Russell Papers, in the Public Record Office.

II. LOCAL

The Baines Papers.

The Cowen Papers, Newcastle Public Library.

The Leader-Mundella Papers, Sheffield University Library.

The Melly Papers, Liverpool Public Library.

The Rathbone Papers, Liverpool University Library.

The J. B. Smith Papers, Manchester Public Library.

The Wilson Papers, Manchester Public Library.

The Papers of Charles William, 5th Earl Fitzwilliam, in the Northamptonshire County Record Office.

The Whitby Elections Collection, Pannett Park Museum, Whitby.

III. RECORDS OF SOCIETIES

The Liberation Society, London County Record Office.
The Peace Society, Browning Street, London, S.E.17.
The National Reform League, Bishopsgate Institute.
The Leeds Reform Committee, Leeds Public Library.
The Rochdale Reform Association.
The Scarborough Liberal Association.

Index